'Jo Wagstaff shows us a revolutionary new ~~...~~ working based on authenticity, wisdom and self-awareness. Using cutting-edge, evidenced-based tools and practices and insightful stories and guidance, she shows us how to escape the trap of hustling, stressing and burning ourselves out trying to prove our worth; and provides a clear path to a life of true success — a life where we are able to achieve great things but more importantly also find meaning, purpose and deep satisfaction in life. The world is in need of this kind of wisdom. This is a book whose time has come'.

— **Melli O'Brien, Co-founder of Mindfulness.com**

'Jo Wagstaff has captured my attention like few others, with her real-life examples mixed with her personal journey and experiences. I recognised myself in many of her stories and felt supported on my journey to live more true to my purpose. More importantly, I've realised we are never done with self-development and self-interrogation, and I absolutely loved her tools and journaling prompts. It has allowed me to gain more clarity on what I am about holistically, and it has given me the strength and inspiration to embrace all of me'.

— **Peggy Renders, Chief Customer Officer, Telstra Enterprise**

'This book starts like an *Eat Pray Love* of the corporate world, but it takes you somewhere deeper and more practical. It offers teachings, wisdom and guidance through one's own history, upbringing, and present life. Thank you, Jo, for opening your heart and offering your story so that we can all learn how to be true to our authentic selves. *Lead Like You* is a must-read for anyone on a journey of self-discovery, be it career-orientated or not'.

— **Karen Taylor, Chief Executive Officer, Hourigan International**

'What a gift *Lead Like You* is. Through Jo Wagstaff's story, guidance, and insights, you feel seen, understood, and held. But, more than that, Jo shows you a path through the challenges, the glimmers of good on the other side and the gifts from lessons you learn along the way'.

— **Mel Ware, Head of Marketing and Brand, Zurich Australia**

LEAD LIKE YOU

LEAD LIKE YOU

How Authenticity Transforms
the Way Women Live, Love, and Succeed

JO WAGSTAFF

WILEY

First published in 2024 by John Wiley & Sons Australia, Ltd
Level 4, 600 Bourke St, Melbourne, Victoria 3000, Australia

Typeset in Adobe Jenson Pro 11.5pt/14pt

ISBN: 978-1-394-24870-4

 A catalogue record for this
book is available from the
National Library of Australia

Cover design by Wiley

Disclaimer
The material in this publication is of the nature of general comment only, and does not represent professional advice. It is not intended to provide specific guidance for particular circumstances and it should not be relied on as the basis for any decision to take action or not take action on any matter which it covers. Readers should obtain professional advice where appropriate, before making any such decision. To the maximum extent permitted by law, the author and publisher disclaim all responsibility and liability to any person, arising directly or indirectly from any person taking or not taking action based on the information in this publication.

Printed and bound by CPI Group (UK) Ltd, Croydon, CR0 4YY

C9781394248704_260324

For all the women I have had the privilege of working with.

Thank you for your vulnerability and trust in undertaking this journey with me.

Thank you for sharing who you are and showing me who I am.

CONTENTS

PREFACE

Thank you for picking up this book and, with it, accepting an invitation to explore a revolutionary new way to live, love, lead and succeed.

Have you noticed how we are living with the relentless demands of a world that never stops asking for more, exhausting ourselves in pursuit of elusive ideals and often unconsciously striving to prove our worth? Never feeling it is enough, we give everything in search of 'success' while often struggling with stress, guilt, self-doubt, and burnout.

For much of our lives, our need to prove ourselves, earn our worth and feel safe in this world can stop us from living and leading true to ourselves. In my experience working with thousands of professional women in many countries and across all levels, I have learned that we are not alone. Many of us have not learned how to be in a relationship with ourselves. A relationship that encourages us to believe deeply in our authentic selves and our strengths and capabilities and empowers us to step into our own lives more fully and to lead true to ourselves.

We often look outside ourselves for validation, but transformation really begins when we look inside ourselves. When we begin to gently and compassionately understand why we do what we do, what unconsciously drives us, and what meaningful success looks like for each of us. Living and leading lives true to ourselves is the foundational ingredient to thriving at both work and in life.

Let's dismantle the illusion of societal expectations and the internal and external forces that limit our lives and instead discover how to embrace our inherent worth as woman and as leaders. This book invites you on a transformational inner journey to return to yourself and the life you want to lead, one that is true to yourself.

This roadmap has been crafted in three parts:

◆ Know yourself: This is the opportunity to deeply reflect on why it can be so hard to live and lead true to ourselves and what may be limiting you.

◆ Care for yourself: Self-compassion, practical self-care, and boundaries as the essential foundations for radical resiliency and inner confidence.

◆ Be yourself: Gain clarity on your values, purpose and vision and the power of authenticity to transform how you live, love, lead and succeed.

This book offers many vulnerable and relatable stories, psychological research, and tools to deepen your awareness and understanding of yourself. It also invites you to pause throughout for conscious reflections and evidence-based conscious practices. May it empower you to slow down, to centre your sense of self, to take back your innate power, to nurture and nourish yourself, to find your truth, speak your truth and live your truth, and stop trying to earn your worth, as you realise that you are born worthy. Worthy of creating the life you want. Worthy of leading from within.

I offer my story, heart, experiences, successes and failures, shared wisdom, and a vision for a new day where men and women feel equal and united, where we all know our innate worth. Where life and leadership aren't about a relentless grind but about leading and living with vitality and authenticity. Where we stop the hustle to earn our worth through our careers as a way of feeling valued or justifying our existence and instead achieve what is important to us from a place of wholeness, purpose, and fulfilment. Where we all feel safe to be our true authentic selves. Where we begin to take care of our poor over-activated nervous system. Where we reclaim the feminine principles of living deeply connected to ourselves and to each other. To live in the ebb and flow of life and be nurtured and nourished by the gift of simply being and allowing more gentleness, compassion, and beauty to saturate our lives. Where we step fully into our authentic power and live and lead true to ourselves.

May we do this together.

INTRODUCTION

I sat in my corner office on the top floor of one of the most beautiful office buildings in Sydney, staring out over the Sydney Harbour Bridge and Sydney Opera House. My assistant handed me a stunning black lace Collette Dinnigan cocktail dress and strappy Jimmy Choo shoes to change into.

I rode down the lift and slid into a black limousine that was waiting for me and was whisked off to Bondi Beach. There, I was welcomed into James Packer's magnificent beachfront apartment, where I joined my male colleagues for a cocktail party. James sat on the board of our company, and at the time, he and Kerry Packer were major shareholders in the business I worked for, as well as one of the wealthiest families in Australia.

I was thirty-two years old, the youngest on the team by some years, and the only female on the executive leadership team. We were a top 200–listed financial services company in the middle of a merger. I had spent the afternoon arguing with investment bankers and lawyers about how we were going to communicate the merger to our staff, shareholders and clients. I had some good wins and was feeling pumped.

It was a heady experience being surrounded by so much masculine intellectual horsepower. I had always been both attracted to and intimidated by intellect — especially intellectual men. And with that, I often underestimated and undervalued my own skills, talents and intellectual capacity. The men I was working with were, unquestionably, some of the brightest around.

I was also attracted to power, and unconsciously, I associated male intellect and success with that power. And I wanted some. I found it exciting to both be a part of and, at times, to go up against it. Ultimately (and I say this with great self-compassion and no awareness of it back then), to try to manipulate them, and in some way, take my power back.

I was desperate to feel safe, to feel equal, to not feel powerless. To feel seen and acknowledged, to belong, to feel enough. Alternatively, I would try to compete with them, try to be like them — just one of the boys, living my masculine traits of doing, striving, achieving, competing. I would tell myself I had to toughen up and hide my feelings. I would often stay silent about things that really mattered to me. I vacillated between what I would call my 'immature feminine' and my overly identified, extreme 'immature masculine'.

It didn't help that I had no qualifications, which meant I spent my working life feeling like an imposter. And here I was, in the financial services industry, which was arguably one of the most male-dominated and intellectually challenging at the time. I made my way to the top echelon by the age of thirty-two.

I remember how awe-struck I felt as James took me for a tour of his home. I had *made* it.

I had a husband who had been a vet and was now an investment banker — what a combo! A gorgeous, healthy, fourteen-month-old son. We were building a beautiful big home on the leafy lower north shore. I had all the material things I could want. I drove a brand-new BMW, for which I had paid cash with my last bonus. I wore all the designer labels and sat at the front of the plane when I travelled. Finally, I had everything that I believed I needed to be happy, to thrive, to feel important and powerful.

I vividly remember excusing myself from the group, walking past a huge, stunning fish tank and entering the powder room. I looked at myself in the mirror, but this time was different. It wasn't a superficial glance to check if I looked attractive enough. I looked deep into my own eyes, and said out loud, 'You've made it honey. You did what you set out to do. You showed them.'

But looking back at me were the saddest, loneliest eyes I had ever seen.

In that moment, while I was not yet ready to admit it to myself, I saw the truth. I had dishonoured and abandoned myself in my need to feel liked, loved, important, successful, powerful and, ultimately, safe, particularly in a very male-dominated world. It had been a high price to pay.

That was the day it all began to unravel.

That year, my marriage ended and my dad got sick and died of cancer. I found new ways to numb my grief — both the grief of the present and the past. I worked harder. I drank more. I used drugs for the first time. I spent a small fortune as a way of pretending I was thriving. I found the most dysfunctional relationship I could as an unconscious way of punishing myself and replaying my attachment pattern, which had been established in my childhood.

To the outside world, even to my family and close friends, it still looked like I was thriving. I was so high functioning. I was the consummate swan, looking like I was gracefully gliding across the pond to the outside world. But underneath, I was kicking my feet a hundred miles an hour and barely staying afloat. Living on adrenalin and high-functioning anxiety.

And the 'universe', for want of a better term, knew that. As long as I stayed busy and used money and success to avoid myself, I was never going to stop and face what I needed to face. Myself. My truth. My needs and wants. My dreams.

A couple of years later, I was offered a lucrative voluntary redundancy and walked away from my corporate career thinking I was financially secure and just needed a 'bit of a break'. But I was never good at resting, and at one point in my on-again off-again 'break' I tried spending a week at a health retreat. They had a labyrinth, and while I was not particularly spiritual at the time, I decided to do a bit of a ceremony for myself. Late at night, under a full moon, I walked the labyrinth, which slowly wound its way to the top of a small hill.

At the top, I got down on my knees and prayed. This was not something I had ever done much of and I had no real sense of what to pray to, so I prayed to the moon. In that prayer, I surrendered. I turned my life and will over to a power greater than myself. I said, 'I am all yours. I don't know what I want or need. I don't know what is wrong with me. I just know I am deeply unhappy and I am tired. Oh, so tired. Please show me the way. I surrender.' In hindsight, I love that I prayed to the moon, as it is said to be a feminine symbol. Ultimately, that is what I had lost touch with: my feminine nature.

Within weeks of my surrender, the share market crashed, and with it, the second tranche of the options I had received disappeared. They had been considered a 'sure thing', and given this, I had bought a home in Balmoral Beach, one of Sydney's most expensive beachside suburbs, in advance of them vesting. Outside of my son, the most important thing to me, the only way I truly felt safe in the world was by having money. It gave me the illusion of control. Having a home was also super important as I craved the stability I had not had as a child.

In a moment, both my home and much of my money vanished. The rug was pulled out from under me. I was fully on my knees, with nowhere to go. And in hindsight, thank god!

I had spent much of my life searching. When I look back now, I am not even sure what I was searching for. At different times, money, control, validation, success, excitement, freedom, power, safety, family, love. But most of the time, what I was really doing was running away from myself: from my feelings, my fears, my hurts, my reality, my deep sense of unworthiness. I was also often denying my true self, including my own values, dreams, purpose, femininity, strengths and talents.

Now it was time to come face-to-face with it all. I had worked so hard to try to earn my worth and self-esteem and it hadn't worked. The life I was leading was not sustainable.

As a woman living in a patriarchal culture, and as a female leader working in a patriarchal culture and industry, there were so many ways I had abandoned myself and been silent. I had lost my way, which is so hard when you think you are meant to know your way and be perfect within it.

I spent the decade following my surrender coming home to myself. Reclaiming my strong feminine. Rediscovering the love and life I needed to truly thrive, rather than barely survive. Learning how to live, love, lead and succeed true to myself.

This is the story of me realising my intrinsic worth. Of learning I am enough. You are enough. We are enough. Just as we are.

My sincere hope is that you will find meaning in my story and the stories of many other women and that they support you to find your authentic voice, your value, radical resiliency and both fulfilment and meaning as a woman in the workplace and in life.

Ultimately, this book offers a roadmap to help you explore your story and realise your worth. It is about exploring the groundbreaking concept that true and sustainable success is not about working harder, but is about living and leading true to yourself. About leading your life and career from the inside out, from a sense of wholeness. About how you show up for yourself and how you show up with others.

This is the roadmap that, when consistently and compassionately practiced, will show you how to reclaim your true self and the life and career you want to lead. It will empower you to embody your inner confidence, calmness, and purpose. This is the roadmap for the inner work of extraordinary sustainable leadership, not just in the office but in every facet of life.

Content warning

As we commence on this journey of self-awareness, care, authenticity and empowerment together, it is important to look after our emotional wellbeing. Please be advised that some chapters explore subjects that may be uncomfortable for some readers, such as sexual abuse and childhood trauma (Chapter 1), birth trauma and postnatal depression (Chapter 2) and substance use (Chapters 3 and 5).

PART I
Know yourself

CHAPTER 1

Why is it so hard to live true to ourselves?

Have you, like me, ever struggled to live true to yourself? At work, in life? To step fully into your power and create and lead the career and life you most want to live? Why can it feel so damn hard?

We human beings are very complex creatures. There are a number of factors, both internal and external, that can make it hard to speak up, believe in ourselves, love ourselves, and live and lead true to ourselves. Some of these factors are cultural, some biological and some come from our childhood and the subconscious beliefs we developed then.

In this chapter, we will begin by exploring the role our upbringings and histories play in shaping how we feel about ourselves, and how we show up and behave in the world as adults today. This is where I begin my work with all my clients; by supporting them to increase their awareness, understanding and acceptance of themselves. I share my own stories here as an invitation for you to reflect on how significant events, people, experiences and potential traumas from your past may have shaped you today.

How our histories shape us

We all have different histories and family roles that set up our patterns of behaviour and shape how we show up in the world and go about trying to find our self-worth. As children, we are all born worthy of love. But when this is not consistently mirrored back to us, however subtly, however naively or accidentally, this sets up a slippery slope for our self-worth. Our childhood attachment histories seriously impact our ability to speak up, to live true to ourselves and to develop a strong sense of self-worth.

If we felt safe in our families, felt we were able to be our own person and have our own thoughts, feelings and beliefs without being shamed, criticised or ignored, it would feel more natural for us to ask for and meet our own needs as adults. If we didn't feel protected, felt we had to compete with siblings, or felt like we had to 'earn' our family's love, then our fear of abandonment, rejection or enmeshment will severely impact our innate sense of worthiness. It impacts our natural ability to be true to ourselves, to speak our truth, to love and believe in ourselves. All of this is very likely to shape how we show up in our life, work and careers.

Many of us struggle with a feeling of dissatisfaction within ourselves, our work and our lives. Many of us feel pulled in a million different directions in a world that is constantly demanding more of us. How do we stop working so hard to prove ourselves — trying, striving, perfecting our lives, constantly busy, trying to be 'good enough' at everything we do?

I have worked with thousands of people who have struggled with this same question. If only there was a simple answer!

As a result of how my upbringing has shaped me, I have found it almost impossible to be true to myself, to believe in myself and, ultimately, to love myself — although it has often not seemed that way to others. I often move from one extreme to another. At one extreme, I will bury my feelings, needs, values, dreams and words to please people, which results in me feeling resentful, and then in turn, behaving passive-aggressively. Then, I can move to the other extreme of finally speaking up, but I'm full of anger, judgement and blame, which means nobody can really hear what I am saying. Slowly, gently, I am finding a middle way, a way that creates understanding and unity rather than more conflict and separation.

It starts at the beginning

As I share my story, I encourage you to reflect on your own childhood with gentle curiosity and great self-compassion, and consider the pivotal experiences, events and significant people that may have shaped your patterns, beliefs and behaviours, which all influence how you show up in the world today.

I was born to two twenty-year-old, newly married, impoverished university students. They were still children themselves, with desires, dreams and plans of their own — and those did not include me.

My mum had travelled overseas on an exchange program twelve months earlier, and aspired to complete her degree and apply for a job at the United Nations in New York. My dad, having been head prefect and captain of the First XV Rugby team, and forever overwhelmed by the pressure he felt from his parents to be 'someone' in the world, aspired to finish his degree and go overseas as a diplomat at one of the New Zealand Government agencies. They had both been the golden child in their families, the ones who were going to do well, and they felt responsible for making their parents proud.

As you can imagine, my parents and grandparents were not very excited initially when I came along. I had thrown a spanner in the works! There was a lot of disappointment and shame around my mum's pregnancy, and in New Zealand in 1970, abortion was illegal. Many girls were sent to special homes for expectant mothers in their last trimester and had their babies taken for adoption. My grandfather wanted this, but thankfully, my dad stepped in and said they would get married and do their best to give me a family. Research now suggests that, even in the womb, we can pick up and take on our parents' emotional states.[1] So, there they were, in an unplanned marriage with a newborn baby, aspirations derailed, no money and very little support — not an easy place from which to start your adult life.

I was also born underweight and had to stay in a special unit where I was mostly on my own. I imagine that was a very lonely existence for me, a little baby needing to be held and comforted and to bond with my mum.

Today, attachment theory tells us this is not the way to set up a secure attachment between baby and parent, which is what we need to establish our worth, have healthy functioning adult relationships and thrive in life. We initially learn how to love, both ourselves and others, from how we experience love (or the lack of it) in our childhoods.

Thinking back, I didn't have a very good run with hospitals. At the age of two, my young parents took me camping with their friends, and mum's girlfriend fell over while carrying me and landed on my leg. It took them two days to take me to the hospital. Perhaps I had already learnt the importance of staying quiet and not making a fuss. Finally, the doctor confirmed it was broken, and suggested I stay in the hospital, while my parents went back and finished their camping trip.

It is hard for me to fathom now what that must have been like for me. My mum told me the nurse said I was very well-behaved (no surprise there), but I can't imagine any two-year-old not wanting to be with her mum and dad after breaking a leg.

When I was two-and-a-half, my darling little brother came along. I loved him with all my heart. From a very young age, I felt responsible for looking after him and protecting him. When I was five, my dad got a job offer, which he thought was a great opportunity to further his career, and we moved to Sydney. I felt devastated about this move, as it meant leaving my grandma Patsy (my dad's mum), who often looked after me, in New Zealand. Being with her gave me such a sense of comfort. She was my safe place, so moving to what felt like the other side of the world ripped my little heart out.

When I left, I remember her hugging me and giving me a beautiful necklace made of different coloured stones. When I got to my new home in the leafy suburb of Wahroonga, I hung it around my lime green–painted iron bedhead so I could look at it every night.

One morning, only two weeks after we had arrived in Sydney, I walked out of my bedroom and saw my dad sitting on the ground crying. I don't remember seeing him ever cry before this. He opened his arms, and I ran to him.

He whispered in my ear, 'Patsy died'.

In that moment, my heart felt shattered. I felt lost. My family was not religious at all (in fact, my dad was a staunch atheist), but after she died, I started getting down on my knees each night in front of the necklace she gave me and praying to my grandma Patsy. I imagine this was my way of trying to stay connected to her.

Then everything changed again

A couple of years later, at the age of seven, our family moved to live in Adelaide, again due to dad's work. One afternoon, just as I was starting to settle into this new life, Mum and Dad asked my brother and me to come into the lounge room. I remember feeling both excited and nervous. Did they have something wonderful to tell us? Perhaps we were finally getting that puppy I had always wanted. Or were they going to tell us we were moving to another state or country again? I didn't want to move again.

But instead, as we sat staring at them on the couch, they told us that they were separating. While they both looked scared and sad, my dad looked completely devastated. I remember feeling confused and wondering what this would mean. I was angry that, once again, just as I started to feel settled and safe in my new home, everything was going to change. I was scared that maybe I had done something wrong. I had tried so hard to be good, to be perfect, to act happy all the time, but Dad was still leaving. Something froze in my heart that day.

The breakdown of my parents' marriage, which I suspect had never been a good one, had a profound impact on me, particularly when my dad decided to leave Adelaide for a few years and work interstate and overseas. As a young girl, it felt impossible not to take this personally. And as a parent myself now, I don't think it was okay either.

My dad was so caught up in his own pain and his own needs that he was rarely, if ever, available for ours. He was also quite introverted and struggled with relationships and communicating in general. And he was deeply, bitterly angry at the world. Actually, mostly at his mother, although nobody in my family can explain why that was.

Don't get me wrong, he could be very charming and was very intellectually interesting and loved to philosophise. But he had a temper on him that could go off at any time. He said things that cut me to the bone and could annihilate my sense of self in one sentence, which is a problem when you are still trying to develop one. He could be both emotionally and physically violent.

I loved him as only a child can love their father, and at the same time, feared him, never knowing which dad I was going to get. The charming one, the distant one, the angry one, the one who always left? When he was living interstate, I would miss him desperately. He would tell me he missed me too and then when I saw him, he would often be cold, distant or simply awkward.

He seemed to be forever leaving, and even when he was with me, not emotionally present or available. I learnt to try to please him, to try to make him happy, to do anything to stop him from getting angry at me and, especially, at my little brother who he took a lot of his own insecurities and regrets out on. He would never say sorry or acknowledge his feelings and behaviours and their impact on us.

To further complicate my relationship with him, my dad also had a good heart, albeit a sad one. I know he did not intend to cause the damage he did. I know he loved us. I experienced, firsthand, just how hard it was for him to love and be loved.

I am also forever grateful to my dad for introducing me to his love of the ocean and nature. The only times I felt truly close to him were at the beach, exploring the rock pools, playing in the waves, and camping and walking in nature. That was when he was most at peace, where, for short periods, before his internal pain and anger kicked in, we were able to connect. The ocean and nature have become my great loves too.

The challenges of instability

By the age of twelve, I had been to four schools, lived in three different cities and eight different houses. On the upside, my resiliency training had started early. On the downside, I had very little physical, emotional or financial stability in my younger years. I had to learn to both make friends quickly and be prepared that I would leave them, so not to get too close.

I struggled to focus at school. I was always way too young compared to the rest of my class, being just sixteen when I matriculated in my final year of high school. I didn't have the emotional maturity or support I needed. I was swimming in pain, fear and anxiety, but didn't know it. Perhaps it stemmed from the lack of stability I had experienced. My dad was often impatient and irritable when I could not work out how to do something. I still remember physically cringing and my heart beginning to beat super fast as his voice began to rise. He would seethe with frustration and contempt as he snarled, 'Are you stupid?' I soon learnt I needed to get things right to avoid his disapproval.

From my struggles at school and the reactions of my teachers and parents, I took on the beliefs, which ultimately became ingrained in me, that I was both stupid and unlovable as I was. From a young age, I felt I had to find a way to 'make up' for being stupid. I felt I had to find a way to be worthy of my parents and other people's love. I had to prove myself.

In hindsight, I was far from stupid, and I know now that I am smart, tenacious and resilient. I quickly figured out that if I looked good, worked hard to look successful and was a 'good girl', I had a chance of proving I was worthy of attention, acceptance and love.

It used to surprise me how often I heard similar underlying, albeit sometimes unconscious, feelings from my clients. They were different stories but very similar feelings: perhaps an older sibling who was super smart that they unconsciously competed with, or being brought up in a family or community that put a lot of emphasis on education/ intelligence/good marks at any cost, or a pervasive message of the importance of hard work over anything else, or judgement around failure or not looking good in the eyes of others. These are all experiences that set up, often unconscious, beliefs and assumptions that can still run our lives.

My relationship with my dad created a huge abandonment wound in me. It's a wound that I now accept will never be fully healed, not by anyone or anything outside of myself. It is a wound that I have learnt to love, nurture and honour when it gets triggered. I am eternally grateful that, with a lot of therapeutic support, it no longer runs my life. But for most of my life, it did. It created a pattern of how I behaved in all my relationships, the type of people I unconsciously chose, and especially my relationships with men, personally and professionally. It set up my attachment dynamic.

My mum was twenty-eight years old when my parents broke up. Since Dad did not financially support us, Mum was left on her own to find work for the first time and support us. She did an amazing job of creating a new life from scratch. Life was not easy for her. Adelaide was an incredibly parochial city at that time, and if you were not in a relationship, it was hard to fit in. For years, I held onto the hope that my parents would get back together. I believed deep down that they really loved each other, and if Dad wasn't so difficult, they would get back together. It felt easier to believe in a fantasy than to accept the truth.

From the time my parents broke up, my mum's career became very important to her. She also struggled with depression at times, like her mother did, and I have too. As a result, I felt like I needed to try to look after her emotionally. While I now understand why her work was important, at the time it had a big impact on me, as did Dad's decision to leave the state. I made up the story that work was more important than I was, that work was more important than being a mum, that making money was more important than family, and I grew up way too early by taking on a lot of responsibilities.

I felt very responsible for looking after my brother, like I was his mum. In a lot of ways, it felt like it was him and me against the world. Every Christmas holiday, my mum would put us on a plane to go to stay with our Auntie Trish and then our grandparents in New Zealand for six weeks.

While those holidays were filled with many wonderful adventures in nature and great times with my cousins and friends, they were also deeply painful times for me. It was a long time away from home. I already felt like I had lost my dad, and now I felt like Mum didn't want us either. Would she even be there when we got back? Even now, the Christmas holidays can bring up great sadness for me and an old sense of loneliness.

My maternal grandfather, Bob, was also incredibly difficult. He had been through World War II as a young man, was old school around manners (Children should be seen and not heard), and was quick to get verbally and physically harsh (not unlike my father). I often felt unsafe in that house, and often late at night, my grandma would find me sitting at the bottom of the stairs, shivering in the cold and crying because I did not want to go to bed. I wanted to sit in front of the fire with her arms wrapped around me.

I loved my nanny, even though she constantly complained about her life. Nanny and Bob were also constantly talking about other people's achievements, wealth and looks; about how much Mr Jones earnt in his job; what promotion the neighbour's son Peter had just got; how successful Evelyn was; how much money Dr Smith was making; how much weight the neighbour down the road had put on — constant comparisons, judgements, criticisms and super racist statements.

My mum had grown up with this, and there is no doubt in my mind that it played a big part in the lens through which she and I started to see the world. It was why I felt so much pressure to perform, look and be perfect, and be successful. It seemed that is how people got love and approval in our family.

Eventually, Mum started a ten-year relationship with another man, and we moved in with him. He was a heavy daily drinker, very emotionally unavailable, and often sexually inappropriate in his comments to and around me as a then-teenage girl. There was not a lot of good, healthy, functional male role modelling or relationship modelling going on in my life. And I remember Mum telling me, from a place of genuine care due to her own bad experiences, 'You should never rely on a man to look after you'. This fuelled my belief that I could not trust or rely on someone else, which can create a lonely way of living. And while my mum worked hard and became very externally successful, she also had many of her own insecurities and patterns from her upbringing, which became mine.

That said, Mum was a trailblazer in her career, and I am very grateful that she taught me how to look after myself and how to set goals and be independent, and she always encouraged me in my career.

Learning to 'earn' my worth

As with many of us, one of the key messages I 'heard' in my family was that I had to earn my worth. Not consciously, not because my parents were trying to be cruel, but because they did not know any better themselves. They were simply doing what they had been taught by their parents.

It is a strong and pervasive message in society. There are many ways we can learn how to earn our worth. Mine were to please others, work hard and be successful, and try to be (or at least look) perfect.

Throughout much of my career, my need to prove myself and earn my worth has had me say 'yes' many times when I really wanted to say 'no'. It has had me stay when I wanted to leave. It has had me burn myself out in the hope of controlling the outcome I wanted. It has had me abandon my needs and my family's needs for those of the organisation. Not only was I not being truthful with others, but I was also often not being honest with myself. To be fair to myself, most of the time I didn't know any of this, as I was living in survival mode.

I was eighteen when I was offered my first real job. I was beyond excited to earn my own money, to feel independent and move forward in life. I had decided to study for a hotel management certificate because it sounded achievable and kind of glamorous. At the end of my training, I was offered an internship at the Adelaide Hyatt Hotel. After my internship, I was offered a role as the local marketing coordinator for another international hotel chain.

I felt like I had really landed on my feet. This was the beginning of a new life for me. I loved and looked up to my boss. She was everything I wanted to be: kind, attractive, successful. I started to dress like her, and outwardly, I looked confident and like I had it all together. Yet, inwardly, I had very little sense of self.

It all seemed to be going so well — until it wasn't. My boss and I were situated in a small building that was separate from the hotel. My desk sat outside her office. One day she had gone out to see a client while I was in the office alone and 'Scott' walked into our building. Scott was a senior member of the hotel's management team. He was incredibly handsome and charismatic — but was also more than ten years older than me and married with a couple of small children. There was no question in anyone's mind that he held all the power.

Scott gave me one of his usual flirty smiles and, after I told him my boss was out, he came around the desk and stood behind my chair. He started rubbing my shoulders and asked me how my job was going.

I froze and had no idea what to do. Part of me loved the special attention — after all, I had wanted to feel special my whole life. Yet, I knew it was wrong. What option did I have? Should I say, 'No, take your hands off me', and potentially lose my job — a job that was giving me a sense of worth for the first time in my life? Should I say 'yes', encourage him and use him to feel safer and more secure in my job, and get back some of the power I felt had just been taken from me? Or do neither and sit in the fear and uncertainty of what might happen next?

Before I had a chance to decide, my boss walked back into the office. I was sitting there frozen, still with a smile on my face, as I had learnt to do many years ago. He removed his hands, but she saw. And I saw that she saw. Later, she asked me if something had been going on. But the way she asked it and the tone she used made me feel like it was somehow my fault. I felt like I was being accused of something that, at the time, I did not even understand.

As I reflect on it now, I am not sure who I felt most upset and disappointed with: the man who felt he owned me because I worked for him, or this woman who I loved and admired who was now looking at me in a way that made me feel grubby.

Looking back as a woman in my fifties now, with great self-compassion, I am probably most disappointed with myself. I stayed quiet and abandoned myself, in the same way I had felt abandoned by every person I had ever loved. This was a pattern that played out in my life repeatedly. Of course, at the time, I felt like I was protecting myself, and perhaps I was. Perhaps I would not have been believed, perhaps I would have lost my job. He was certainly more 'important' than I was. Or at least, that was my assumption — an assumption that has run me all my life and has stopped me from being true to myself, over and over again.

For much of my life, my need to prove myself and earn my worth to feel safe in this world has stopped me from living true to myself. I am deeply grateful that I eventually woke up and began the journey of coming home to myself, the journey of cultivating my worth from the inside out rather than the outside in.

Whatever our histories, many of us have not learnt how to be in a relationship with ourselves that encourages us to learn and grow and believe in ourselves. A relationship that empowers us to step fully into our lives. We often spend so much time looking for the answer outside of ourselves. But before we look outside ourselves, we can begin by looking inside ourselves. We can begin gently and compassionately understanding ourselves and what it looks like for each of us, individually, to live true to ourselves as the foundational ingredient to thriving, at both work and in life.

Conscious reflection

What did 'earning your worth' look like in your family, school, community? Can you remember times you may have abandoned yourself in the hope of being liked, loved, successful?

How trauma shapes us

I have worked with hundreds of clients in the corporate world who have experienced trauma, but who show up as very high-functioning and successful executives. I have noticed that few of my clients have referred to their experiences as trauma. Instead, many of us walk around unconscious of, or in denial of, our trauma, despite it having a significant impact on our relationships with ourselves and others.

In its simplest dictionary definition, trauma is a deeply distressing or disturbing experience. It can be physical, mental, emotional, spiritual or all four. It can include very common events, such as divorce, accidents, the loss of someone close to you, an illness, a difficult birth experience (for you or your child), neglect, witnessing something terrible happening to another, etc. Or it can be more extreme events, such as physical and mental abuse, domestic violence, war, rape, torture, and so on.

In addition to divorce, neglect, and emotional and physical abuse by my father, I also experienced sexual abuse as a child. It is still hard for me to write about, to comprehend that a human being can do this to a child. I know, intellectually, that those who sexually abuse are sick, and statistically, they were likely sexually abused themselves, but that does not make it okay — nothing makes it okay. It is the ultimate betrayal on every level: physically, mentally, emotionally and spiritually. It disconnects us from ourselves and often prevents us from being able to believe there is a power greater than ourselves that is good and loving.

When I was sexually abused, I decided not to tell anyone. Somewhere deep within me, I believed either nobody would believe me, or if they did believe me, they would not stick up for me. That would have been almost as devastating as the abuse itself. So I stayed silent. I have since learnt that this is very common for victims of sexual abuse. We often take on the shame of our abusers. Furthermore, my abuser also threatened my life if I were ever to tell anyone. Through much of my teenage and adult years, I slept with a knife under my bed because of this threat.

The only way I could hold this level of pain was to deny (even to myself) that it had happened. It was not until my early forties, after I had stopped all the things I had previously used to run away from and numb my pain (workaholism, dysfunctional relationships, food, alcohol, sleeping pills, recreational drugs) and had been in therapy for a few years, that I finally felt safe enough to admit what had happened. To say it was painful to start to get in touch with, first the body memories and then eventually the flashbacks, is a major understatement. I had told myself for so long that it was not true as a way of coping. My head can still try to tell me that sometimes, as coming into my truth has, at times, felt annihilating. But as trauma expert Dr Bessel Van Der Kolk's book title so beautifully expresses *The Body Keeps the Score*.

I spent years trying to avoid it. But as I have learnt the hard way, we can't go over, under or around the pain of our past. We can try — and I gave it a damn good try! Ultimately, we can only go through it. This is so important, because if we don't learn to embrace all the parts of ourselves, especially the parts we have tried to silence and disown, we will struggle to heal and feel integrated and whole.

I now vividly remember, at the time of my abuse, leaving my body and watching what was unfolding from the top of the ceiling, fully dissociated from what was happening. Yet, I was also feeling angry at the body I saw on the ground, my body, which was frozen and not fighting. As I went on to deny my truth, I also had no outlet for my hurt and the anger and rage that covered it up. So, I turned it in on myself. I spent years, most of my life, unconsciously blaming and hating myself. Not just for my sexual abuse, but for everything else that had unfolded in my childhood.

Because of the abuse, and the people who didn't protect me from it, my trust in human beings completely shattered. And my trust in myself also shattered because I didn't fight back, and I blamed myself.

But now I see that I *did* fight. While my automatic freeze response kicked in during the act, afterwards, there was something incredibly strong inside me that said, 'This will not beat me. I will show them.'

Remember in the introduction when I stood in the mirror and said, 'You showed them'? I believe that is what I meant. I would never let 'them' beat me.

But spending your life unconsciously fighting for your life, your sense of self and your identity, after having it all annihilated, is absolutely exhausting. It is about just surviving from day-to-day. What I really needed was to learn how to thrive. And when you have a history of self-neglect, self-abuse and caring for others more than you do for yourself, then it is a long journey home to develop deep self-care, to love yourself and thrive.

Although it has felt like it at times, my experience of sexual abuse does not define me. When I occasionally get really triggered, it can still feel like it does. It has, however, had a huge impact on me, especially on my ability to trust myself and others.

This book is not about sexual abuse, and yet it is an important part of my story. This book is about the many different things that can impact our ability to show up fully in the world. To be true to ourselves, to believe in ourselves, to love ourselves, to feel worthy. This book is about finding a path forward to freedom, to thriving despite whatever trauma we've experienced in the past.

But my childhood was normal

Some of you may read my story and resonate with it based on your past experiences. Some of you may have had more traumatic and difficult experiences than mine. And some will read my story and, while perhaps feeling compassion, may say to yourself, 'But my childhood was "normal". Nothing big happened in my childhood.'

Approximately 50 per cent of people have childhoods in which they develop secure attachment to caregivers.[2] People who are securely attached from birth are much more likely to believe in themselves, be true to themselves, love themselves and speak up and assert themselves.

For the other 50 per cent of us, our attachment patterns affect our ability to feel secure in our own innate sense of self, including in the workplace.

I have worked with a lot of women and men who have told me they had happy, 'normal' childhoods. Interestingly, I would have told you that myself fifteen years ago, as denial has been a key survival behaviour for me. Then they start to talk about growing up in South Africa and the level of almost unconscious fear that pervaded their lives. Or having a parent that, while they intellectually knew loved them, was not around much as they had to work a lot. Or having a parent who was emotionally absent or focused on others and therefore unable to be there for them. Or having an alcoholic parent. Or living through a nasty divorce. Or losing a parent when they were young. Or being bullied at school or by siblings. Or their parents had significant money issues and were therefore always anxious. Or they had a parent who couldn't regulate their emotions and struggled with high levels of anger or anxiety and/or depression and unconsciously expected their child to look after them emotionally. Or their parents were often yelling at each other, so it was hard to feel safe in their own home.

I could continue, but you get the point. Many of these examples can create a feeling of sometimes subtle, sometimes not-so-subtle unconscious neglect and abandonment. Or, alternatively, a fear of enmeshment, where it was hard for you as a child to be your own person because you felt you had to look after everybody else emotionally. Some traumatic events are considered big-T trauma, some small-t trauma.

Defining trauma

Big-T trauma is often referred to as events that are life-threatening or severe, and can be associated with post-traumatic stress disorder (PTSD). Examples of these might include, physical and sexual assault, witnessing or experiencing a violent crime, a serious car accident or natural disasters.

Small-t trauma, is typically less severe but is still distressing and can create a sense of fear or helplessness. It can have a profound impact on an individual's self-worth, security and trust. In addition to the examples above, these might also include bullying, emotional abuse, humiliation, the end of a significant relationship or significant life stressors. Small-t traumas, especially when experienced over a prolonged period, can contribute to the development of complex PTSD.

It is important not to be rigid in our assessment of where the line is for big-T and small-t trauma. It is often subjective, and how events impact individuals, and how they respond, can be influenced by their coping mechanisms, personal experiences, the availability of social support, their resilience, and the context of their environment. Importantly, any trauma and difficult events we experience as children and as adults need to be approached with a great deal of sensitivity, validity, compassion and understanding.

I hear many stories of subtle neglect, which research tells us can have greater consequences than abuse,[3] perhaps because abuse is so much more obvious and subtle neglect is quiet and pervasive.

This is not about trying to make our parents wrong or blaming them or others. (Although, in my experience, I needed to go through that before I could come out the other side and feel genuine understanding and compassion for them.) I needed to learn to hold my love and appreciation for what my parents gave me *and* feel my deep hurt, grief and anger at what they were not capable of giving me, and its impact on my life.

This is not about becoming or creating a victim mentality. In most cases, our parents and caregivers and teachers did the best they could. Yet, we were victims in childhood. We were often powerless over what we did and didn't receive back then. We were often powerless over the beliefs, assumptions and patterns that these set up in us and how they shape our lives today. Becoming aware of these is an important part of understanding why we do what we do, and what may be limiting us and stopping us from living an authentic and meaningful life, which is a crucial part of deepening our self-awareness and self-understanding.

When we grow up in even a slightly dysfunctional family, we often take on family roles and then play them out repeatedly in our adult lives, including our work lives.

At some point in my younger years, I decided it was my job to be the responsible one, the 'caretaker', the 'rescuer'. I had lost my dad and was terrified my mum would leave us too, so I did everything possible to look after her emotionally.

I learnt not to rock the boat and to appease people. I subconsciously worried hyper-vigilantly about how everyone around me felt so that I could please, caretake and be perfect. Subconsciously, I was trying to control my environment, to emulate my mum, and ultimately, to enmesh with her and become her so she would love me. Within that, there was no space for me to become my own person. I took on the family roles of the caretaker and the hero, except for two periods in my life when I did the opposite and fully rebelled in my despair, powerlessness and rage. At these times I took on the role of scapegoat, both as a teenager and when my marriage to my son's dad broke up.[4]

Our experiences as children literally lay down neural pathways that create our default thinking and behaving. Feelings that are not able to be felt or expressed in our childhood, such as anger, fear and hurt, literally get stored in our bodies. Our inner work is to uncover, make sense of, feel and heal these feelings, thoughts and the beliefs and assumptions they created in us in order to change the subsequent unhealthy behaviours they create and to learn how to soothe our often overactivated nervous system.

This is about understanding and healing the patterns, roles and beliefs that are set up in our childhoods so we don't keep repeating them, and so we don't hand them down to our own children. As adults, we are not powerless. In fact, it is our responsibility as adults to do the inner work we need to do and not hand these beliefs down to our children. Hurt people hurt people, and continue to hurt themselves.

It is through awareness, understanding, self-compassion and self-acceptance that we can heal our pain and feel liberated and empowered to create a different life for ourselves. To slowly, gently and with great self-compassion change the behaviours that stop us from speaking up, from being our authentic selves, from believing in ourselves, from thriving. If we truly want to be free from the bondage of self, we must do our emotional inner work. That starts with coming into reality around our truth. We cannot recover if we don't know what we are recovering from. We need to know our story to heal it. And to heal it, we need to feel it.

We are not meant to do it alone

I have grown immensely and come a long way in learning to love the person I am, including appreciating the gifts that have come from my upbringing. I am also aware of the limitations my past has created in me, including as a parent, partner, friend, colleague, leader. The very deep and often unconscious hurt and fears that are set up when we don't have a secure background create unconscious patterns in us all. When unseen and unhealed, they continue to harm us and those around us.

I also have come to understand that the patterns that were created in our childhood relationships can only be healed in relationships. I deeply believe that we cannot heal ourselves on our own. And in my experience, our healing relationships must be very secure. Personally, the only place I have found that is in therapy.

When our trust is broken in our childhood experiences, whether that be obviously or subtly, it needs to be rebuilt within a relationship. I spent every week (for the first couple of years, twice a week) in therapy with a somatic psychotherapist named Robyn for almost nine years. Robyn loved me back to life. She reparented me in a way a child needs to be parented: with no judgement, no criticism and no expectations. She was present to and encouraging of my feelings. She mirrored back my goodness. She role modelled good boundaries. She supported me to feel the depth of the fear, grief, hurt and pain that has been held

21

in my body all these years. She supported me to find a sense of self and to start to embody that. She taught me how to reparent myself, to soothe myself, to become my own best friend.

Our body never forgets. It still holds all the feeling memories we were not able to have and hold as children. Ultimately, we can't heal without doing our emotional inner work. While coming to understand my story has been important for me, as I was in a lot of denial about it when I first started, I have seen myself and many others get caught in this never-ending dialogue of our story. We can use this to stay in our heads, to just find another way to escape the difficult feelings we hold in our bodies. I have seen within myself, repeatedly, that under my blame, shame and judgement, sits my anger. Under my anger sits my fear. Under my fear sits my hurt. And almost every behaviour is about protecting me from feeling hurt again and from feeling the depth of the hurt that is stored deep within me. But this is a lonely and unfulfilling way to live.

Psychotherapy has been my greatest gift of self-love. Even when I have struggled financially, it has been the one thing I have never stopped. Somewhere deep inside, my soul knew that I could not do this alone. It is the one gift I have consistently chosen to give myself. The gift of ongoing self-compassion, self-awareness and growth.

I still go to therapy now. I have done group therapy, couples' therapy and individual therapy. Robyn retired and I have been in therapy with a contemporary relational psychoanalyst for the last five years. This has been harder. This is where I have had to come face-to-face with all those parts of me that I never wanted to see. This has been the deeper shadow work — where I get to see all the unconscious patterns that are running and limiting my relationships and life. I don't go to therapy because I feel broken or need to fix myself. I go to therapy because I am humble enough to know I need support. Learning to be in a relationship with myself and others is a lifelong journey, and many of us were never taught how to navigate it. I go to therapy to rewire my neural pathways. To create a new lens through which I see and experience life now. To rewire the relationship template that was laid down in my childhood. To learn how to be in a loving, interdependent relationship with myself and others.

I can sit in my pain on my own quite easily now. Where the deep healing and rewiring happens is when I can sit with someone who can hold the depth of my grief, anger, shame and terror and I can learn to find the 'edge'. This is where I can feel the depths of the hurt without it consuming me, and at the same time, let in my own self-compassion and the loving compassion and presence of the person I am with. In contemporary relational psychoanalysis, I get to fully and safely explore that. To explore my edges, my shadow, my blind spots, my relationship with myself and others. I get to practice doing it differently in therapy, which allows me to show up more fully in my everyday life.

When we first begin, it can take years to develop trust with a therapist that allows us to go to the depths that we need to go to heal. And, I believe, the therapist needs to have been there themselves. The first question I always ask a therapist is how much therapy have they done themselves? Are they still doing therapy or having supervision? I would not see a therapist who had not done many years of their own healing work. It is a deeply humbling, confronting and richly rewarding process.

For me, this has been the journey of learning to accept and love my flaws. To see my strengths and all that I bring to the world, just as I am. To learn how to be a kind and loving parent to myself. To learn how to lead my own life: one that is true to myself. To step into my authentic inner power. This has been the journey to find my worth, the journey to learn to live and work in a new way and, as a result, I have had the gift of working with many hundreds of women in our Authentic Woman Leadership Program as we have guided them on a similar journey and watched them find themselves, and step into their power and create the leadership and life they desire, all of which we are going to explore together.

CHAPTER 2

Learning to get our needs met

In my personal experience, and from working with many hundreds of executive women and men, overwork often comes from a place of unworthiness, of needing to constantly be liked, striving to prove ourselves, or needing to be seen as the expert. It comes from trying to get our core needs met from the outside in, from our work. As this chapter unfolds, we will peel back the many layers, masks and beliefs that drive our limiting reactive behaviours in a desire to feel loved, accepted, wanted and important. We will reflect on why we may work so hard and what needs we are trying to meet.

It is so easy to get stuck in old ways and old beliefs, including how each gender should behave. It is also easy to get stuck in old identities, often unconscious of our own biases, against women, against men, against ourselves. Letting go of old behaviours and negative thoughts by becoming aware of who we are at the core is a slow process. It is key to finding a new relationship with ourselves and the world.

As we peel back these layers and are confronted with the truth about ourselves, we begin to understand that we were simply trying to get some very human needs met. As we apply great compassion to ourselves we see we wanted to feel safe, valued, worthy and loved. And we can feel relief knowing we are not alone in any of these needs, or in the misguided ways we go about trying to get those needs met.

Why are we working so hard?

There are some obvious and simple answers to this question. We have mortgages to pay, food to put on our families' plates, a lifestyle we want to enjoy, a desire to feel valued. We may have career dreams and ambitions and want to be successful in what we do. Yet, as I worked with more and more clients, I realised that I was not alone in feeling quite exhausted from working too hard and trying too hard: trying too hard to be liked, to be the best at everything I did, or to be the smartest person in the room. So many of us are exhausted from looking outside of ourselves for external validation, and yet often never feel very satisfied with ourselves or our work and lives. At some point, I realised this dissatisfaction was my soul calling me to a new way of being in the world.

One example of seeking external validation in my own life was how I handled pregnancy and childbirth. I loved being pregnant. Now, twenty-two years later, I still have the diary planner where I used to mark off when I was ovulating and suggest to my then husband, Troy, that it would be a good date to 'try'. As usual, I left nothing to chance! We were lucky and got pregnant quickly and were both incredibly happy about it. I luxuriated in being pregnant. I used to wander around our home, gently rubbing my huge belly and singing and talking to the baby within. I was in awe of my body and its ability to hold this incredible gift that was growing inside of me.

I vividly remember feeling beautiful — a strong feminine, womanly beauty — perhaps for the first time in my life. It came from a strong sense that this is what I was put on this Earth to do and the awe that my body was doing it all for me. The fact that I was able to bring a baby into this world felt miraculous to me.

At this same time, Troy and I decided we would build a house. In hindsight, it was probably not a great idea. Everything that could go wrong, did. It probably didn't help that we both had very demanding jobs, me running a large team in a wealth management company and

Troy taking on a new senior role in a global investment bank. We found a little rental property near where we were building and set up a temporary home.

Neither of us saw the level of stress that was building. We had taken on too much and were struggling to handle it. Troy was beyond stressed in his all-consuming new senior role, often coming home from work after midnight. He was really struggling with the pressure he was under. Eventually, together, we decided the best thing for him to do would be to leave investment banking. It wasn't worth the toll it was having on his mental health and wellbeing. We decided that he would be a stay-at-home dad for a while. Although I wanted to and did support him in this decision, as a first-time mum and in late-stage pregnancy, I felt extremely vulnerable. I wanted to be a mum more than anything, but now I felt I needed to take on the responsibility of looking after us financially as well.

My labour was traumatic for me. It lasted twenty-two hours, and I ended up having an emergency caesarean. As we headed into the operating room, I was extremely exhausted and scared, and I remember the doctors and nurses laughing and making light of something. It brought up all my past trauma as I remembered how scared, alone and out of control I felt in that hospital as a little girl. My nervous system was in overdrive: my fight, flight and freeze response had been fully activated.

I imagine this was the beginning of the postnatal depression I went on to experience. As I reflect on it now, I don't even know if it was postnatal depression or if my postnatal symptoms were a trauma response to all that had unfolded in the lead up to and during my son's birth. I wish with all my heart that my beautiful son Hugo could have arrived in the world at a time I when I felt supported, peaceful, calm and connected to him. But, instead, I was struggling from his first breath. Our children's tiny little nervous systems get regulated by us, their parents. Given that mine was completely dysregulated, it was no surprise that Hugo struggled to feed, settle and sleep for the first nine months of his life.

Within my postnatal depression, I could still feel my love for Hugo, but it often felt clouded by fog under which was a deep self-loathing. Life felt dark and hard, and I felt totally out of my depth, out of control, and very disconnected from myself, my life and my family. I didn't know how to make Hugo or Troy happy. I felt like I couldn't do anything right as I struggled to breastfeed, to soothe Hugo, to sleep, to be a 'good' wife.

I was overwhelmed. I believed I was a failure as a mother, and I told myself they didn't really need or want me. I now know that the desire to feel needed and appreciated is strong in me, but only when I have some kind of control over those needs and know how to meet them.

Conscious reflection

I notice that while writing this story, over twenty-two years later, it still brings up much shame, pain, grief and regret for me. I notice my reluctance to pause and invite you to reflect on your own experience in case it does the same for you. However, I have learnt repeatedly, that it is only through being with ourselves and honouring our feelings through our struggles that we find peace. So, I encourage you to gently stop and reflect on your own experience of work, birth and mothering. Or for those who were not able to, or chose not to, be a mother, what does this bring up for you? What may still need some loving attention within you?

To regain my sense of self-worth, I turned back to my work. Two days after I got out of the hospital, my boss called to ask for my help. Thank god! Someone needed me and in a way in which I knew I could deliver and feel valued. Within three months I was back at work full-time, albeit with flexible hours. Going back to work at this time is one of the biggest regrets of my life. Work will always be there. The first few years of a child's life are precious and fleeting. I remember going into the office toilets each day with a breast pump, relieving my aching breasts and expressing milk as tears rolled down my cheeks. I was so deeply sad and scared, and my hormones were out of control. I told myself I was doing this for the money because I felt responsible for looking after my family financially at this time, and there is some truth in that was a big pressure for me. But nothing in life is ever just about the money. It's what the money represents: in my case, at the core, it is always about safety, which often looks like control/power, and validation. At work, I felt important, valued and needed, and I knew what to do. Plus, I was terrified of losing my job, so saying 'no' didn't really feel like an option. Looking back, deep down I subconsciously resented Troy for being at home with our son, while at the same time I felt pretty sure that was the best option for Hugo, as I felt like such a failure as a mum. My dream of motherhood had been shattered and I was heartbroken. In hindsight, this also marked the beginning of the end of our marriage, which very sadly happened fourteen months later.

Each day, I put on my power suit, drove into work and solved problems. I did whatever anyone needed me to do, and I tried to do it perfectly. I loved my job, loved the people I worked with, loved the opportunities I was given and the sense of accomplishment that came with it. But underneath all of that, I was also running away from myself and using work to numb out all my fears and insecurities. Once again, I used work to justify my existence and try to prove my worth and value in this world.

Conscious reflection

Pause for a moment and ask yourself, *Why am I working or trying so hard?* Be completely honest with yourself. Dig deeper than the surface responses of practical physical needs. What are the subconscious forces that make you so driven? What are you truly wanting most of all?

Three unconscious strategies for getting our needs met

How we think, what we feel and how we make meaning of things determine how we act in the world. By the time we start exhibiting certain behaviours, many things have happened. We have had certain thoughts and feelings, and probably placed meaning on a situation through our own perspective, which is usually based on old and often limiting beliefs and assumptions. This perspective of ours, how we interpret the world, can be influenced by many things, including, as we have previously explored, our upbringing as children.

Leadership Circle framework

I have done a lot of work with a company called Leadership Circle,[5] which uses Kegan's Adult Stages of Development framework as a key overlay. When I start working with a new client, we begin by undertaking the Leadership Circle Profile 360° Assessment to gain clarity on how we are perceived to be showing up in the workplace by others and ourselves. Part of the assessment provides insights into whether we are operating from a socialised or self-authoring state of mind, as well as our core coping strategies as human beings. Based on the work of psychoanalyst Karen Horny, the Leadership Circle framework groups together three reactive patterns that can drive our behaviours. These behaviours ultimately come from our internal assumptions and beliefs set up in our childhood.

In its simplest form, we adopt certain strategies as children to get our needs met and to feel loved, safe, secure and worthwhile. These strategies are in response to the type of environment we grew up in, and they become patterns for us in later life.

The first is a *complying tendency*. As kids, we are hardwired to want to be close to our caregivers. So we often start (unconsciously) moving toward them by complying. That is, we do what we think they want us to do.

The second is a *controlling tendency*. If the first strategy of complying doesn't work for us, and we don't get the love and attention we are hardwired to want to receive, we may then go the other way, again quite unconsciously. We will move against people and the world to try to control our environment and those around us.

The third tendency is a *protecting tendency*. If neither of the first two strategies feel safe or work, we may learn to move away from others, especially emotionally. We may withdraw and distance ourselves or over-intellectualise as a way of protecting ourselves from feeling vulnerable.

All three of these tendencies are quite natural reactive strategies to the difficulties life threw at us as children. We needed to stay safe and to feel loved, and as we practise them over and over again, they become natural, hardwired, reactive patterns within us as adults. Now, as adults, we may move between all three tendencies, depending on the situation, or we typically have a favourite we use more often. When we are in these patterns, we are reacting from fear and anxiety, rather than responding openly to life from a place of purpose and passion. We are looking outside of ourselves for our sense of self and identity, rather than coming from a calm and connected place within us.

There are wonderful gifts and strengths that come out of each of these patterns. And as with all gifts, if they are overplayed or overused, they can become our greatest limitations and strongly impede our ability for authentic expression, healthy relations, self-empowerment and sustainable success.

Let's explore all three strategies in a little more depth. As I go through the three tendencies below, I encourage you to reflect, with great self-compassion, as to which resonates with you, particularly in times of stress.

Complying tendency: Moving toward

The complying tendency can turn us into chronic people pleasers and social chameleons, trying to be whatever we think other people or circumstances require for us to be liked and to fit in.

When we are overly activated in this complying tendency, we may show up to others as being conservative; looking to please them and not speaking up for ourselves; being very focused on belonging, whatever the cost; perhaps behaving passively, always letting others take the lead; or being indecisive, not being able to make decisions ourselves. In this case, our safety and self-worth tend to come from winning approval from others, by trying to live within what we think others expect from us. This comes from feeling an internal insecurity, of not feeling worthy or loved, fear of rejection, not feeling needed, feeling alone and unprotected.

When we develop a strong sense of our inner self-worth and learn to give ourselves approval, the gift this tendency brings is our natural ability to be of real service to others. The positive expression of this tendency is offering love and support from an unconditional place, a genuine ability to respond to the needs of others, an intuitive ability to be there for people, being loyal and having strong interpersonal skills.

However, when this tendency is out of balance, we can start to become aware of when our strengths are now being overplayed, and we are driven from a fear of not being liked. It often shows up as us not meeting our own needs. Or we feel like the victim, always blaming others, being overly needy because we have never learnt how to meet our own needs. From this place, we disempower ourselves or give up our power to others. We don't set boundaries, we avoid conflict. We may find ourselves trying too hard to please or rescue others or being passive and not taking responsibility for our part in creating our vision for our lives. We may not hold the boundaries we need to empower ourselves, or find ourselves not holding others accountable or speaking up about what is important to us. We abandon ourselves in the hope of others liking and valuing us, while not really valuing ourselves within that.

This used to be my go-to pattern to try to get people to like or love me. I can still be this way when I am feeling particularly fearful. In these instances, I still say 'yes' even when I want to say 'no'. I take on more than I have the capacity to do. I struggle to get clear on my own needs and wants. I don't speak up, and instead, end up feeling resentful of others. Or, if I do speak up, it can come across as passive aggressive, where I make others wrong rather than clearly asking for what I need. I sit and listen to people for hours, even if I am not interested or really need to be doing something else. I didn't have a deep sense of my own self-worth, and what was okay and not okay for me. And I couldn't stand the anxiety that came up when I went against what someone else wanted.

When we are over-activated in our complying tendency

Over the years, I have worked with literally hundreds of women and men who struggle with this tendency. I recently worked with an executive named Kate, and as with all my clients, I felt such deep compassion for and resonance with her struggle. She has a senior customer-facing role in a large global company and seems like she has a super-successful career. However, when I started working with her, she was exhausted. Exhausted from trying to please everybody around her: her boss, her staff, her clients, her internal stakeholders and her family. She did a great job. People really liked her and thought she was wonderful and continuously came to her to ask her to help them with things. She felt valued, needed and liked.

As we slowly unpacked it all, deep down she felt terrified that if she stopped saying 'yes', she would lose her value and not be liked. Her sense of self and value were intrinsically linked to people liking her and seeing her as the person who would always help and would always be there for them. She was the same at home, with her family members and her husband — always putting aside her needs for theirs. There was always a very legitimate reason why their needs were more important than hers. If her husband asked her what she wanted for dinner, her answer was, 'Whatever you want'. If her friends asked where she would like to go on holidays, she would always answer, 'Where do you want to go?'

Kate had grown up with a mum who suffered from depression, and Kate had spent her childhood trying to take care of her. Trying to make her happy, trying to work out what she might need and give it to her before she got upset or depressed. Once that happened, there would be no time or attention for Kate. She had never been taught to find and honour her own boundaries and needs. Nobody was ever there for her.

As we explored further, she realised she didn't want to feel that ever again, so she did everything she could not to feel those old feelings. Quite understandably, as a child, she started living her life based on the assumption that her value came from helping others. To do this, she had to ignore her own needs, her own boundaries, her own inner voice. She perfected this complying tendency as a way of hoping to get her needs met. But now, as an adult, it was exhausting and was stopping her from creating the life she wanted.

I have sat in this internal wounding, the feeling of the deep unworthiness that drives this tendency and behaviours within us. It is a deeply painful wound in me. How can we believe and trust that we are lovable as we are, not for what we do for others, when we were never taught that as a child?

Conscious practice

Who will you be if nobody likes you? You will be alone. You may not survive. And as children, we would not have survived. How do we sit with our own fear of abandonment or rejection?

We do it slowly, gently. We learn how to not abandon ourselves. We teach ourselves, by the way we treat ourselves and how we allow others to treat us, that we are worthy of love as we are. We learn to like ourselves and validate ourselves rather than looking outside of ourselves for this. We practice respecting ourselves first. We practise finding our voice, trusting ourselves, setting boundaries, honouring our needs and being self-compassionate with the anxiety this brings up within us when we practice new behaviours.

If you relate to this complying tendency, begin by gently becoming aware of when you start to lose yourself in the needs, demands and expectations of others, perhaps looking to others to make decisions for you, or to direct your thinking and actions, or doing and saying things so they will like you.

When you notice this:

- ◆ Pause and accept, perhaps saying to yourself: 'I notice I am feeling lost and unsure of myself right now, and that is okay.'

- ◆ Take three deep breaths into your belly.

- ◆ Feel your feet firmly planted on the ground. Rest your shoulders back and down. Feel your spine running down your back.

◆ Notice what you are feeling and name it, for example, 'I am feeling anxious'.

◆ Grab your journal and pen and answer the questions: 'What's at risk if I say something that others don't agree with? What do I think is the best thing to do right now? What is my opinion/ decision/choice/need?'

◆ Empower yourself by sharing it with others. It doesn't matter whether they agree or disagree: success is you sharing your clear request or opinion.

◆ Hold yourself gently if it feels uncomfortable, and reassure yourself that your intention is to grow and learn.

This is about slowing down and spending time getting clear on what we think and what we need, while becoming more aware of when our often-compulsive need to be liked or overplayed relationship strengths may be running us. This is the practice of taking back our power and building more trust in our own capabilities and opinions and then sharing these with others.

Controlling tendency: Moving against

When we are overly activated in the controlling tendency, we may show up to others as being a perfectionist; being overly driven; being aggressively ambitious at the cost of others; and/or being autocratic, always telling people what to do. Here, our safety and self-worth are dependent on being in control, having a sense of power and achieving. This comes from our need to establish self-worth from outside ourselves, from our achievements.

When we have developed a strong sense of our inner self-worth, the positive gifts this tendency brings includes a focus on continuous improvement, high standards, getting into action and creating results.

However, when this tendency is out of balance and is running us rather than us managing it, it's driven by anxiety, our fear of failure and the need to control. In this, we can start to become aware of when our strengths are now being overplayed. This often leads to fault-finding, a compulsive drive to achieve, being demanding and forceful, and winning at any cost. We may find ourselves trying to have power over others, trying to force our own extremely high expectations onto others, trying to control others to avoid our own fear of failure or feeling disappointed. We often avoid letting go of control or trusting others, constantly trying to prove ourselves, often at the expense of others. We can ignore other people's boundaries and disempower them with these behaviours and the energy we bring into the room.

I also know this one well. In fact, as I learnt to stop complying, I found I started to unconsciously try to control my environment and myself even more, as a way of not feeling the anxiety I was having from no longer pleasing everyone. If I just 'got it right', if I was just 'perfect', if I just 'achieved' everything I needed to, then maybe I could feel secure, loved and accept myself, and hopefully others would too. I was still looking for approval outside of myself, looking to prove my worth through my success. 'I will show them.'

I am still not sure who 'them' was, maybe my parents, maybe my grandparents, and probably anyone I thought was judging me as being worthless or a failure, which of course, in hindsight, included myself. If I could control how you saw me, then I could feel safe in a world that felt unsafe for me.

I started my career in sales. The combination of me wanting to please everyone, being super driven, and wanting to do everything perfectly made me a very successful salesperson. And as we may intuitively imagine, the combination of wanting to please, be perfect and be driven is the number one recipe for burnout! This is the tendency my workaholism was born out of. Rather than trying to move toward people to get them to like me, I subtly moved against people to try to control everything around me, so I could feel safe and secure and in control of my life and how people saw me. I have seen this tendency literally run many of my clients' lives, as it did mine.

When we are over-activated in our controlling tendency

Janet is a senior leader I have worked with for many years. She is married, has four children and works with several charities in her spare time. After I got to know her well, I realised she cared deeply about her team, clients and her organisation. But when I first met her, nobody knew this. She was so super driven. Her eye was always on achieving the results the business needed, at what others perceived as being at the cost of her team and her family. She had extremely high expectations of herself and of everyone around her. Nobody dared make a mistake. In meetings she would talk quickly, take up a lot of the space and have strong opinions. Her energy came across as intense, demanding, and at times, aggressive, as she was always in a hurry to move on to the next task. Failure was not an option for Janet, and this drove her.

Nobody really got a chance to get to know her. Her way of showing she cared was by making sure the team achieved the results they needed to be successful. She often micro-managed people's roles so they would understand where they were going wrong. But nobody felt cared for by her; they thought she only cared about the results. People generally found her intimidating and unapproachable, as it always felt like she was in a rush and not interested in listening to their point of view.

As we explored what was going on within her, Janet came to gently understand the internal anxiety that was driving her desperate need to feel in control and to not fail at any cost.

Janet's parents emigrated from Europe with nothing. They literally arrived in Australia with only the clothes on their backs, speaking very little English, wanting to start a new life and yet not sure how they were going to survive. Her parents both worked two jobs to try to make ends meet and create a life for their kids. When Janet and her brother came along, there was very little time for them. Janet soon learnt that to survive in this world, she needed to work super hard.

This is how her parents showed they cared, and they regularly told her that they were working 'to give her a better life'.

At school she felt different from the other white Anglo-Saxon kids and believed if she worked hard at school and got good marks, then she would be able to prove she was as good as them. She never again wanted to be as poor as she was as a child. She needed to make her parents proud, so all their hard work did not go to waste. She felt responsible for their happiness, and she needed to prove that she fit in in this country. To do this, she needed to take control of everything and everyone around her and be successful.

Underneath, Janet did not want to feel the anxiety and loneliness that drove her perfectionism and super high standards. Her sense of worth came from being seen by others as successful, perfect and in control because, as a child, she and her parents had felt so out of control. It was heartbreaking for Janet when she started to see the impact of her behaviour on others, when she realised that both her team and her family often did not feel cared for by her. This awareness was the beginning of a great change in her. She realised she needed to learn to slow down, manage her anxiety, and open and allow others to see how much she cared. Through our coaching and by consciously practising showing up more authentically and managing her reactive tendencies, when she undertook another 360° feedback process twelve months later, her feedback had transformed, and she was seen as a leader who not only empowered the team to achieve the necessary results, but who cared.

We are all perfectly imperfect

I am not exaggerating when I say I was shocked to realise that, as a human being, I was not meant to be perfect. We are not meant to get everything right. We are not meant to know how to do everything before we have done it. Our worth, our safety and our security are not dependent on what we do or don't achieve or how we do or don't look to others. We are worthy of love and acceptance for simply being who we are. True safety and security come from within us, from a deep inner *knowing* that we will be okay no matter what happens.

I can still struggle to sit in the fear of failure and unworthiness that drives this tendency and behaviour. It is deeply uncomfortable to sit in financial fear, fear of losing my job or my business, fear of being seen as a failure, and the depth of how unsafe I would feel without the security these things bring me. My entire sense of safety came from what money represents to me: control. The vulnerability that sits under the idea of not being able to care for myself is excruciating, as I don't believe for a moment that anyone else ever will.

Conscious practice

How can we help our nervous systems believe and trust that failure is a part of life, that there is nothing to prove, that we are lovable as we are, not for what we achieve or accomplish or accrue, when we were never taught that as a child?

We do it slowly, gently. We slow down. *Oh my god, that is hard.* We set boundaries around work. We take the focus off what other people are and aren't doing and bring the focus back to ourselves. We learn to soothe our nervous system when it gets activated. We trust in the goodness of life and our capabilities without having to prove them to others. We create space in our life for things that are not accomplishments and do things purely for joy — this can literally feel like letting go of an addiction. We risk trusting others to live their own lives and do things their way. We teach ourselves, by the way we treat ourselves and how we allow others to treat us, that we are worthy simply as we are.

If you relate to this controlling tendency:

◆ Begin by creating space to slow down regularly throughout your day: perhaps put a reminder in your phone or calendar between every meeting.

◆ Take a one-minute conscious pause, breathing deeply into your belly. Notice if you are in overdrive and where you are holding that in your body. Name it.

(continued)

- If your anxiety is high, accept and acknowledge it and allow some movement in your body. Perhaps go for a walk around the block or even do some star jumps to help move and release your energy, which will also help your thinking patterns to shift.

- Notice if you are overly focused on the task and goals and forgetting about the people around you and their needs and opinions. If so, sit back in your chair, hold yourself back and allow more space for others. Talk less. Listen more. With compassion, notice the compulsion in you to jump in and take over and practise doing the opposite.

Rather than control running us, this is the practice of learning to consciously manage our often compulsive need to control as it arrives in us. Instead, we slow down and invite others in, expand our focus and create collective results by tapping into the many gifts of this tendency.

Protecting tendency: Moving away

When we are overly activated in the protecting tendency, we may show up to others as being arrogant, critical, distant, withdrawn or aloof. We often feel a deep lack of belief in ourselves, which we may or may not be aware of. We come from a place of feeling inferior or superior. Our safety and self-worth are dependent on a variety of external behaviours, such as being right, being overly intellectual, presenting as unemotional, always being rational or being cynical.

When we have developed a strong sense of our inner self-worth, the gifts of this tendency include remaining detached and observant; a special ability to take a wider perspective; and caring deeply for a few people or causes.

However, when this tendency is out of balance, it is often driven by a compulsive need to move away from others; to avoid staying in connection with, listening to and understanding others; putting up walls rather than boundaries; and not fully participating in the relationships we really need to. This is ultimately due to our own fear of vulnerability. When we are highly activated in our protecting tendency, we may find ourselves withholding power from others with behaviours that come from a place of superiority over others. This could include withholding important information or withdrawing and distancing ourselves from others through fear of being overwhelmed by other people's needs and expectations.

I relate to this one too. It's my final go-to when the other two tendencies don't work. For those who relate to this tendency, it is often the hardest to shift for that reason. As I stopped complying and I practised letting go of control of others and myself, I found I wanted to protect myself more. I wanted to withdraw, distance myself and observe life from the sidelines a little more, or sometimes act intellectually superior and judgemental.

This tendency can also show up as being very critical, of myself and others, as a way of protecting myself from feeling my own vulnerability. If I find all of the faults in me and in you, then there can be no surprise disappointments. It is not okay for you to disappoint me and it is not okay for me to disappoint you, so we had better get it right. It was a surprise for me to learn that criticism and judgement of others, and of myself, is just another form of control, a way of trying to feel superior to others. And under that superiority are our own fears and insecurities.

Writing this book goes against every pattern I have! It feels so incredibly vulnerable. What if I get something wrong? What if I receive criticism? My heart literally aches as I feel into the wound that sits under this tendency, as that is precisely what we are trying to protect: our deep insecurities, our hurts, our many disappointments, our grief, our aching hearts. It is too hard to feel it, so we lock it away behind reason and logic, being a know-it-all, being short and prickly, being critical and distancing ourselves from our feelings and from others.

Instead, I gently breathe into this protecting part of me and accept I will likely get something wrong—how can I not? That is okay, because it creates an opportunity for authentic dialogue, and I will learn something new and grow and evolve. I get to include and transcend any 'wrongness'.

When we are over-activated in our protecting tendency

My precious client Gabriella managed much of her work and life from this protecting tendency. She is also a very successful executive who, when she was at her best, always delivered, and people often had a great deal of respect for her ideas and opinion. She always did what she said she was going to do and was a deep thinker. The problem arose the moment she felt threatened, for example, if someone was not listening to her or suggested she may not be right. Her value, her worth, was based on what she knew, on her being right.

Although she ran a sizable team, she also tended to work on her own a lot, feeling like she was the only one who could work things out. She would work it all out and then come to the team with the solution. It was very hard for her to let others help. When she was feeling particularly insecure, she would often become arrogant and belligerent, and name-drop or provide evidence of how important she was. People experienced her as very aloof, distant and hard to get to know. People respected her opinion, but they did not feel motivated to work for her or with her, and her behaviour often triggered deep insecurities in others. They found her intellectually intimidating, so they did not offer their views or perspectives, as they found that often when they did, she would vehemently debate their ideas or shut them down. She loved a good debate but did not realise how antagonising, harsh, critical and often disrespectful she was to others' ideas, although this was not her intention.

While her behaviours showed up differently to Janet's, Gabriella also cared about people and the business she was running. But she often did not allow herself to feel this care, and definitely did not think to show this care to the people she worked with. She felt people should just know she cares because she looked after them in other ways, like with promotions and pay rises. She felt it was important for her to stay emotionally distant from others but had not previously recognised this because she unconsciously wanted to stay distant to her own emotions. Dealing with people often felt like hard work, as she didn't know how to meet their needs, and their needs often felt never-ending to her.

Distance, criticism and, at times, arrogance were her form of boundaries. In truth, they were walls not boundaries, but she did not know how to be close to people and not feel swamped by their needs and, unconsciously, her own emotions. Just as she was mostly unaware of and ignored her own needs, she didn't know how to hold boundaries around others, so she distanced herself instead.

The way Gabriella explained it to me, she grew up 'on the wrong side of the tracks'. Her parents were very absent, both physically and emotionally. Her father could be violent and raged a lot, particularly when she 'got things wrong'. Her mother was often unwell and very needy. There was no soft safe place to turn to, so she turned to herself. At school, she found she was quite smart, and she did not need to work particularly hard to get good grades. Although she was preoccupied with surviving a rough home life, she knew she could count on her intellect. The safest place for her was in her head, making sure she got things right, working things out before they happened. When she was in her head, she didn't have to feel her fear, pain and loneliness. Her identity became tied to being right, and she shut herself off from what would have been overwhelming emotions for her to feel as a young girl.

The hardest part of this tendency is that, when we are in it, we are often numb to our own needs for connection, care and relationships. We have such high expectations of our intellectual selves, and we expect the same from others. At the core, Gabriela's fear of vulnerability, of feeling stupid, hurt and, ultimately, her deep unacknowledged grief made it very hard to act any other way. She felt she needed to protect herself or she might have to feel the emotional devastation of her upbringing. But, when we numb our grief, we also numb our ability to feel true joy and connection with ourselves and others.

Conscious practice

As with all the tendencies, stepping out of our protective tendency is very uncomfortable. This will likely be a lifelong practice for all of us who know this tendency. How do we do this?

By allowing ourselves to be more vulnerable, feeling our vulnerability, and learning to trust and rely on others. We allow ourselves to feel and show our care for others, while also holding our boundaries and not allowing others' needs to overwhelm us. We allow ourselves to not know everything, to get things wrong, to allow others to be right. We create space for non-thinking and learn to live less in our heads and more connected with our bodies, living from a place of lightness and fun. We connect with our feelings, desires and fears. We learn to let go, just a little, and gently come into our heart, even when it aches.

If you resonate with this tendency:

◆ Begin by allowing yourself not to be the expert in the room.

◆ Practice sitting in a group and genuinely listening to others' views and opinions and paraphrasing them back, so they feel you have really understood what they are saying.

◆ Look for opportunities to invite other people to make decisions, showing your respect for their thoughts and opinions. It doesn't mean you can't ask questions and coach them to find the best solution, but hold yourself back from making them wrong and you right—let them learn and grow from their own mistakes if necessary.

◆ Learn to say 'sorry'. There is nothing more powerful for people to hear us say than, 'I am sorry and I can really see the impact my behaviour had on you'.

◆ This is the practice of vulnerability and staying engaged in relationships with the people around us. Of learning to manage our protecting tendency rather than it running us, allowing us to tap into the gifts of our intellect and wisdom, without shutting others down and out.

The root of all three tendencies

All three tendencies, when highly activated, come from a place of insecurity within us, from a place of believing we need to be a certain way or a certain person to get love, respect, success and safety in this world. Within this, our focus is on the outside in — on what people think of us — rather than the inside out where we are true to ourselves.

When we're coming from the inside out, we're coming from a place of knowing ourselves and our strengths, caring and respecting ourselves, believing in ourselves and our purpose and vision. We also see our foibles and that we are imperfect beings, but at the core, we know we are enough exactly as we are. We have nothing to prove, nobody to please, nothing more we need to know or do. We learn how to step into our own inner power and how to empower others.

While I have found myself moving through all three patterns, and I can still move in and out of them depending on the situation I am in. You may only resonate with one or two patterns. I have found it interesting how, often when we change, we move out of one unhelpful pattern into another equally unhelpful one to compensate! Hence the importance of our ongoing compassionate self-awareness journey, being our own best friend as we become aware of beliefs that no longer serve us.

These patterns of behaving stop us from feeling the fear, anxiety and vulnerability that would come up if we weren't using them. So, it makes sense that we keep doing this as our brains are psychologically hardwired to avoid these feelings. Changing our responses and behaviours is not easy. It is a practice and one that, in my experience, gets easier the kinder and gentler we are with ourselves.

Awareness. Acceptance. Action. Afterburn.

To change these patterns and behaviours, ultimately, we need to build our inner self-worth, self-belief and self-trust. We learn to focus inwards rather than looking outward as we become our own supportive inner coach.

Awareness

It starts with awareness. Awareness of the vision and values we hold for ourselves and our lives, and becoming aware of our reactive patterns and how they may be limiting us. By witnessing them within ourselves, and importantly, what triggers them within us, we can begin a gentle practice to deepen our awareness, build our capacity to hold our triggers and regulate our nervous system, rather than react to a situation or person.

In this way, we become more aware of the physical sensations, the emotions, the self-talk, the behaviours and the underlying beliefs and assumptions that are at play when we are in our reactive tendencies. While our core triggers will likely always be with us, as we do our inner emotional work, and build our capacity to manage our stress, we are able to come back to ourselves much more quickly and respond with a level of emotional maturity that supports how we want to show up in our relationships and lives.

In this first stage, it is all about becoming aware when we are triggered. We may not be able to do anything different initially other than perhaps notice that we are feeling triggered; however, as our awareness grows, we will slowly build the capacity to regulate our nervous system and be able to respond differently.

Conscious practice

When we notice we are triggered, we can take the following steps:

1. Take three deep breaths into your belly.

2. Bring attention to your body and notice what is going on internally. What sensations can you feel? Where do you notice these sensations? Perhaps your heart is beating fast, or there is tension in your throat or chest, or your face feels hot. Here we are building the capacity to notice we are triggered, notice the

sensations in our body, and start to allow ourselves to feel the underlying feelings.

3. Notice and name what you are feeling and soothe these underlying emotions by talking kindly to yourself, inviting and acknowledging the sensations and emotions without over-identifying with them, and letting yourself know you will be okay. 'I notice I'm feeling scared/anxious/angry/hurt right now, and that is okay.'

4. This may mean stepping away from the situation you are in, going for a walk, jumping up and down, shaking, dancing, or moving your body to help discharge the flight, fight or freeze energy of the trigger.

5. Once the charge moves through your body, reflect on your self-talk and what limiting beliefs and assumptions are driving your reaction in this situation. Ask: 'Do I feel a need to comply, to control or to protect myself here?'

Acceptance

Next, we accept, with self-compassion, that these patterns are psychologically and culturally hardwired into us. They are not easy to change. It takes curiosity, practise and lots of mistakes. The practice of total acceptance can be all it takes to allow change to happen within us. Psychologist Carl Rogers eloquently said: 'The curious paradox is that when I accept myself just as I am, then I can change.' In my own journey, I have often tried to jump from awareness to practising new behaviours and entirely skipped the acceptance part. It doesn't work! Often because, with acceptance, comes another layer of inner emotional work. We now create space to acknowledge and grieve the unmet needs that sit under our compulsive tendencies, with fierce self-compassion. Many of us have criticised ourselves and made ourselves 'wrong' all our lives. This self-criticism drives the never-ending internal belief we continue to tell ourselves that we are not enough as we are and stops us from allowing our grief.

Personal and professional development can be just another form of self-abuse, like an addiction to constantly try and fix ourselves so we don't feel broken. Acceptance is a very important step to self-understanding and, ultimately, self-forgiveness. Deep healing can take place in this acceptance of our feelings, but it is a gift we rarely give ourselves. It doesn't mean we don't have regrets. It doesn't mean we don't wish we could have done something differently — we would if we could. It means, 'Now I understand why I did what I did, and why I do what I do. And now that I understand, I can apologise and make amends, including to myself. With this kind understanding of myself, I can find some space and freedom to begin to choose to behave differently.'

Conscious practice

Once you have paused, checked in with your body, named and soothed, moved your body and reflected on what is going on for you, now we practice:

6. Put one hand on your heart and one hand on your belly, allowing a deep sigh. Acknowledge to yourself why you are triggered, why you want to either comply, control or protect yourself. Acknowledge with self-compassion, self-respect and care, the underlying beliefs and assumptions that drive these behaviours and the role your histories have played in these. Let yourself know it is okay; in fact, it makes perfect sense to that part of you that is scared and has activated its nervous systems.

While we may not always like our behaviours and want to do it differently next time, we can also allow ourselves to feel our feelings and be human.

Action

Thirdly, we gently and regularly practise new empowering, purposeful actions. We commit to practising uncomfortable new behaviours and start responding differently.

> ## Conscious practice
>
> Having paused, checked in with your body, named and soothed, moved your body, reflected on what is going on for you, and allowed yourself to acknowledge and accept your reactive behaviours, you can now move on to:
>
> 7. Practise choosing a different empowering response to your normal reactive pattern. If your inclination is to always say 'yes' to comply, practice saying 'no' to be true to yourself. If your inclination is to be driven and perfect so you feel in control, practise slowing down, taking your attention off others and letting go. If your inclination is to withdraw or be superior, practise being curious about what you can learn from someone else.
>
> Always remember to practise self-compassion as we lean into these new behaviours.

It is important to be clear on our vision for ourselves, our lives and our values to help keep us on track.

For a long time, my purpose was built around wanting to be a good mum; to not hand down my own limiting beliefs and behaviours to Hugo; to be a present, available parent. He is in his twenties now and is on his own journey. I hope I have taught him to love and respect himself and others. He certainly seems to have a much better sense of self-worth than I did at his age. I am, of course, aware that for the first six to eight years of his life I was pretty tied up in my own bondage of self, and that will have affected him. This is the journey of self-forgiveness and self-acceptance that I am still on. Perhaps it is why I am writing this book.

Now, my purpose comes from a deeper place of self-love, to feel the freedom that comes from being true to myself, being in loving relationships and being of authentic service to others. Some days I don't want to practise new behaviours. Some days it would feel so much easier to just do what I think others want me to do, or distance myself instead of showing up to a conversation that needs to be had, or go into overdrive and demand rather than surrender an outcome that is out of my control. I do my best one day at a time to practise living true to myself and the values I espouse — to 'practise what I preach' — and take purposeful action.

When we know what we want to bring into being, what we are moving toward and why, then it makes it easier to keep showing up in the way we want to be in the world. We will explore all of this together in detail in Part III.

Watch out for the afterburn!

Lastly, to support us to change these patterns, is the practise of simply *being with* and allowing our thoughts (especially the inner critic and negative self-talk), rather than trying to push the thoughts and feelings away by ignoring them or numbing them out. As the common saying goes, 'what we resist persists'.

The hardest part of practising new behaviours is simply being with the uncomfortable feelings that arise when we go against our old patterns. I refer to this as the *afterburn*. We have been doing a certain behaviour our whole lives because we deeply believe that behaviour is going to give us the outcome we want: to feel safe, loved, accepted and respected. And then, suddenly, we do something else. Even though we have come to rationally understand that these behaviours are now limiting, and even sabotaging, us from getting exactly what we most want, we are still going against everything we have built our lives on. Hence, when we start to practise new behaviours, it is very uncomfortable, and it often gets harder before it gets easier. The critical voice in my head often gets louder before it gets quieter.

I can experience a lot of anxiety, often mixed in with some guilt or shame. Change is uncomfortable! When I have made a really big change, the inner critic and obsessive thinking and feelings can feel quite debilitating at first. We can learn to acknowledge what feels uncomfortable in us. To make time to slow down and be with those feelings and notice our self-talk, which is often enflaming our anxiety and guilt, perhaps put our hand on our heart and belly and offer ourselves self-compassion, rather than often compulsively getting busy over the top of our anxiety and guilt. Until it passes. And it always passes. With each practice it gets easier, and we come more deeply into alignment with ourselves.

This is where deep inner confidence, calmness and connection begins to grow from. Slowly, gently.

CHAPTER 3

Learning to dance in relationships

I have a long history of being attracted to emotionally unavailable men. It was hard to face the truth that they were just a mirror of my own emotional unavailability. For a long time, I was not emotionally available to myself, to my son or to others. I have eventually realised that if I am in a relationship with an unavailable man, rather than trying to change him, my focus needs to be on my own inner work. That is my pattern to heal.

I have worked with many highly successful women who have struggled, or are struggling, in their intimate relationships. The struggle often comes from a place of great unworthiness (perhaps a relationship where they are overly responsible and their partner under responsible or vice versa), which often creates a power imbalance and the use of control, subtle and not so subtle.

I don't pretend to be a professional expert in attachment theory, or the dynamics that play out as a result. However, I have worked closely with trained therapists in this area, and I have experienced and closely studied my own attachment dynamics. I want to give you a little more detail and point you in the direction of some resources should you want to explore this further for yourself. It has a huge impact on our relationship with ourselves and with others, as well as our ability to thrive in all areas of our lives, including at work. I have found enormous freedom, especially from self-judgement, by better understanding why I do what I do, as well as why others, especially those close to me, often do what they do.

Learning to dance

Our individual attachment styles are set up in childhood. Dr Susan Johnson is a pioneer in the field of attachment theory, and she explains that foundational revolutionary research offers us a whole new basis upon which to view the impact of our childhoods on our current relationship styles. This research was originally conducted by psychologist and psychoanalyst John Bowlby. It revealed that, while other people can provide food or attend to the basic needs of a child, it is the emotional connection between a child and their primary caregiver that is so essential for the child's survival and development.

The primary caregiver is the person who is responsible for providing the main (and most) care, both physical and emotional, to a child in their first twelve months. As we move forward, I will use the term 'mum', but obviously, this person may be a father, grandparent, foster carer, etc.

Decades of research reveals that how our mum meets our core needs correlates to the attachment styles we have as adults. How we relate and connect or distance and avoid. How meaningful and healthy, or not so, our relationships are. In other words, we attach to our romantic partner and those we are emotionally close to with the same attachment pattern that we developed as an infant.

I love Dr Johnson's analogy of learning to dance. Our caregivers teach us a certain way of dancing in our relationships. If our mum was not able to self-regulate and regularly meet our needs in childhood, we can learn ways to dance that really don't support us in developing a secure attachment in our adult relationships. Sometimes we get stuck in those dance steps, so just as we are starting to pull our friend or partner close, we end up pushing them away. This significantly affects our ability to create the secure and fulfilling relationships we innately long for.

As babies, the urge to seek proximity to our mum is hardwired into our brain. As John Bowlby's original research progressed, it was revealed that, in the first twelve months, our mum's sensitivity and responsiveness to our needs, and their ability to be present and offer consistent empathy and understanding, is crucial in developing our sense of security and confidence that our needs will be met.

Some of the ways our mum can show this sensitivity and responsiveness are by how quickly she responds to our distress, her attempts to relieve our distress by offering us comfort, and her tender and soothing physical contact. If this relationship between mother and child is set up securely in our first year, we feel safe to turn toward our mum when we are frightened. We protest if separated, yet we feel safe enough to explore our world. Sadly, when Hugo was a little boy, I was not aware of this. He struggled to settle, and when I got some professional advice, I was told to leave him to cry, going in only every few minutes to pat him gently on the back and then walking out and leaving him again. I wish with all my heart I had known differently.

If you have done any reading or courses on secure parenting, you may have come across a group called the Circle of Security,[6] which is based on decades of attachment research. It breaks down and beautifully simplifies the three main needs we look for as children, and continue to look for as adults.

The first is, *going out on the circle.* This means that, as a child, we felt safe and supported, and we can go out and discover our world, knowing this exploration was encouraged, that mum is right there watching over us and delighting in this exploration.

Second is what's referred to as, *coming in on the circle.* This is about Mum filling our emotional cup. This is done by mum 'welcoming' and 'delighting in' our return. She offers protection, comfort, understanding and helps organise our feelings for us.

I recently saw a girlfriend do this beautifully with her toddler. Her daughter came to her in tears, struggling with sharing her toys. Mum opened her arms to her daughter, cuddled her and simply said, 'I can see you're sad that it's not your turn'. Her little one had a big cry and held on tightly while her mum was simply present to the cuddle. What surprised me was how quickly the toddler released her pent-up emotions then, feeling safe and secure, ran off to explore again.

The third of our basic three needs, according to this attachment style of parenting is known as, *hands on the circle*. When we are children, we need our mum to be bigger, stronger, wiser and kinder. We need to feel we can trust her to understand what we need when we are feeling lost, confused or out of control. We need someone to hold healthy boundaries and loving limits for us, someone to be in charge in a kind way.

'Good enough' parenting

As children, we all know how uncomfortable it can be to be held too tightly when we want to be out exploring, or kept at a distance when we need emotional support. As children, we need an emotionally mature, responsible and loving adult who can differentiate our needs, and be available to meet them. We need someone who can regulate their own nervous system and teach their child how to regulate theirs through role modelling.

Whether this relationship is working well is strongly affected by our mum's state of mind and nervous system: basically, our mum's ability to be emotionally available and present to us as children. There are so many factors that can seriously impact our mum's ability to offer us this, including the messages our caregivers received as children themselves.

Conscious reflection

As challenging as it may feel, at least for me, when we take a moment to reflect back on our own childhoods, as well as our own parenting, we can gently, with compassion, become aware of which of these three core needs were regularly met and which may not have been. And importantly, we can now learn to give these to ourselves and to those people around us.

As we know, no parent is perfect. No parent can meet their child's needs all of the time, and it is important we allow ourselves to be imperfect without beating ourselves up. It is when our main caregiver can meet our physical and emotional needs *enough* of the time, that it allows us to develop a secure attachment, which sets us up for healthy, meaningful relational connections throughout our life. One great parenting book on this that I recommend is *Good Inside: A practical guide to becoming the parent you want to be* by Dr Becky Kennedy.

Our culture has often taught us to be ashamed of needing comfort and support. But these needs are inescapably hardwired into our brain. With securely attached relationships, we are healthier, stronger and, ultimately, more independent. It is easier to go out into the world and take the world on when someone has our back, and we know we are not alone.

Secure attachment to those we love provides a solid foundation for mental health and wellbeing. Yet, perhaps not surprisingly, we don't all get what we need from our parents or experience secure attachment as children. In fact, many recent research studies suggest that only approximately 50 per cent of people have what is termed a *secure* attachment style in adulthood. And of those within that 50 per cent, half of them are what are called *earned secure attachment*. They have learnt (through awareness, therapy and support from secure attachment role modelling) how to experience secure attachment later in life.

Understanding your attachment style, the dance we do in our relationships and how it affects our interactions with our partner and others we are close to, is an important piece of self-awareness in a healthy relationship. It's also an indicator of our ability to speak up, and to love and believe in ourselves.

As children, our sense of safety, security, worth and love comes from outside of us. We need to have that role modelled and mirrored back to us by our caregivers, our family. Research shows us that we need at least one person who is truly there for us to develop a healthy level of attachment.

Dancing blindly

When my son Hugo was just sixteen months old, his father Troy and I separated. I am not going to go into detail out of respect for both Troy and Hugo, but what I will share is that, while I believe both people contribute to relationship breakdowns, in hindsight, I did not know how to be in a healthy, functional relationship. If I could have done it differently, I would have. I would have done anything to keep my family together, but I honestly didn't know how. I had come from a broken home, and I did not want that for Hugo or myself, but it was all I knew, and sadly, it was also my second failed marriage, the first lasting only nine months when I was in my early twenties.

I was completely devastated at the loss of this dream, and from that moment on, my life began to spiral out of control. It was hard to tell from the outside, as I was still very successful at work, earning a lot of money and using that money to mask what was unfolding within me.

Two months after Troy and I broke up, my dad and stepmum visited me in Sydney. I vividly remember sitting on my couch in a stunning waterfront apartment with 180-degree views of the Sydney Harbour Bridge, looking like I was living the life, as my dad sat in front of me and told me he had advanced bowel and liver cancer. He had had it for some time, and this was the first I was hearing about it, which I felt angry about, even as I felt scared and devastated. He died less than six months later.

I had always had a very complex relationship with my dad. Even though he was an extremely difficult man to love, I still loved him with every fibre of my being. It was hard to ever get things right for him. He had a very quick and nasty temper and was impatient, easily irritated and supercritical.

What do you do when you have such overwhelming and complex feelings trying to get your attention? For me, I fell right into many tried-and-tested behavioural patterns to dissociate from my complete overwhelm, numb my pain, and try to find some much-needed comfort. Sadly, in my pain and unworthiness, and still feeling that

Hugo was better off without me, I left Troy to continue to be Hugo's primary caregiver for the next year, which he did an extraordinary job of, especially as he was going through his own grief and had to finish renovating the house we had started together on his own.

I also focused on other people, rather than staying with what was going on for me. There was no better distraction from myself and my feelings than focusing on others. It was a way of trying to feel some kind of control when my emotional life felt so out of control. I flew back and forth to Adelaide to visit my dad and to try to work out how I could 'fix' his cancer. I got caught up in any drama that my friends were having. I worked even harder, if that was possible. I also managed to find the perfect man to help me try to run from my pain and myself.

One evening, a few months after Dad had died, I was at a barbecue and met a man we'll call Tim. He was very handsome and charismatic. He had been trying to make it as an actor all his life, so he didn't have a job or any money, but boy, could he make me feel good. I was newly divorced, feeling incredibly insecure about being an over-the-hill single mother who nobody would want, while also in incredible pain and abandonment over my marriage ending and my dad dying. Tim admired my success, showered me with attention and told me I was beautiful. I was so deeply insecure that his attention was like a drug. I wanted more.

As I left the barbecue that night, a mutual friend said, 'Stay away from Tim. He has a lot of problems and I promise you, he will never be able to love you.'

In my distorted thinking, I thought: 'game on'. I had spent my whole life trying to get my father to want me, so this was a very familiar game. I would be able to change him, I would be able to love him and look after him — the way I am sure I wanted to be loved and looked after in that moment.

So, into rescue mode I went, using my money and a successful career to give me some sense of power and control. It's now obvious to me that Tim never would have stayed with me if I hadn't had money. He used me to live a lifestyle he had no interest in working for. And I used him to try to feel better about myself and, I suspect, to punish myself. All of which came from a place of great unworthiness.

Tim was a true party boy and I had never been a party girl, not nearly to this level. Sure, I enjoyed a good time, a few drinks and a good night out, but I had never tried drugs, other than perhaps a bit of marijuana back in my high school years, which just sent me to sleep. I remember one night when I was married, Troy and I were offered some ecstasy at a New Year's Eve party. 'No way', I said. 'That stuff can kill you'. I was very conservative around the ideas of sex, drugs and 'high-end' partying. In fact, I didn't really know any of it existed. Tim was a high-functioning drug addict, sex addict and gambler, but I didn't know any of that in the early days.

Conscious reflection

Have you ever lost yourself in a relationship? Or prioritised your partner over yourself? Or avoided yourself or areas of your life that you knew needed attention? As confronting as it can feel to acknowledge these parts of ourselves, when we bring self-compassion to self-awareness, there is enormous freedom that comes from facing the truth and learning to honour ourselves and our needs.

While Hugo was with his dad, Tim introduced me to a whole new world, parts of which were exciting and felt liberating, parts of which were terrifying and overwhelming. I paid for it financially, mentally, emotionally and spiritually. I was offered and tried almost every drug there is other than heroin. I snorted cocaine off toilet seats in nightclubs at ungodly hours of the morning. I took uppers and downers. Drank excessive amounts of French champagne. I picked Tim up after he had been beaten by his drug dealers and shoved into the boot of a car. I paid off all his debts, a few times. I believed him when he told me he was not being unfaithful, even though I had seen text messages that said otherwise. I called him many times when he would disappear on two- or three-day benders and would not pick up his phone. I begged him to call me, then asked him to leave, before forgiving him when he asked to come back. I was anxious to feel close and desperate not to feel my deep abandonment wound that was triggered almost daily with him. I had no boundaries, internally or externally.

All that time, I was trying to numb my own pain and grief and hide from my own inner demons. Numbing through drugs and alcohol, numbing through trying to fix and rescue Tim, caught up and distracted from my own pain by the constant drama that surrounded him and continuing to numb with work, as I was still very focused on trying to achieve my worth there. In and amongst these very turbulent years, when Hugo was with me, I spent very little time with Tim and tried so hard to show Hugo how much I loved him, but looking back, I wish with all my heart I could have done it differently. When Hugo was not with his dad and stepmum, I was grateful I could afford a very precious nanny called Tanya, who looked after Hugo while I was at work and became a very important member of our family. Hugo had so many women in his life that loved him.

This was undoubtedly the most emotionally painful time of my adult life. As I reflect back on it, I see the deep attachment wounds that were driving my behaviours, which ultimately were replaying the patterns set up in my past. While I am grateful for my awareness and understanding of myself now, I am still learning to forgive myself for what I did not know or understand then, to forgive myself for what I put myself through in my own self-abandonment — and especially for not being capable of being more fully available to my son, and the breakdown and incredible loss of relationships that were important to me.

Very slowly, I have become aware of my conditioning and the impact of trauma on our ability to be in healthy relationships. I gained an understanding of attachment theory. I have become more capable of seeing my own unconsciousness and innocence, and the powerlessness that comes with this. Perhaps most importantly, I have taken responsibility for my own healing. I have committed myself to raising my consciousness and minimising the impact of my past on the present and on those whom I love. I am committed to breaking the relational cycles that are handed down through generations in my family and all families. Now I can sometimes even allow myself a level of pride for doing what is arguably the hardest work we can ever do. When we heal the mother, we heal the children. If I were to leave this Earth tomorrow, this is the legacy I most want to leave, and within it, find some peace in my heart and being.

How do you dance?

According to attachment experts, there are four main attachment styles. While I am generally not a big fan of labels, the more we understand our own style and that of our loved ones, the more we can change unhelpful patterns and create more secure relationships. In my personal experience, this is a lifelong journey. When I began a new relationship with the man who is now my husband, we decided to work with an expert in this area to help us grow toward creating secure attachment in our relationship. It is a very gradual process! I also work with my own therapist with the intention of creating healthy, authentic and meaningful relationships with those I love and those I interact with on a day-to-day basis. The goal is to empower myself, to learn how to truly love and be loved.

I will use an explanation of the four attachment styles from Dr Karen Baikie, clinical psychologist and certified Hakomi therapist. As we look at these, I invite you to hold yourself with great self-compassion. Please offer yourself warmth and kindness. It can be hard to recognise some of these patterns within yourself and it's okay, we all have them, it's part of what makes us human.

We may relate to certain aspects of each attachment style at times, and they may change depending on who we are in relationship with. This is normal. Yet, we also have a default, or dominant, attachment style, the one from which we operate most of the time, especially when we are stressed or our brain is in our threat system (more on this in Chapter 4). However, each of these styles should be thought of as a continuum of attachment behaviours, simply a way of describing and understanding an individual's behaviour instead of an exact description. In my experience, understanding your dominant attachment style helps you to understand your own dance steps, reactions and interactions in romantic and other emotionally close relationships. It can help you understand both yourself and others better. No meaningful change can occur without awareness and acceptance of our histories and patterns.

As we become more aware and do the work to heal our needs, we will begin to have more choice about how we interact within our relationships, rather than reacting unconsciously from the dance we have been taught.

1. Secure attachment: The rock of reliability

A child develops a secure attachment when they grow up with a caregiver who is emotionally attuned to them and validating, as well as sensitive and responsive to their physical and emotional needs and in their interactions.

A securely attached child shows distress when their caregiver leaves the room, but is able to manage that distress reasonably well in order to refocus on their environment. When the caregiver returns, the child turns to the parent and reaches out, immediately wanting to be close. The child responds well to the caregiver's support, folding in for a hug, which eases their distress. The child recovers quickly from the distress, and returns to their environment, ready to play with the caregiver.

An adult who develops secure attachment in childhood grows up to have a strong sense of themselves, as well as desiring to be close to others. They generally have a positive view of themselves as people, in a solid and balanced way, but they also feel positive about their partners. They feel comfortable both when alone and when with others. They develop trusting, lasting relationships, have good self-esteem, share feelings easily and enjoy good social support.

People with secure attachment are like emotional anchors. They feel comfortable with intimacy and independence, striking a healthy balance. They trust their partners and themselves, believing that they are worthy of love and care. In relationships, they communicate openly, express emotions freely, and handle conflicts with understanding. Secure individuals form strong, lasting bonds without fear of abandonment, as they know they can rely on their partners and themselves.

2. Insecure ambivalent/anxious preoccupied: The yearning for connection

A child develops an insecure ambivalent attachment when they grow up with a caregiver who is unpredictably responsive. The key element in the development of this attachment style is inconsistently attuned parenting.

An insecure ambivalent child shows distress even in anticipation of any separation, and then more intense distress when the caregiver leaves. The child is fearful while the parent is gone. When the parent returns, the child is clingy and difficult to comfort. The child initially seeks out the parent, but then often resists close contact, and may even push the parent away when being held.

Adults who grow up with this style are often insecure and self-critical. They often seek approval and reassurance from others, yet they still hold much self-doubt. These adults are often fearful and distrustful in their relationships because they feel sure that they are going to be rejected. They are not close to others and worry that they are not loved. As a result, they tend to behave in ways that make them seem clingy and overly dependent on their partner. They are often left feeling emotionally desperate in their relationships and become distraught when a relationship ends.

People with this attachment style seek a lot of closeness and reassurance, often feeling anxious about their partner's availability. They are highly attuned to changes in their relationships, and might become overly concerned about potential abandonment. This can lead to clinginess, intense emotions and a fear of rejection. Individuals with this style may tend to overthink situations, seeking constant validation to ease their anxieties.

3. Insecure avoidant/dismissive avoidant: The island of independence

A child develops an insecure avoidant attachment when they grow up with a caregiver who is emotionally unavailable and, as a result, is insensitive to and unaware of the needs of their child. Generally, these parents show little or no response to a hurting or distressed child. They discourage crying and encourage independence. As a result, their children are very self-contained and tend not to need much from anyone else.

An insecure avoidant child shows no great distress when their caregiver leaves the room. The child stays focused on their environment and doesn't stop playing. When the caregiver returns, neither the child nor the caregiver really seeks each other out. The parent may not even pick up or greet the child, and the child doesn't seek out the parent. The child can be comforted equally well by a parent or a stranger.

Children who develop insecure avoidant attachment generally grow up to be loners and have a dismissive avoidant attachment style. They tend to be inward-focused and isolated, good 'thinkers' who suppress their feelings. They are often emotionally alienated from themselves and others and may see emotions and relationships as relatively unimportant. They avoid conflict and distance themselves from stressful situations. They may have intimacy problems, as they tend to be unemotional in relationships and don't share their feelings with others.

This style typically prioritises self-sufficiency and independence. They might downplay the importance of emotional connection, appearing aloof and distant. While they enjoy casual relationships, they may struggle with deeper intimacy, avoiding vulnerability. They often emphasise self-reliance and might be uncomfortable with emotional expressions, seeing them as a sign of weakness. This style can make forming lasting emotional bonds challenging.

4. Disorganised/fearful avoidant: The pendulum of confusion

A child develops a disorganised attachment when they grow up with a caregiver who is either frightened or frightening in moments of stress with their child. The caregiver may be abusive or neglectful. The parent may act in ways that do not make sense, perhaps being unpredictable, confusing or erratic, which frightens the child. Disorganised attachment is generally caused by abuse from the caregiver, or because of a caregiver who has unresolved trauma and loss in their own life.

A child with a disorganised attachment expresses odd or ambivalent behaviour toward the parent. The child may initially run up to the parent but then suddenly pull away. The child's first impulse may be to seek comfort from the parent, but as they get near the parent, they feel afraid to be close, which is the key element of the disorganised style. The child may appear dazed, confused or apprehensive.

An adult who develops disorganised attachment in childhood grows up to be somewhat detached from themselves or dissociative. They want to be in relationships and are comfortable until they get emotionally close. They then get triggered by the closeness, with suppressed feelings from childhood emerging in the present, causing them to relive old trauma. These adults do not have a solid, coherent sense of themselves, nor do they feel very connected to others. They may struggle to learn healthy ways to self-soothe, and may also rely on others to regulate their emotions.

For those with disorganised attachment, it's difficult to open up or seek help. Given that they were unable to trust their primary caregivers during childhood, they often have difficulty trusting people as adults. They have a hard time forming and sustaining healthy, consistent relationships. They can also struggle with regulating their emotions and managing stress. Because they fundamentally view the world as an unsafe place, they may even display aggressive behaviour.

This style often results in a constant internal tug-of-war between the person's desire for closeness and fear of getting hurt. They crave intimacy but also worry about being rejected or betrayed. This conflict can lead to a push-pull dynamic in relationships, as they may alternate between seeking connection and withdrawing. These individuals might exhibit unpredictable behaviours, struggling to find a stable footing between their conflicting emotions.

Resolve your trauma to heal your attachment style

Research has shown that it is not necessarily how bad someone's childhood was that affects attachment between them and their child, but how much they've been able to process the pain of their past and make sense of it. The more someone has resolved the trauma and conflict from their early lives, the better they will be able to form a secure attachment with their child and within their relationships.

I love reading about secure attachment and remembering we can 'earn' secure attachment by doing our inner work and working together with our partner and/or a therapist. No matter which style you resonate with, anyone can work toward a secure attachment style through awareness, therapy and support from secure attachment role modelling.

If you're interested in exploring this further in your own partnership, Stan Tatkin's book *Wired for Love: How understanding your partner's brain and attachment style can help you defuse conflict and build a secure relationship* is very powerful.

Secure attachment traits

In their book *Attached: The new science of adult attachment and how it can help you find—and keep—love*, Amir Levine and Rachel Heller explain that securely attached individuals are:

♦ *Great conflict busters.* During a fight they don't feel the need to act defensively or to injure or punish their partner, and so prevent the situation from escalating.

(continued)

◆ *Mentally flexible.* They are not threatened by criticism. They're willing to reconsider their ways, and if necessary, revise their beliefs and strategies.

◆ *Effective communicators.* They expect others to be understanding and responsive, so expressing their feelings freely and accurately to their partners comes naturally to them.

◆ *Not game players.* They want closeness and believe others want the same, so why play games?

◆ *Comfortable with closeness, unconcerned about boundaries.* They seek intimacy and aren't afraid of being 'enmeshed'. They find it easy to enjoy closeness, whether physical or emotional.

◆ *Quick to forgive.* They assume their partner's intentions are good and are therefore likely to forgive them when they do something hurtful.

◆ *Inclined to view sex and emotional intimacy as one.* They don't need to create distance by separating the two—sex comes with emotional intimacy.

◆ *Treat their partners like royalty.* When you've become part of their inner circle, they treat you with love and respect.

◆ *Responsible for their partner's wellbeing.* They expect others to be responsive and loving toward them and they also offer this love and responsiveness.

I love this list of traits as a guide for how we can practice showing up in our relationship. Although when I read the final one, I couldn't help but think that, in today's post-modern world, women are learning to be *responsive to* their partner's wellbeing rather than *responsible for*. We are more comfortable with requiring men to be responsible for articulating their own wellbeing needs, rather than taking on the mental load of both figuring it out for them and then magically fixing whatever is missing. Just as we need to be responsible for articulating our needs.

Attachment in the workplace

Attachment theory was originally thought to play out primarily in our family and intimate relationships, but in 1990, Hazan and Shaver began researching how it applied to social dynamics in the workplace. Since then, there have been numerous studies into attachment theory at work, including how we may experience our organisation as an attachment figure and experience grief, emotional distress and/or feelings of abandonment when an organisation no longer offers a secure base.[7]

Our attachment styles can influence how we interact with colleagues, superiors and subordinates. Aside from secure attachment, anxious/ambivalent attachment and dismissive avoidant attachment are the two main attachment styles relevant to the workplace.

1. Anxiously attached in the workplace

A person with an anxious attachment style in the workplace tends to crave close relationships and worry about rejection or abandonment. In the workplace, this style may manifest in the following ways:

◆ *Seeking excessive reassurance:* We may frequently seek reassurance from managers or colleagues to validate our competence and worth.

◆ *Overthinking and self-doubt:* We may be prone to overthinking situations, especially in relation to work performance, which can lead to increased self-doubt.

◆ *Difficulty handling criticism:* People with this attachment style may take constructive feedback as personal attacks, leading to emotional reactions and difficulty in accepting and integrating feedback.

◆ *Strong emotional reactions:* We may experience heightened emotions, such as stress and anxiety, in response to workplace challenges or interpersonal conflicts.

◆ *Over-dependence on colleagues:* We may rely heavily on the support of colleagues or superiors, sometimes to the extent of hindering our own autonomy and decision-making.

2. Avoidantly attached in the workplace

An avoidant attachment style in the workplace typically manifests as valuing independence and having difficulty fully trusting others. In the workplace, this attachment style may be observed in the following behaviours:

◆ *Distancing ourselves from others:* We might keep our interactions with colleagues and superiors formal and professional, avoiding emotional intimacy.

◆ *Unwillingness to seek help or support:* We may be hesitant to ask for help or support, even when needed, due to a fear of appearing vulnerable or reliant on others.

◆ *Difficulty collaborating:* Our preference for independence might lead to challenges in working effectively in teams or collaborative projects.

◆ *Emotional detachment:* We may appear emotionally distant and might find it challenging to connect with colleagues on a deeper level.

◆ *Struggle with providing emotional support:* We might find it difficult to offer emotional support to colleagues in times of need, as we are more comfortable with practical assistance.

3. *Securely attached in the workplace*

A secure attachment style in the workplace may manifest as:

◆ *Strong work relationships:* We tend to be more comfortable with intimacy and independence, forming close, positive relationships with colleagues, managers and subordinates.

◆ *Open communication:* We feel safe enough to express our needs, feelings and concerns, and are usually receptive to feedback and can handle constructive criticism without becoming overly defensive.

◆ *Adaptability:* We are typically more resilient when confronted with change because we have an inherent belief that we can rely on ourselves and others for support.

◆ *Healthy boundaries:* We have strong personal and professional boundaries and balance our work and personal lives effectively.

◆ *Positive view of self and others:* This often translates to increased confidence in our abilities and trust in our colleagues. We tend to be able to handle conflict in a constructive manner, focusing on resolution rather than avoidance or escalation.

It's essential to understand that attachment styles can be fluid and influenced by various factors, including life experiences and personal growth. Those of us with anxious or avoidant attachment styles can work toward developing more secure attachment patterns, often characterised by trust, empathy and effective communication.

In the workplace, fostering a secure and supportive environment, through creating a culture of trust, providing regular feedback, and prioritising work-life balance can also positively impact employee wellbeing and collaboration.

Hold your heart gently

I always feel the need to take some very deep breaths and put my hand on my heart as I read this kind of material.

Thankfully, we can heal the past. There is quite a lot of research that says our attachment style naturally changes when we begin to do things differently in our lives. Just as we have learnt through the power of neuroplasticity that we can change the way we think and feel, we can also change our attachment wiring. Through practising new behaviours, we can literally rewire our brain with compassionate self-awareness and slowly learn a new way to dance. And through establishing a consistent and secure relationship with a therapist with whom we feel safe with, we can face into, feel, making meaning of, learn to trust and heal the past.

It starts with us. We can become aware of which style we are operating out of and begin to make different and conscious choices, such as taking risks with safe people, reaching out to others, and creating more safety and trust. We can learn our part in the dance and practise new dance steps. We can learn how to assert our needs and how to self-soothe. In intimate relationships, we need a partner who respects our needs and can make them a priority, while also knowing their own needs and doing their own inner work.

Bowlby, the brain behind attachment theory, gave us a huge gift: a brilliant framework for understanding how secure attachment is *real love* in action. Attachment theory also offers us the opportunity to lay the foundation for a life of secure attachment in our children. What I love about this parenting model is that it offers self-compassion in action. There's no such thing as a perfect parent, and *good enough*, not perfect, parenting is all that is needed to create these healthy foundations. I will be forever grateful that Troy prioritised this above all else with Hugo in his earliest years when I was lost in my pain and that, later, after my recovery, I was also able to make this my focus too.

I recently asked Jo Flynn (a therapist and a good friend) how we forgive ourselves when our parenting is not 'good enough'. I have struggled with this because of how emotionally unavailable I feel I was to Hugo in his earliest years. I loved her response: 'The answer is simple. We do it cognitively, we do it somatically and we do it in good company. There is no other way'. And she offered the following practice.

Conscious practice

How to forgive ourselves for imperfect parenting

We start cognitively by having the courage to name our limitations (real or perceived). For example, our self shaming might say, 'I have been a *bad* mother. I just shouted at the kids for no apparent reason other than I was stressed.' Or 'I realise I was not there for my child at a time they really needed me'. That, in itself, is a hard concept to face: that we are less perfect than we would have liked. Less perfect than all those other mums on Facebook who are so shiny and serene.

Next, we notice where we are holding this self-judgement in our body. We sit with where it hurts, rather than explaining it away. We hang out with that tender place in our bodies, just breathing, for as long as it takes for the energy to settle down. We don't fight it or flee from it or fix it, we just breathe into the core of where it hurts to know that we have been less than perfect.

Now, if we can do that in good company, with a friend or coach or therapist, then the degree to which we embrace that limitation, tenderly and compassionately, is the degree to which our own forgiveness naturally arises in our body. We actually cannot do that healing work on our own—it just spins around our brains in a racetrack of self-recrimination. But a good friend, coach or therapist will help us hold the space to tell a new, deeper, wiser truth. We can include and transcend our 'mistakes'.

We can also apologise to our children when we are 'not good enough' and invite them to share their experience with us, without us defending, but simply being present and acknowledging the impact on them. This invites a genuine repair to take place in our relationship with them.

When I began my relationship with my psychotherapist, which enabled me to begin to experience a secure attachment for the first time in my life, I identified as having a fearful avoidant/disorganised attachment style. I had a low sense of self and found it very hard to trust others. This was not only because of the attachment style set up in my early childhood, but also because of the trauma I experienced.

This understandably set up a very fearful attachment within me and toward others. Through therapy and my ongoing self-awareness and mindfulness practices, I now have a much more positive view of myself. However, I can still find it hard, particularly when I am under stress, to trust in others, and can still tend to have a more dismissive avoidant style or overly independent view of relationships. My inner work these days is on learning to trust myself and others.

As I mentioned at the beginning, my intention with this chapter is simply to bring our attachment styles into our conscious awareness, as they affect all our relationships in all aspects of our lives.

May you begin to bring gentle and compassionate awareness to your own attachment styles, and seek support and have the courage to dance a more secure dance. May you learn to deeply love, value and believe in yourself, in the relationship you have with yourself and with others.

CHAPTER 4

The many forces that hinder our authenticity

I love the quote by Mary Shelly: 'I do not wish women to have power over men; but over themselves.' It speaks so beautifully to the journey of us coming into a relationship with our own innate feminine power — and it is not lost on me just how difficult this is.

I viscerally remember the day I sat down with my own executive coach to receive my very first 360° feedback. As part of the assessment, I invited my two managers, a group of peers, my direct reports and a group of other stakeholders to provide me with feedback on how they experienced my leadership. I was about to come face-to-face with what people thought of me, and I was beyond anxious.

Thankfully, my coach was a very compassionate woman. She began by exploring the current context of my life and work before taking me back to my past. Through this lens, I was better able to make meaning of the feedback I received with understanding and self-compassion.

While there were many things to digest, the four most profound for me included:

◆ The level of self-doubt that drove me. People thought so much more of me than I thought of myself.

◆ The impact of my perfectionism and overdrive on myself and others. It's exhausting all round and pushes people away.

◆ When my overdrive and perfectionism is combined with my need to please. This was the perfect recipe for living on the edge of burnout.

◆ Perhaps most surprising, I wasn't hiding anything from anyone. In the feedback, everybody saw my need to please and try to be perfect and overwork. It's ironic that in trying to hide my perceived imperfections from others, I had been hiding them more from myself.

Off the back of this, it became very clear to me what I wanted to change, the new practices and behaviours I wanted to put in place to support me to grow my inner confidence. I needed more trust in myself. I wanted to be less intense and controlling, to stop trying to please others and to start living and leading true to myself.

That was when I started to realise just how hard change is. Change sounds so simple, especially when we are clear that we want it. But there are so many internal and external forces that hinder our desire to grow and live and lead true to ourselves, some of which we have explored in previous chapters. In this chapter we will explore other factors, including how our brain and nervous systems are wired, the identity we have formed, the challenge of adult development, the impact of the patriarchal society we live in, the narrative we have created, and (within all of this) how our template, the way we see the world, has been laid down. Knowing all of this has really helped me understand and have more compassion for myself and others.

Our brain is wired for survival

Let's start with our brain: a masterpiece of contradictions. All our past experiences, traumas, patterns, beliefs, identity issues and our environment condition us to think, feel and behave in certain ways. Through these filters, we find our comfort zone, the lens through which we see our life. A way of thinking, feeling and behaving that feels 'normal' for us.

The tricky part of this is that part of our brain, our amygdala, is hardwired for survival. So, when we think, feel, say or do something new and different and outside our comfort zone, our brain can get triggered automatically to work against this new way of behaving. Ultimately, this part of our brain can work against our desire to speak up and be true to ourselves, depending on how we were taught to see ourselves by our caregivers and community.

I see it in myself and my clients daily. Recently, one of my clients identified that she was a chronic people pleaser. She often said 'yes' when she wanted to say 'no'. I asked her to practise doing the opposite, just for a fortnight. She was gobsmacked at how hard this was to do. This seemingly simple change felt impossible to her. When she tried this, she noticed that she compulsively said 'yes', and that she always came up with a reason why she couldn't say 'no'. When we dug underneath it all, she realised it was because she believed that if she said 'no', she would not be liked or loved. Her survival brain automatically kicked in to stop this from happening and *made* her say 'yes' to protect her. What would it be like for you to try this in your own life: at work, at home, with friends? Would you find it easy or challenging? Are there some areas of your life where it would feel harder than others?

Much has been written about how the brain works in this regard, and modern neuroscience is forever developing its understanding of our adaptive brain,[8] so I won't go into a lot of detail. At its simplest, our amygdala, which sits within the limbic systems of our brain, is triggered into fight, flight or freeze when it detects a threat. This was very helpful when we lived on the land, hunted for food, and saw a tiger coming our way, but now it can often be stress that triggers our amygdala hijack (when our amygdala triggers a flight or fight response even when there is no threat).[9] And, in fact, research now suggests that living with chronic stress may lead to an overactive fear and anxiety circuitry within us.[10]

So, if we do anything outside of our comfort zone that our brain considers threatening, then it will naturally try to avoid it or fight against it. That doesn't exactly support our innate need to speak up and truly be ourselves if that goes against our comfort zone, does it? If, because of our histories, we have not internalised and embodied our innate worth, our brain also works against us speaking up and holding our boundaries.

We also have what's called 'negativity bias'. Dr Rick Hanson is a neuropsychologist who has spent significant time researching this. He sums it up with, 'Our brains are Velcro for the negative and Teflon for the positive.'[11] Our brain is naturally wired to focus on the negative, which can make us feel stressed, worried and disconnected, even though there are many positive things in our lives.

Why on earth would our brains be wired this way? To keep us alive. 'Mother Nature', says Dr Hanson, 'evolved a brain that routinely tricks us into making three mistakes: 1) overestimating threats, 2) underestimating opportunities, and 3) underestimating resources'. Again this was wonderful when we were roaming the savannahs keeping an eye out for that sabre-toothed tiger, but not so good for supporting us to speak up and out, and live true to ourselves in a modern world.

Our internal threat, drive and soothing systems

Professor Paul Gilbert, British clinical psychologist and the founder of compassion-focused therapy, suggests that we have three major emotional regulation systems: our threat system, which is there to protect us; our drive system, which aims to get our needs met; and our soothing system, to provide rest, healing and connection.

Our threat system

When our threat system detects a risk or danger, all our attention is focused on that threat. As mentioned earlier, anything that challenges our comfort zone is interpreted by our brain's threat system as dangerous.

Any situation where the demands involved may exceed our perceived ability to cope sets off our threat system. The emotions we experience when our threat system is activated are unpleasant: frustration, defensiveness, anger, anxiety, disgust, etc. These emotions are accompanied by physical sensations, such as increased heart rate, perspiration, shallow rapid breathing, churning gut, dry mouth and tense muscles.

When activated, our threat system pumps adrenaline and the hormone cortisol through our bodies to prepare us for fight, flight or freeze. While originally useful to handle physical threats, this system is equally responsive to emotional assaults, despite its intended purpose.

In terms of our emotional responses to threats, *fight* comes in the form of self-criticism or self-blame (e.g., 'You never get things right'). We direct our aggression to that part of ourselves we feel threatened by. *Flight* becomes fleeing from ourselves, perhaps by numbing out with food, alcohol, work, sex, you name it. And *freeze* becomes an over-identification, where we often get stuck in rumination, thinking about our perceived inadequacies repeatedly. Or we catastrophise situations (e.g., 'I'll never love again').[12]

One of the many challenging aspects of our threat system is that it's activated when we're simply *imagining* danger or feeling emotionally insecure. In fact, that's exactly the nature of anxiety. When we don't know what the future holds, we make up all kinds of scenarios — and usually the worst-case ones.

This is because of our new brain's capacity for memory, reflection and projection. We can now project into the future with fear and negativity, and trigger our threat system into action, even when, right here, right now, we're perfectly safe and all our essential needs are met.

When I was younger, I had a friend who helped me a lot with this. I would ring her in a fluster, feeling full of anxiety. She would remind me to take a big deep breath and do a conscious practice.

Look around and ask yourself: Am I safe? Yes.

Is there any threat at that moment? No.

Can you meet your basic human needs today? Yes.

My body was simply pumping with adrenaline and cortisol because my threat system had been activated. Often, for me, it was due to feeling overwhelmed with all that had to be done that week, and going into a worst-case scenario without even realising this was what was going on.

Another aspect of the threat system to keep in mind is that many sociologists refer to this time in history as the 'age of uncertainty'. Within this, we're constantly bombarded by information and societal messages that rev up fear and uncertainty.

Our drive system

As the name suggests, this is the system that gives us the energy and motivation (the 'get up and go') to engage with the world, to act, to seize opportunities and rise to challenges.

The job of our drive system is to get our needs met. It is activated by our wants and desires, such as hunger, sex, possessions, social relationships, success, status and power. When we're in our drive system, our attention gets narrowed and focused on the rewards that come from fulfilling these needs. Consider the reward of feeling joy as that delicious chocolate melts in your mouth, or the vitality we can feel when we're involved in a work or community project that we love, or the excitement we feel when we're given a promotion.

Emotions generated by the drive system are very pleasant, but they don't last for long. In the drive system, our behaviour is active. We're very much in *doing mode*, and our doing can feel like striving toward something—like getting the grocery shopping done, running an extra kilometre this week, achieving our work targets, or consuming something (shopping, anyone?). When our drive system is active, it pumps the hormone dopamine through us, which gives us a wonderful feeling of gratification and satisfaction.

One of the challenging aspects of our drive system is that we can get caught up in too much *doing*, and it becomes difficult to turn it off. All those dopamine-fuelled feelings of gratification and satisfaction can become quite chemically addictive. Our culture is also filled with messages that demand and reward busyness.

In some circles, how busy we are has become a way to show how important we are. The message being that we're leading a full and worthy life if we're busy. The idea that the ideal employee, mum or friend is always available, completely booked and in demand every hour of the day is becoming dangerously ingrained in our belief system and culture. And technology means it's now possible to be contacted 24/7 — as if that's a good thing!

It helps me to have this broader societal perspective to keep my drive system in check. For example, one small thing I do is power off all my devices at least an hour before bedtime and have a screen-free day once a week. So, yes, I do need to take action and get things done, but then I need to stop and refuel, and that leads me to our next system.

Our soothing system

The job of our soothing system is to provide us with rest, healing and connection. Our soothing system is all about relationships, care and *safeness*, which is different from *safety*. Physical safety is what the threat system seeks.

Safeness is where we can truly feel at ease and welcomed just as we are. When our soothing system is switched on, our attention is open and evenly divided between our internal and external worlds, between ourselves and others. We experience pleasant emotions that are long-lasting and of a different quality compared with the short-term pleasant emotions we experience in the drive system.

Our soothing system pumps the hormone oxytocin, which gives us feelings of warmth, contentment and ease, and we enjoy affection and connection with ourselves and other people. In this state, we can simply enjoy *being*. Our behaviour is caring, kind, peaceful, relaxed and playful.

Although we may not readily associate relational connection with survival, our soothing system is critical for survival. As humans, we are wired so that we can't survive, let alone thrive, without being able to seek, receive and give care and support to ourselves and to one another.

The challenge with the soothing system is that culturally, and often within our own belief system, it can be undervalued and even discouraged and disparaged.

I call it the myth of emotional self-sufficiency. I know this myth well. When it comes to intimate relationships, for example, I was plagued with a constant nagging inner voice that said: *Why do you need an intimate relationship so much? You ought to be able to fulfill your own needs. You should be content with yourself. You should be more self-sufficient. What's wrong with you?*

Dependency and interdependency

I bought into the cultural myth that people who need others are simply needy, that a deep longing for a relationship is immature, and that caring for and about others is co-dependent. This myth says we should be able to meet all our own needs, and that if we just loved ourselves enough, we wouldn't need anyone else. It's the myth that shames us for feeling lonely and wanting a loving connection with others.

The definition of dependence is 'a reliance on something or someone'. The definition is neutral, but for so many of us, the word *dependency* is a dirty word.

We are biologically hardwired to be interdependent. We are connected beings who require involvement with each other to meet our physical and emotional needs, and to grow and thrive. Caring connections with others help us deal with stress, find emotional balance and heal.

They also give us a secure base from which to venture out of our comfort zone. Knowing we are not alone gives us more courage to be curious and independent.

For human beings to be at our strongest, we need to be connected, to recognise our need for closeness and know how to get our needs met. This involves our relationship with ourselves and with others. And our soothing system requires a particular way of relating with ourselves and others with warmth, kindness, care and compassion.

Clearly, all three of our brain's regulation systems are necessary. The ideal is to balance the three, because our threat and drive systems are typically activated too frequently and too easily and take turns being dominant, while our soothing system is typically under activated and insufficiently developed. With the three systems balanced, our next aim is to work toward making our soothing system more readily our default system, the place we go easily and naturally when our threat or drive systems are legitimately not needed. When our threat and drive systems are overactivated and running our lives, it's a lot harder to live and lead true to ourselves.

Adult stages of development

Professor Robert Kegan sits on the Harvard Graduate School faculty and was trained in lifespan psychology before becoming the pre-eminent researcher in the field of adult development (rather than child or adolescent development). His Adult Stages of Development framework, which we looked at in Chapter 2, has had a profound impact on me, as through this lens I came to understand that all human beings struggle to self-actualise, reach our full potential, and live and lead true to ourselves.

According to his research, approximately 58 per cent of the adult population does not make the transition from what Kegan describes as the socialised mind to the self-authoring mind.[13] Or, in other words, 58 per cent of us orient our sense of self from the outside in, looking to people, places and things outside of us to tell us how to be.

For me, this very simply answers the question: *Why is it so hard to live true to ourselves?*

Kegan also explains that it is only through transformation that we can fully evolve from one stage of development to another. He defines transformation as, 'evolving the manner in which we make meaning — how we think, feel, how we construct our social relations with others, and how we construct our interior relationship with parts of ourselves', or, in other words, 'the gradual evolutions of our interior individual development'. We all know that transformation isn't easy, which, as a concept, provided me with great relief to finally understand I was not alone in my struggles to grow and evolve, which also allowed me a little more self-compassion.

Kegan also helped me understand that we don't become wiser simply by knowing more. We become wiser by upgrading our 'internal operating system', by evolving our meaning-making. And as scholar and philosopher Ken Wilber describes, at each stage 'we transcend and include' our prior logic and meaning-making.[14]

Robert Kegan's well-researched and widely accepted theory proposes that human beings go through different levels of understanding and thinking as they grow and mature. The first two (impulsive mind and imperial mind) predominantly address adolescence. We are most interested in stages three, four and five, so I want to provide you with a high-level overview. To explain the stages, I draw primarily from Robert Kegan's book, *The Evolving Self: Problem and process in human development*.

Stage 3: Socialised mind

In this stage, the core mindset is, 'I am my relationships; I follow the rules'. According to Kegan, 58 per cent of the population operates at this level.

At this stage, people primarily view the world through the lens of social norms and expectations. They rely on the opinions and approval of others to shape their identity. Think of it like being part of a team or a group where you want to fit in and follow the rules. People at this stage tend to conform to the values and beliefs of their community, and they might have a hard time questioning or challenging those norms.

At this stage, individuals primarily identify themselves through their social roles and affiliations. They seek validation and approval from the groups they belong to, such as family, friends or community. Their sense of self-worth is closely tied to how well they fit into these groups and adhere to their norms and expectations. People at this stage might feel uncomfortable challenging the status quo, as they fear rejection or isolation from their social circles.

Can you imagine turning up to a football game wearing a tutu? That's the level of awkwardness we feel when we're pushing through socialised mind. Everyone else clearly got the memo — they knew we were playing football — while we've turned up ready for ballet. It takes huge courage and self-belief not to change clothes.

Stage 4: Self-authoring mind

In this stage, the core mindset is 'I have an identity; I make the rules'. Kegan says that 35 per cent of the population operates at this level.

In this stage, individuals start to develop a stronger sense of self. They move away from just conforming to social expectations and begin to think more independently. They start defining their own values and beliefs, and they become more aware of their own needs and desires. They start to author their own life story instead of just following the script given to them by others. They begin to question the status quo, as well as to take responsibility for their choices and actions.

During this stage, individuals begin to distinguish their own values, beliefs and desires from those of the groups they are part of. They take on a more autonomous role in shaping their identity and life choices. This is where the idea of self-authorship comes into play. People in stage 4 become more reflective and capable of introspection. They can step back and question whether their beliefs align with their own true selves. This stage often involves a heightened sense of responsibility for one's life and actions, as well as a willingness to assert oneself, even if it means going against social norms.

As Kegan explains in *The Evolving Self*:

> *This is a tremendously empowering and inspiring stage of development, as we come into our own voice. But before we get there, as we transform, there is often a lot of terror, grief, and anticipated loss as we object to the norms we use to adhere to. What will be the results? Will people still love me? Will I be put out of my society, community, organisation?*
>
> *This is the most dynamic transformation in adult development. But is it not the final stage of development.*

Stage 5: Self-transforming mind

At the highest level, the core mindset is, 'I have many identities; I embrace paradox'. Kegan says that only 1 per cent of the population operates at this level.

At this stage, people's thinking becomes even more complex. They realise that their own beliefs and values are not set in stone and can evolve over time. They become more open to diverse perspectives and are comfortable with uncertainty and ambiguity. Instead of seeing the world as black and white, they understand that there are multiple shades of grey. They are able to hold contradictory ideas without feeling the need to resolve them immediately. This stage is about constant growth, adaptation and a willingness to learn from different sources.

In stage 5, individuals demonstrate a remarkable ability to hold complexity and paradox. They recognise that reality is multi-faceted and that different perspectives can coexist. This stage is marked by a deep humility and a willingness to learn from others, even if their viewpoints differ greatly. People in stage 5 are also comfortable with uncertainty and change.

In short, as we evolve through the stages, we shift from being a follower of societal norms (stage 3); to becoming an independent thinker and creator of our own path (stage 4); and finally, reaching a stage where we're open to continuous growth, change and learning from a wide range of experiences and viewpoints (stage 5).

These stages are not rigid and fixed. People can move through them at their own pace, and some might not reach the later stages in certain areas of their lives. The idea is to understand that our human development is a journey, and these stages help us make sense of how we evolve in our thinking and understanding of ourselves and the world around us.

In my own personal experience and from working with many others, we often think we are operating from a higher level of consciousness than we are — denial can be one of the many challenges of working with our own limited consciousness. And it is not a linear process. I regularly notice, especially when I am scared (like at the thought of publishing this book) or doing something new, that I can dip back into my socialised mind, and other times, when I stay focused on my vision, purpose and values, the fear and anxiety (while sometimes still there) no longer runs me, and I feel more trusting and grounded and my life feels more effortless. Given that fundamental shifts in consciousness are incredibly difficult to achieve, this theory clearly points to the great challenge we all encounter when transforming to live, lead and succeed true to ourselves.

Conscious reflection

I encourage you to pause and take a moment to get really curious about where you feel you are on your own adult development journey. You may want to think back to Chapter 3 where we explored our reactive tendencies, which, when over-activated, are caught in the socialised mind (where our sense of self comes from the outside in: other people, places and things) rather than operating as an independent thinker (making our own choices, creating our own path). If you bring in great curiosity and self-compassion, where in your life do you most struggle to stay true to yourself?

Our core beliefs colour how we see the world

As we go through life, we accumulate beliefs from our experiences. We then internalise them, and these beliefs strongly influence the lens through which we see and perceive our lives, and therefore, how we behave in any given situation. They are the 'stories' we tell ourselves from the experiences we have, especially from our childhoods and then we co-create them over and over and over. Some of these beliefs can really support us in our lives, while others can be very limiting, self-sabotaging and even destructive.

Our core beliefs influence all areas of our lives, whether they are beliefs around money, relationships, work or health. It is challenging to see the core beliefs that drive our behaviour because we are usually not conscious of them. Yet, they are constantly unconsciously directing our thoughts, feelings and behaviours.

Some examples for me, which took many years to see, included:

◆ Men are dangerous.

◆ I am not important.

◆ Nobody cares about my feelings.

◆ Nobody really wants me.

◆ I am not enough as I am.

◆ Anger is bad.

◆ It isn't safe to speak up.

◆ Don't rock the boat.

◆ My job is to keep everyone happy.

◆ Work and success are more important than family.

◆ I can't trust anyone.

◆ Men don't like successful women and neither do other women.

◆ What other people think about me is more important than what I think of myself.

Our beliefs are often very unconscious and can feel quite intangible and yet very real. When someone I am very close to did something that I felt incredibly hurt and betrayed by, it led me to discuss trust with my therapist.

My therapist said, 'So she broke your trust'.

'Yes', I said, 'but you can't really trust people, can you? I mean we are all human. We all make mistakes, so we are all going to hurt each other, even just accidentally'.

She responded, 'Yes, we are human, and we do make mistakes, but this was a big betrayal, it wasn't just a small mistake. It had a huge impact on you and people don't just do that every day. It's okay for you to feel hurt and angry about that'.

There lies a very strong and quiet unconscious belief: 'I can't trust anyone'. Given my history, it makes sense that I have this belief and I am often unconsciously just waiting for people to let me down, disappoint me and break my trust.

Not only do our beliefs constantly influence our behaviour, but to further complicate matters, we also have a predictive brain. As psychiatrist Regina Pally explains:

> *According to neuroscience, even before events happen in our life, the brain has already made a prediction about what is mostly likely to happen, and sets in motion the perception, behaviour, emotions, physiologic responses, and interpersonal ways of relating that best fit with what is predicted. In a sense, we learn from the past what to predict for the future and then live the future we expect.*[15]

No wonder we often feel like we are repeating the same patterns over and over! Becoming aware of our core beliefs and how they play out in our lives and relationships is critical to living true to ourselves.

Getting stuck in identity and our narrative

Throughout different stages of our life, we all take on different roles and identities. These roles and identities are often tied to our beliefs and how we generally think about ourselves. They are often how we want to be seen in the world and how we want to see ourselves in the world. These may include examples such as being a good mother, a helpful sister, the perfect partner, an entrepreneur, a leader, our title at work, wealthy or successful, intellectually bright or superior, spiritual, competent, perfect, a good person, and so on. Or sometimes, quite unconsciously, we create an internal narrative that we are a failure, broken or a victim to life.

There is nothing right or wrong with any of these. However, if we over-identify with them, and hold on too tightly to them, it can be very challenging to grow and change. It can feel particularly hard to speak up and live true to ourselves when what we need or want to say consciously or unconsciously threatens our identity. We can often end up feeling stuck.

Part of this is created by the story we tell ourselves about who we have been, who we are now and who we are going to be: our identity narrative. I recently participated in a workshop on narrative identity facilitated by Steve Athey, senior partner at the Full Circle Group. He explained how our narrative identity is made up of our curated past, our experienced present and our imagined future. He invited each of us to tell the story of how we came to be who we are. This is the familiar story we tell about ourselves; the one that comes most naturally to us.

Steve then invited us to explore what we may have been over-privileging or had left out in this story. It is interesting to note, of the millions of experiences we have had in our lives, what we automatically include and what we leave out. For some participants in the room, their stories were focused on being seen as a 'good girl' or 'good boy'; for others, there was a focus on loss and grief. I noticed in mine that I had a story that justified my imperfections, the parts I don't like about myself. I over-privileged what had happened to me, but left out what I had done with those challenges, how I had grown and overcome my past.

He then invited us to explore where we might feel stuck in our story. Where did we notice that in our bodies? What body posture represented this 'stuckness', and what happened when we held that posture with compassion and allowed it to move and transform itself in its own time?

Through this, I noticed part of me was still stuck in my story, my identity of brokenness, shame and unworthiness, which my narrative was reinforcing. As this posture transformed and I sat back, I felt a deep compassion, I felt grounded and I felt my inner power start to emerge within me. I also felt some grief arise as I began the process of forgiving myself for not seeing the woman I had become. And within this, my identity narrative loosened and expanded.

Who am I without my identity?

We can often be over-identified with our roles and identities and feel our sense of self or worthiness comes from these roles and identities. In my experience, when I want to let go of an identity I am deeply invested in and over-identified with, it literally feels like a part of me is dying. It feels like (and ultimately is) a death of self, the end of a way of seeing myself in the world. In that process, we often go through what many refer to as a 'dark night of the soul'. I, for one, can feel so lost when I am in the process of letting go of an aspect of myself that is tied to my identity.

It makes so much sense when we think of it like that, doesn't it? If a part of my identity, or my sense of worth, is tied to being seen as a good and kind person, and then I need to say 'no' to something or someone and they are (potentially) not going to like my no, then that is going to threaten my identity of being seen as a good person. If my sense of identity comes from being seen as wealthy and successful and I lose that or I never get that, then who am I without my wealth and success?

These identity issues have been an absolute minefield for me to navigate. The moment I become aware of my over-identifying with a particular role and identity and consciously practise being less identified or less attached to it, I quickly go and pick up another one.

I have so many examples! Like a little while after the share market crashed in 2008, when I lost that second tranche of equity and had to sell my house, I also decided I needed to sell my BMW. I vividly remember it feeling like I was cutting off my right arm, like losing a piece of myself when I sold that car.

I didn't really understand why at the time, but the more I explored it in therapy, I realised that my whole identity, my whole sense of worth, was tied to my work, to my success, to my wealth, to how people saw me in the world. It wasn't so much the car itself — it was what the car represented to me, what I believed the car said to other people. If I drove a new-model BMW, then I must be important and successful. And in the end, what that actually meant to me was that I must be worthy of your love. My sense of self was over-identified with what I did.

The gift and challenge of being a mum

I also see it as a mother. I love being a mother to my son. I love being part of his life. As he grew up, I loved driving him places, taking him surfing, making meals together, supporting him with his study, sitting and talking, hanging out, watching him grow into his own person. For me, there has been no greater gift in my life than being a mother to my son. My son is a young man now. He doesn't need me like he used to. Letting him go to fully become his own person and make his own decisions and become truly independent has been both an absolute joy and one of the most difficult things I have ever experienced. Partly because my identity was so tied to wanting to be a good mother and needing to be needed, and partly because any loss or significant change in a relationship can trigger all of our past losses. I love how Mia Freedman described it in one of her blogs that captured the zeitgeist for her readers: 'Your son growing up will feel like the slowest break up you've ever known.'[16]

Many men (and women) grew up with mothers who never fully let them go, who want to continue to mother them, who hold on too tightly. Mothers whose major identity is tied to what their children do or don't do with their lives as an extension of their own 'accomplishment' or replacement for their own unmet hopes and dreams. While we can try to paint the picture that we just love our kids, when we are not aware that we are holding on too tightly or *why* we are holding on too tightly (which can often be to avoid our own feelings of loss and perhaps our own deeply rooted abandonment pain), then it actually becomes all about our needs and identities, and not about our children at all.

And it is hard! Because we genuinely and whole-heartedly love them like no other love. We have spent years being needed by them. And many of us can be over-identified as being mothers. We can feel like our sense of self, our sense of worthiness in the world comes from being seen as a good mother. We can also feel bloody lost when they no longer need us like they used to. I know for me, much of my identity in the past has come from my need to be needed.

Conscious reflection

Again, with gentle curiosity and great self-compassion:

◆ What roles and identities resonate most strongly with you in your own life and work?

◆ Where might you be drawing self-worth from? Is it outside of yourself?

◆ Where might you be over-invested or holding on too tightly to your identities or roles?

In the coming chapters, we will explore how we go about becoming more conscious of these identities and in what areas of our life they may support or no longer serve us.

Perimenopause and menopause

Having now gone through it myself and witnessed the struggles of many other friends and clients, particularly those in their mid-forties who get caught by surprise, I can't with any integrity write a book about why it can feel hard to live true to ourselves as women and not mention the potential impact of perimenopause and menopause on our sense of self as we reach midlife.

It still blows my mind how little I knew about this before it arrived for me, and how little it is talked about in many circles. I am not an expert in this space; however, I want to at least highlight the potential impact of menopausal symptoms on our quality of life and work, and encourage you to talk about it and get support to manage this transition if it is close for you.

For most women, menopause will occur between forty-five and fifty-five years of age, and perimenopause lasts four to six years on average.[17] Perimenopause ends one year after your last period.

My understanding is that some women breeze through both perimenopause and menopause, and others struggle enormously with one or both. I personally sit somewhere in between, but only after I realised what was going on, as for a long while I thought I was going slightly insane! Hot sweats, while problematic for sleeping and not ideal when I was in the middle of a meeting, felt like the least of my challenges versus the at-times crippling anxiety and brain fog that affected my ability to function, let alone feel confident and excited about life and work.

Additional symptoms that many women don't know about include decreased interest in sex, menopausal depression, forgetfulness, heart racing or pounding, hot flashes, insomnia/difficulty sleeping, joint stiffness, mood changes, night sweats, urine leakage, vaginal dryness, changes in where our body stores weight (around the tummy), sore breasts, tiredness and difficulty concentrating.[18] Fun, right?

As the British Menopause Society states:

> *Menopausal symptoms affect more than 75% of women ... and over 25% describe severe symptoms. Menopausal symptoms may last for a long time with an average duration of 7 years, and 1 in 3 women experience symptoms beyond the 7 years.*[19]

For me, my symptoms have been very manageable through hormone replacement therapy; however, it took me a long time to explore this as an option because I had not read the new research on the benefits, and I was still under the impression that this was not a valid option. There are many wonderful resources, and one I love is the book *It's the Menopause: Everything you need to know in your 40s, 50s and beyond* by Kaz Cooke, where she talks about the 'confidence crash'; another is Dr Lisa Mosconi's book *The Menopause Brain*.

Wherever you sit in the spectrum of symptoms, or as you head into your mid-forties, may you seek out knowledge and resources to support you and honour this important life transition. When managed well, menopause coincides with a time in life when we can enjoy the wisdom that comes from our experience. It can be a period of great personal growth and self-discovery to a deeper understanding of ourselves and our desires, a sense of freedom from the pressures to conform to certain standards of beauty and femininity and lead to greater self-acceptance and authenticity.

The reality of a patriarchal, white-privileged and outwardly focused society

This is obviously a complex subject to broach. It is so pervasive. It is so obvious and yet so subtle. And as a white, privileged woman, I am also very aware I am offering my views through my own lens and my own unconscious biases.

Regardless of our patterns and beliefs, we have all grown up in a patriarchal society, some of us also in white-privileged cultures. It was only at the beginning of the last century that most Western women were allowed to vote, and there are still too many countries where women do not have the most basic of equalities. It is hard for me to fathom that this is still the case in the twenty-first century. And yet here we are, still fighting for equal pay and equal representation, subtly and not so subtly.

Here in Australia, one out of three women has experienced physical and/or sexual violence. One out of five over the age of eighteen has been stalked. One out of five experiences harassment in the workplace. One woman, on average, is killed every week by a current or former partner.[20] And the statistics in the US, UK and other Western countries are very similar.

#metoo

I was deeply moved and inspired by the #metoo movement. At the same time, I also noticed a very quiet internal conflict arise within me. I had grown up in an era where much of what was now being called out had been normalised. I had normalised if for myself. While I feel quite sick in my stomach writing this, which is likely carried shame, I have sometimes even noticed a defensiveness that wanted to come up within me to protect some of the men I had worked with (e.g., 'they didn't know any better'). Within this, I had to begin to own where I had been complicit, where I had been in denial, as well as seeing my own fears at owning and speaking my truth. I am forever grateful for the incredibly courageous women who found their voices and faced a system that wanted to shut them down. This movement is all about women speaking up and out, sharing stories of sexual harassment, gender discrimination and inequality in the workplace. It's about learning to honour ourselves and our experiences.

In this patriarchal culture, masculine corporate structures, attitudes, microaggressions, biases and prejudices are embedded in our walls.

As Elizabeth Broderick, the previous Australian Sex Discrimination Commissioner, said:

> We're now dealing with 'gender asbestos'. It's in the roofs, walls, and floors of our organisations. You can't see it. Can't touch it. But it exists and it's dangerous. It's more difficult to name and therefore more difficult to do anything about.[21]

The patriarchal culture has not just affected and damaged women. I recently heard author Glennon Doyle sum it up beautifully:

> Telling a boy he must take all the power is as damaging as telling a girl she must take none... Being told you must be big, bold, invulnerable to earn your worthiness is as shaming as being told you must be small, weak, and passive to earn it.[22]

Many of us are stuck in old ways, old beliefs about how each gender should behave. As with all beliefs, we're often unconscious of our own biases against women, men, gender fluidity, race, age etc. Against anything that has us feel uncomfortable and forces us to look at ourselves.

Workplace gender bias

Women often face various biases in the workplace, which can significantly affect our professional experiences and opportunities. These biases encompass stereotypes, unequal treatment and both subtle and not-so-subtle forms of discrimination. Stereotypes may portray women as less competent or not suited for leadership roles, resulting in us being overlooked for promotions or important projects. Unequal treatment can manifest as disparities in pay, where women are paid less than their male counterparts for the same work. Subtle biases, like microaggressions or exclusion from informal networks, can lead to feelings of isolation and hinder career advancement.

The global research and consulting firm McKinsey publishes an annual 'Women in the Workplace' study,[23] conducted in partnership with LeanIn.Org. Its most recent findings explored four common myths related to women in the workplace.

Myth 1: Women are becoming less ambitious.

Reality: Women are more ambitious than before the pandemic — and flexibility is fuelling that ambition.

Myth 2: The biggest barrier to women's advancement is the 'glass ceiling'.

Reality: The 'broken rung' is the greatest obstacle women face on the path to senior leadership.

Myth 3: Microaggressions have a 'micro' impact.

Reality: Microaggressions have a large and lasting impact on women. Women who experience microaggressions — and self-shield to deflect them — are three times more likely to think about quitting their jobs and four times more likely to almost always be burned out.

Myth 4: It's mostly women who want — and benefit from — flexible work.

Reality: Men and women see flexibility as a 'top 3' employee benefit and critical to their company's success.

The impact of these myths, biases and microaggressions on professional women is profound. We can experience lowered self-confidence due to the constant invalidation, leading to imposter syndrome, where we doubt our achievements. Limited access to growth opportunities and leadership roles can curtail our advancement potential. Gender bias also contributes to a lack of diversity at higher organisational levels, which diminishes diverse perspectives and innovation. These challenges can create a hostile work environment, affecting mental and emotional wellbeing, causing some women to leave their careers prematurely. Addressing gender bias is crucial, not only for women's individual success, but also for building inclusive workplaces that foster diversity, equality and productivity.

I also work across many Asian countries and hear about women's struggles to live true to themselves within the cultural demands, hierarchical structures and patriarchal systems they feel they are constantly having to fight against. I hear stories in Japan of women still not being able to have a voice in a client meeting as the client is not interested in what a woman has to say. In other stories from women in India, Korea and Thailand, managers show obvious positive bias toward male colleagues.

Wherever we live in the world, and I deeply appreciate that some countries and companies are much worse than others, I think it is fair to say these cultural nuances and patriarchal systems do not support us to speak up, to believe in ourselves, to live true to ourselves, and to honour ourselves and each other. I see so many of my clients struggle with the fear they will be seen as 'weak' or 'playing the gender card', so they stay silent. And I see so many men feeling defensive and shutting down. It's hard to find our truth and our voice in that environment. It's hard to come together in that. It's hard to listen and hear each other in that. It's hard to heal our collective pain and fears within that.

Moving forward

I fundamentally believe that it is time for us all to learn to believe in ourselves, to step fully into our authentic power and to support each other. This is not easy. We are dealing with long-term unconscious patterns, privileges and biases: our own and those of the women and men we work and live with.

This is not about making men wrong. It's hard and confusing for them too — and they're just as blindly stuck in a system they can't see as we are. This is about knowing ourselves and our own patterns, to know when and why we can be complicit in our silence, in our own denial. To be heard, we need to be grounded in our truth, our power, our strong feminine. We need to hold boundaries. We need to know ourselves, care for ourselves, be ourselves and believe in ourselves.

And, yes, we are likely to piss some people off along the way as we call out old behaviours and unconscious biases. It will feel threatening to all of us.

I have worked with some incredibly respectful and supportive men in my career. And I have also experienced blatant sexism, sexual harassment, white male privilege, unconscious bias, inappropriate behaviours and psychological coercion in my workplaces and at industry events. These have sometimes been subtle, many times far from subtle. Historically, I pretended to myself and with them and others that it was okay, often due to legitimate fears of the ramifications for my career and financial wellbeing if I spoke up. I know for a fact, no matter the policies and procedures that are in place, that it is still happening within the many industries I now work across.

When we learn to live and lead true to ourselves and find our authentic voice, we are threatening a culture that feels 'normal' for many of us at work and at home. We are threatening our old ways of being: our identities, old patterns and beliefs. As we explored on page 76, our brain is literally wired for survival. Speaking up and challenging the status quo threatens our own and others' sense of safety.

Yes, we need to revolutionise the patriarchal structures and cultures we still live and work in and to do this, we need strong male allies:

> ...when men are deliberately engaged in gender inclusion programs, 96% of organizations see progress—compared to only 30% of organizations where men are not engaged.[24]

We need governments to take this seriously and, while it's only the beginning here in Australia, the Respect@Work Bill and the pay transparency directive are further small steps forward. Yes, we need men to do their own inner work to become aware of their biases and be fierce allies. And to support this revolution we, as women, also need to consciously take back our power. For many of us, that is not an easy thing. If we want to be true to ourselves, we will not be able to please everyone. Change can only happen collectively when each one of us takes up the mantle to role model the change we want to see in the world. We need to do this together. I have done life on my own a lot, but we weren't meant for that. Women need women. And for years, I lost touch with that.

Good enough

In addition to all of the challenges we have explored, our cultures often subtly and not so subtly encourage and reinforce the message that 'you are not enough'. Through movies, advertising, magazines and role modelling, we often learn we are not pretty enough, skinny enough, smart enough, fit enough, kind enough, successful enough, etc., accentuating the 'confidence gap' that women often experience. Creating a belief that we are just not enough as we are. There is always something more to strive for. Something more to achieve.

> ## Conscious reflection
>
> I invite you to take a one-minute conscious pause here. Breathe deep into your belly and ask yourself:
>
> ◆ Where do I still not feel good enough at work, at home, in life?
>
> ◆ Where does this belief, and the assumption that sits under it, come from in me?
>
> ◆ What am I worried will happen if I let go of this belief?
>
> ◆ What is the most supportive and encouraging thing I could say to myself next time I notice this belief arising in me?

The paradox here has always been a tough one for me to grasp. If we want to change, we must learn to accept ourselves fully as we are.

Changing our template

Through our attachment dynamics, trauma, childhood experiences, cultures, beliefs and our biological hardwiring, we lay down a 'template', a way of being in the world and our self-concept.

Our self-concept is the intricate tapestry of beliefs, perceptions and ideas we construct about ourselves throughout our lives. This intricate mental portrait not only shapes how we view ourselves, but also influences our behaviours, choices and interactions with the world. Our self-concept can be our staunchest ally and harshest critic, profoundly impacting our self-esteem and overall wellbeing. It is a dynamic and evolving construct influenced by experiences, social feedback and personal growth. Understanding our self-concept is a crucial journey toward self-acceptance, as it enables us to embrace our strengths, acknowledge our limitations and strive for personal growth and authenticity in a complex and ever-changing world.

For many of us, to find our authentic voice and our worth, to believe in and live true to ourselves, we need to become conscious of and gently evolve our self-concept and the stories we tell ourselves. This is where I always start with the women I work with in our signature Authentic Woman Leadership Program.

We start by not giving ourselves a hard time when we are unable to change instantly, when we are struggling to be the best versions of ourselves or when we feel dissatisfied with ourselves or life. We start with a little self-acceptance and self-compassion for what it is like to be a human being in a fast-paced, demanding and ever-changing world.

Let us also recognise that if our sense of safety, security, survival and, ultimately, our worth is tied to our jobs, homes, money, family, friends (anything that is outside of ourselves), we are always going to struggle to speak up and live true to ourselves, to believe in ourselves from an empowered place.

To free ourselves from this old template, we lean into our inner work. This means facing our limiting and seemingly self-sabotaging behaviours and exploring the often unconscious forces creating them. It means diving deep into what Carl Jung called the 'shadow': the parts of our unconscious mind composed of our repressed and denied thoughts, desires, instincts and weaknesses. It means gently exploring the characteristics we project onto others and our triggers, to resolve the subconscious feelings behind them. It means acknowledging, making meaning of and grieving the past so we can manage it, rather than it running us. The past will control us from the shadows if we don't bring it into the light. It means becoming aware of the limiting beliefs and assumptions created from our past, as it is hard to create and sustain new behaviours without understanding where the old ones came from. It means consciously, courageously, consistently and, most of all, compassionately facing the deepest truths about ourselves to evolve and grow.

As we do the inner work, we begin to internalise and embody a sense of safety and security within us, irrelevant of what is going on outside of us. This is 'the work'. This is the journey to freedom. This is the only solution I know.

In the context of our emotional inner work, I love the confronting message of psychotherapist Ron Kurtz:

> If you don't have what you want in life, one of two things is happening. It is not there, not available, which is rarely the case, or you can't let it in due to your template.[25]

PART II
Care
for yourself

CHAPTER 5

The challenge and gift of being our own best friend

One of the most profound lessons I have learnt is that how we see and experience and interact with the world and treat people and allow others to treat us all depend on our relationship with ourself. Learning to be our own best friend is the cornerstone of self-worth, of inner confidence, of inner-calm and connection. Learning to be our own best friend is how we move from surviving to thriving.

At some point in my young life, I decided that the only way to feel truly safe in the world was to make money and become successful and independent, and I did a pretty bloody good job of it for a long time. I was incredibly driven, I pushed myself hard and climbed that corporate ladder quickly. I did whatever I thought I needed to do, even if that often meant abandoning myself. And, if I am very honest with myself, as painful as it is to acknowledge out loud, I abandoned those parts of my life outside of work that needed my attention. I worked long hours, I said 'yes' when I needed to say 'no', I played the politics, I got close to people I felt were important and would look after me, I tried to do everything perfectly. Within this, I found a false sense of control and power.

The consummate swan, I had been paddling like crazy for years to keep my life on track, even though many people would not have known this. My life looked good from the outside (although I was paddling like crazy underneath), and work was a very important part of this for me.

It is tiring to constantly have to prove yourself and protect yourself, living from a place of survival. I once read that feeling powerless is the most uncomfortable feeling for a human being. I can really see all the things I did to avoid feeling powerless, and feeling the loss that comes with it.

Like most of us, I had never learnt how to love myself, how to nurture my relationship with myself. After years of this practice, I had learnt to neglect myself and abandon myself. I had learnt to criticise myself. I had learnt how to put others first. I had learnt how to be 'successful' and how to be resilient. I had learnt how to survive — and I did that well — but I had never learnt how to be my own best friend.

In this chapter we are going to explore how you can become your own best friend, and that, rather than it being a little self-indulgent, how it can actually support you to create a more meaningful and fulfilling life. You will also discover why we often avoid self-compassion, and the crippling impact shame and our inner critic have on our sense of self. We will learn how we can begin to replace this inner critic with our inner coach.

Becoming our own best friend with self-compassion

How would you describe the nature and quality of the relationship you have with yourself? What is more foundational in truly being ourselves, than the quality of that connection we have with ourselves?

Strangely, we are the only ones in our own company 24/7, yet at times, we are probably more horrible to ourselves than anyone else could be. Being our own best friend ultimately means having compassion for ourselves. Having compassion for ourselves is the same as having compassion for others — although it feels much harder for most of us.

Dr Kristin Neff is a pioneer in self-compassion research who defines compassion as 'feeling moved by someone's suffering in a way that our heart responds to their pain'. At its roots, the word *compassion* means *to suffer with*. To feel compassion means feeling a caring desire to help those in pain. Compassion is one of the deepest ways we connect with each other as human beings.

When we're feeling stress and not coping well, self-compassion means to feel moved to take care of ourselves. Instead of just ignoring our anxiety or pain, harshly judging ourselves for it, or distracting ourselves from it (often by overworking, overeating, drinking, or obsessively thinking), we can stop and acknowledge to ourselves: *This feels hard. How can I best take care of myself right now?*

Self-compassion means replacing our critical inner judge with a loving voice of self-care — especially when confronted with our personal weaknesses.

Learning to love myself

While I can understand there would have been some financial imperatives for my parents, through the eyes of a young girl, I felt both my mum and my dad prioritised work over parenting. I heard my grandparents constantly talking about who was successful and who was not, as though a person's worth was built on what they did or did not accomplish. This created an embodied experience of anxiety and fear born from not having enough money, and the stress and tension that created in our household: a fear I still carry in my body today.

I used to say that what I loved about money was that it gave me choices, but I now understand that it gave me a false sense of security and control. Until something is taken away from us, I am not sure we ever really understand our relationship with it — and that includes money. When I had money and 'success', I felt like I didn't have to rely on others. I didn't have to ask for help, I could stay separate, I could distance myself from my often unconscious fears, hide from my insecurities. It felt easier to hold boundaries, as I told myself that money would keep me safe, even if it meant others didn't like me or would possibly abandon me. I thought I would finally feel free to choose what I wanted to say 'yes' and 'no' to. (Chapter 9 will cover our relationship with money in more depth.)

Conscious reflection

What is your relationship to money?

- ◆ Other than the obvious (e.g., it pays your mortgage, puts food on your table and so on), what does money represent to you?

- ◆ If you lost it all, assuming you could still meet your basic needs, what would that mean for you, about you?

Toward the end of my tumultuous relationship with Tim, I decided to take a very lucrative financial package and step away from my corporate career in financial services, and I believed now that I was financially secure, life would be simple. That decision brought on a tremendous amount of relief, knowing I would never have to do anything I didn't want to do again. I would never have to feel anxious or uncomfortable again. My nervous system could finally rest. I would never have to people-please or prove myself again. I could finally feel safe and free. Little did I know what a gross delusion this was, especially as I chose to step straight back into work.

The next year was as tumultuous as my relationship with Tim was. I didn't want to go back into financial services. Even though I had loved the people I worked with and the products we created, I felt burnt out by my experience there and I didn't trust myself to do it differently. Yet, my first step was to talk my way into a role in a completely different industry, one of Australia's largest listed marketing and communications groups. It was a role they created for me. I honestly can't tell you why, other than I think the boss at the time liked the idea of bringing in people with different experiences and thinking.

But with no specific remit and none of the agencies within the group financially aligned with my role, it was never going to work. It was an incredibly misogynistic boy's club culture, and I was one of a handful of token senior females. They didn't know what they wanted me to do, and I didn't know what I was meant to do, which, when you are a driven, people-pleasing, perfectionist, is a very scary place to be. This job, which only lasted nine months, was a complete disaster on every level. The role was set up for failure and the organisational culture was extremely toxic. And while I was definitely not at my best at this time of my life, sadly, when we agreed to amicably part ways, I fully blamed myself and was covered in a deep sense of shame. Given the share market was at an all-time high, and the final tranche of my shares were due to vest in the next six months, perhaps it was time to semi-retire at thirty-seven.

I spent the next six months watching the share market dramatically decline, and my shares, which were 'almost' guaranteed to vest and were going to 'set me up for life' literally disappeared. With this, my financial situation completely changed. All that false safety I had been feeling suddenly disappeared. While I was far from destitute, I now had to rebuild my life and career on my own, with a young son.

I felt lost. Much of my identity and self-worth were completely wrapped up in my title, my success, my material things, what I did and how I looked. I was unconsciously obsessed with how people saw me. How would they know I had been successful, and was therefore worthy of their love and respect, if I didn't have my houses, cars and outfits to show them? Who was I without these things? Why would anyone love me or want me if I didn't have these things? At this stage of my life, with all that had transpired, my anxiety and insecurities were at an all-time high and my self-worth was at an all-time low.

I spent weeks curled up in the foetal position in my bedroom. I am not sure I have ever felt more alone: on my own, co-parenting my young son and no job or self-worth. It felt like everything had been taken from me. In retrospect, this was really the beginning of a new life for me. The gift in all of this was that I hit my rock bottom. I was desperate for change, and desperation can be a wonderful catalyst for deep change. It has often led me to a surrender of the old way of doing something and a willingness to try something different.

As part of a desperate search for change, I started to see an acupuncturist. Each week I would come in with a new, often painful story about a romantic entanglement, what to do about work, or the bad choices I had made after drinking too much. It was in this space that he introduced me to several support programs. This was a very important part of my surrender, to finally put down all the things I was using to numb out and run away from myself, which had escalated through this difficult period of my life.

While it can look different for everyone, what numbing out and escaping looked like for me was overworking, binge drinking and attracting dysfunctional relationships. I used workaholism to avoid what was going on inside of me, which looks very acceptable to the outside world. But it was slowly destroying the rest of my life.

Binge drinking gave me the illusion of having control over alcohol, but in truth, it had control over me, and I regularly used it to numb my thoughts and feelings and escape my reality. At the end of a hard week, I 'deserved' to let my hair down and have some fun. Drinking became a habit that did not support me to be who I wanted to be. I had to stop and honestly reflect on my relationship with alcohol, how and why I drank. I used it to manage my stress, and I could not always guarantee my behaviour or my ability to stop after just one or two drinks. I gave it up many times but could never fully stay away.

I needed help and support to do this, and I am grateful that, at the time of writing this book, with the support of a higher power and a supportive community, I have not had a drink or drug for over fifteen years.

I also habitually attracted dysfunctional, often drama-filled relationships, especially with men, but also within some of my friendships. I remember reading Melody Beattie's beautiful book, *The Language of Letting Go*, and another one of hers, *Codependent*

No More. Both shattered my world and opened my eyes to why I did what I did in relationships.

When we use anything to escape our feelings, our thinking, our lives and ourselves, and we take that thing away, we are still left with what we are trying to escape from. Unless we treat the underlying cause, we will just find something else to pick up and escape with (sugar, fatty foods, social media, TV, exercise, etc.). Otherwise, we become very irritable, restless and discontent, typically making lots of 'rules' and becoming obsessive compulsive or super controlling in all areas of our life as we try to control our dependencies without recognising or healing what creates them.

To surrender my dependencies and my control, I realised I needed a spiritual practice, a higher power that was not my overthinking, nor another human being, as I had used other people's opinions of me as my higher power for much of my life. This higher power of my own understanding helped me connect to my higher self and begin to change the relationship I had with myself and the world. I also started therapy, to face into my history and the feelings I had been running from my whole life.

Slowly but surely, I have learnt how to see myself, love myself, care for myself and (mostly) forgive myself. I love a quote by Kamilla Tolnoe: 'The past is what you were, not what you are'. I have dug deep to honour and heal my past, to make a living amends for how I behaved in the past and to become the mother and human being I am today. I genuinely like who I am these days. This has definitely allowed me to trust myself and show up differently in the world.

But isn't it just self-indulgence?

Often, the concern that arises when we start practising self-compassion is, how on earth are we meant to grow and become our best if we're always so quick to accept our weaknesses and shortcomings? To be warm and kind toward them? Isn't this all a little self-indulgent?

I battled with this when I first began to learn about and practice self-compassion. I didn't really understand the difference between self-compassion and self-indulgence. I found it difficult to allow myself self-compassion because I thought it meant I would become lazy and unmotivated.

Being compassionate with ourselves means we want to be authentically happy and healthy in the long-term. Rarely does self-indulgence support this. Self-indulgence typically helps us feel better in the short-term, usually by distracting us or numbing us from whatever it is we don't want to feel or don't want to do. Self-compassion has our longer-term interests at heart and gives us a way to soothe and comfort ourselves in the moment when we're having a hard time. It takes discernment to know when our intent is distracting or numbing versus genuine self-care.

When we want to change something about ourselves, most of us use the self-critical approach. We often shame ourselves into taking action and maintaining discipline. I don't know about you, but this approach has backfired on me time and time again because it meant I couldn't face the difficult truths about myself. I was so afraid that if I really acknowledged a hard truth about myself, my inner critic would go into overdrive.

For example, I've been on more than twenty diets in my life. Each time, I told myself I just hadn't found the right one yet. It wasn't until I started practising self-compassion that I was able to be more honest with myself and realise the inner work that my food habits were pointing to. No diet was going to fix the root problems. I needed to look inside at the difficult emotions I was pushing down with food. I needed to explore why my worth was so attached to my body image and how I looked to the outside world. I had to trust myself to be caring and warm and kind toward my failings and imperfections before I was able to really see this difficult truth.

Our own criticism and harsh self-judgement can be kind of tricky to see at first, and unconsciously stops us from seeing the hard stuff we don't want to see about ourselves. In contrast, self-compassion is a powerful catalyst for change because it creates the safety we need to see our dysfunctional behaviours and patterns more clearly, without shame and blame. With self-compassion, our motivation for change is because we care about ourselves, not because we think we're worthless or unacceptable as we are.

How shame cripples us

Oh, the pain of shame. Guilt says, 'I did something wrong', but shame says, 'Something is wrong with me'. Guilt says, 'I made a mistake'. Shame says, 'I am a mistake'. Shame is about who I am; guilt is about what I did. If your parents said, 'What you did was not okay', that is about your behaviour. If your parents said, 'You are a bad girl for doing that', that is shaming. As humans, we can learn a new behaviour, but shame will have us believe there is something innately wrong with us.

Shame fuels perfectionism and control, as it tells us that it is not okay to make a mistake, to not know how to do something, to not be perfect. As children, we internalise the messages we receive from family, teachers and friends, which become our internal voice and the way we speak to ourselves as adults. I, for one, have a very harsh inner critic who is very good at shaming me. As shame, authenticity and vulnerability researcher Brené Brown says: 'Shame corrodes the very part of us that believes we are capable of change.'

When our feelings are shamed as children, albeit often unconsciously, we often feel like there is something innately wrong with us for having them. Having and talking about feelings was not something that was encouraged when I was growing up, culturally or in our family. My granddads were both World War II veterans and their message was very much one of, 'you just suck it up and get on with it', passing that message on down the family line. I interpreted the message as, 'If it looks good on the outside, nobody will ever know what is really going on.'

Shame has often been a very common tool for controlling children: to make them feel wrong for their feelings and their behaviours (which they often learnt from their parents' role modelling). Often, because the adult didn't know how to deal with the child's feelings or behaviours themselves, they say things like, 'Don't cry', 'It's not okay to be angry', and 'Children should be seen and not heard'. When our feelings and reality are denied as children, then we learn to deny our feelings and reality as adults.

Conscious reflection

Take a moment to think back over the messages you received as a child, especially around your feelings and behaviours. Did these messages encourage you to be open and honest and embrace all parts of yourself and your feelings? Or did they tend to shut you down and shame parts of you or certain behaviours?

We are not looking to blame our parents here; they were also influenced by their pasts and their experiences growing up. This is about growing our own awareness and better understanding and having compassion for why we do what we do.

In my experience, the greatest antidotes to shame are self-compassion and connection. Self-compassion enables me to find distance from my inner critic, soothe myself and very slowly rewire how I think and talk to myself. Connection works because shame and connection cannot coexist. When we receive genuine understanding and empathy through connecting with another human being and realise we are human and imperfect just like everybody else, then the shame dissipates.

Shame has been one of the major hindrances to my ability to love and believe in myself, to find my voice and place in the world. My inner critic often causes me to give away my power. It can make it hard for me to take on constructive feedback. It can make it hard to say 'no'. It can make it hard for me to take risks, especially if I don't know how to do something and might make a mistake. It can make it hard for me to be vulnerable and ask for help.

Ironically, my shame is genuinely there to try to protect me from feeling hurt and disappointment. But ultimately, it also stops me from accessing the self-acceptance, self-love, joy and freedom I have longed for all my life.

> ## Conscious practice
>
> Think of a habit or something you keep doing for which you berate yourself.
>
> ◆ Take a moment now to offer yourself some understanding, kindness and compassion.
>
> ◆ Consider a loving action you can take for yourself.
>
> ◆ Repeat this the next time you notice yourself doing it again.
>
> I've found this to be incredibly hard to do—and incredibly powerful. Coming from a loving perspective allows me to shift my unhelpful ways far more effectively. Whereas berating myself seems to keep me stuck in whatever it is I'm doing that doesn't serve me.

An additional valuable insight I've acquired from my self-compassion journey is that showing myself compassion equates to acknowledging and embracing my innate humanity. Life doesn't consistently align with our desires. We inevitably face setbacks and losses, make errors, confront our limitations and deviate from our aspirations. This constitutes the human experience, a shared reality amongst us all. By embracing this truth wholeheartedly rather than consistently resisting it, we can cultivate a deeper capacity for self-compassion, extending it not only to ourselves but also to every individual within the human community.

Why do we resist self-compassion?

I recently coached a wonderful woman named Pauline. She was full of passion and energy and was extremely ambitious. But for some reason, nothing was working for her. She kept being overlooked for promotions. People questioned her integrity, as they experienced her as a real people pleaser and, therefore, did not feel they could always trust what she said. She took too much on, and therefore did not finish what she started and appeared unreliable. Her need to be liked and her inability to say 'no' and stay focused on what was important, rather than other people's urgencies, meant it was almost impossible for her to achieve her own goals.

But no matter how hard she drove herself, she never felt like it was enough. On those days that her body was exhausted and she could not get up early, she would berate herself, 'You will never be successful if you can't be disciplined'. And on those days that she did get up early and set herself up well for the day, other people's needs and requests meant she never got done what she needed to get done. She kept unconsciously sabotaging herself by pleasing others and then wondering why she couldn't achieve what she wanted to achieve.

As we explored her background, she recognised that she had a mother who would never let her sit down as a child. She was told there was always something to do. Her mum never slept more than four hours a night and was always busy, and demanded the same from her. She was also super critical and nothing was ever good enough. Pauline internalised her mother's critical voice and this became her own internal self-talk. She learnt that the only way to feel loved or hear any vague kind of praise from her mum was to try and achieve a lot.

Pauline, now in her forties with her own family, was still unconsciously busy in her own head, trying to get her mum's approval, saying 'yes' to everything everyone wanted and working herself into the ground to do it. She was completely out of touch with herself, her boundaries and her needs. She was regularly abandoning herself, her son and her husband, unconsciously saying 'no' to them while she said 'yes' to the work.

Even though I knew it would feel very counterintuitive and uncomfortable, I invited her to start to slow down, get clear on her own goals and priorities, and become more aware of what was driving her and what she was saying to herself. I invited her to practise self-compassion, self-support and self-acknowledgement. She wanted to see the research proving that if she stopped berating herself and instead was kind to herself that she could still achieve what she wanted to achieve. She was worried if she acted on self-compassion that she would become self-indulgent and lazy.

While Pauline was incredibly honest with me about her fears of ultimately changing her relationship with herself, she is not alone in them. I hear them often.

In *The Handbook of Self-Compassion*, Dr Kristin Neff explains that we're typically much more critical of ourselves than anyone else, and we're much less compassionate toward ourselves than we are for people we care about.

Self-criticism is a natural human behaviour coming from a brain hardwired for survival. When we make a mistake, we feel threatened. As we looked at in Chapter 4, this triggers our internal fight, flight or freeze mode. As Neff explains, these primal reactions can be turned on ourselves in three ways:

- Fight comes in the form of self-criticism, directing aggression to that part of ourselves we feel threatened by (e.g., 'You screwed up again').

- Flight means numbing out with food, alcohol, work, etc.

- Freeze is getting stuck in rumination, running our mistakes over and over in our minds.

In short, self-criticism activates our threat system, but with self-compassion, we can override our threat system and switch into our soothing system.

When dealing with the failings of others, it's easier for us to be understanding, supportive and encouraging. It's so important we learn how to do this for ourselves. This is part of caring as much for ourselves as we do for others.

As human beings, we're wired to be compassionate. It's in us naturally; we evolved to be a compassionate species because it had evolutionary advantages. We were far more likely to survive as a tribe where everyone protected and supported each other than alone in the wild. When you have never done it before, learning to practise self-compassion is not easy. We can come up with a million reasons to not give it to ourselves. After working with many women (and men), here's a list of common reasons I have heard for not wanting to practise self-compassion:

◆ It doesn't appeal to me at all to meet or feel my pain and disappointments in life.

◆ I feel ashamed to have compassion for myself while so many people have a lot more serious problems. I don't deserve it.

◆ I might become self-centred, lazy or too easy-going.

◆ When I tell my friends that I'm doing self-compassion training, they will think I'm a wimp or weird or soft.

◆ I feel some trepidation. This is new, and I'm not sure it's a good idea and I don't know what I'll uncover.

◆ I don't have time for all this fluffy emotional stuff.

◆ I fear I won't be as productive or successful.

I had a bit of all these reservations when I first encountered self-compassion, and they can still come up for me now. These barriers often point to inner fears or defences, or to misunderstandings about self-compassion. As Dr Neff says in her book, *Self-Compassion: The proven power of being kind to yourself*: 'Self-compassion is not the same as being easy on ourselves. It's a way of nurturing ourselves so that we can reach our full potential.'

Mindfulness teacher Tara Brach adds in her book *Radical Acceptance*:

Feeling compassion for ourselves in no way releases us from responsibility for our actions. Rather, it releases us from the self-hatred that prevents us from responding to our life with clarity and balance.

Proven benefits of practising self-compassion

Here's just a short list of what researchers are finding to be the benefits of practising self-compassion:

- less anxiety and depression

- reduced stress and overwork

- less perfectionism

- fewer control issues

- more resilience

- increased happiness, optimism and gratitude.

Self-compassionate people:

- feel greater motivation to make amends and avoid repeating moral transgressions

- are more motivated to improve personal weaknesses

- are more likely to take responsibility for their past mistakes

- are more likely to set new goals for themselves after not meeting goals.

Replace the inner critic with the inner coach

You may be blessed to have good, supportive friends and family. But when you wake up at three in the morning with your head full of a problem or ruminating about something you said, you are really all you have to help and support yourself, to soothe yourself emotionally. So having the regular practise of self-compassion is vital.

The research also tells us that self-compassion works primarily because it deactivates our threat system and activates our soothing system, which encourages feelings of safeness, calmness and warm connection. By increasing our feelings of safeness and connection and reducing feelings of threat and isolation, self-compassion gives us much greater emotional balance. This supports us when we're triggered and feeling difficult emotions. It also supports us when there is simply nothing we can change in a moment of pain. So rather than eat, drink, overwork or toss-and-turn in bed to resist our pain, we find greater strength to be with our pain without being overwhelmed by it.

One of my biggest fears was being overwhelmed by my feelings, especially sadness, anger, loneliness and fear. In hindsight, this makes so much sense, as in my childhood these feelings did feel completely overwhelming for me, and nobody was there to help me make sense of them or help me hold them. So, I came up with all kinds of strategies to avoid these strong emotions. This process of loving self-compassion, of offering myself soothing, has been profound. It's created great peace and clarity, as well as a new level of connection to myself and others. I've discovered the fear of overwhelm, coupled with the toll of my avoidant strategies, was a much tougher road than embracing this new way.

Self-compassion, like meditation, activates the same social circuitry that gets activated in a child who has a very safe, empathic, loving parent. Since many of us didn't have this kind of parent, you might say self-compassion is a way of re-parenting ourselves. Research from Dr Paul Gilbert also shows that self-compassion builds a strength in us that helps us cope with adversity. In one study of people going through a divorce, the researchers scored how self-compassionately people were talking about their divorce experience. They found that the level of self-compassion was by far the strongest predictor of how well they were coping nine months later.[26]

Similarly, the researchers looked at veterans returning from Iraq and Afghanistan, and found that a soldier's level of self-compassion was more predictive of whether or not they developed post-traumatic stress disorder symptoms than the level of combat exposure.[27] The evidence is becoming more and more incontrovertible that self-compassion is a way to cope with stressful situations and difficult emotions, and it leads to genuine resilience.

Our innate sense of worth comes from knowing we are okay no matter what happens outside of us. That I am innately a good person, no matter what I do or don't do. That I don't need to prove that to myself or to anyone else. Ultimately, it is my relationship with myself that sets the tone for every other relationship in my life. My relationship with myself is the foundation for my self-worth. To feeling confident, calm and connected.

My coaching clients often share stories of being in the middle of a difficult meeting, or having an argument with someone at work, or feeling frustrated with their child, or about to go on stage for a big presentation, and hearing my caring voice telling them to stop and take a deep breath, put their hand on their heart to self-soothe and feel the connection to themselves, encouraging them with words like, 'You got this'. I love it when I hear this supports them, as this often feels like the first stage — my voice replacing the negative self-talk that so many of us grew up with.

I also encourage them to find their own inner coach. Rather than it being my voice, inviting them to find *their* voice that is supporting and encouraging them. This is where the real power is. Nothing outside of ourselves (including people) can take our inner strength, calm and support from us. The world can do what the ever-changing world does, and we can stay constant, consistent and stable as our own best friend. This is real stability, an inner stability that so many of us unconsciously crave that becomes less about what we achieve and more about how we achieve what is important and meaningful to us.

The swan does not only need to look graceful on the surface. When we learn to be our own best friend, life takes on an ease and grace that often makes us unflappable. Not every day (we are human after all), but with practice, we can live most days from a place of inner ease, grace and stability.

CHAPTER 6

Finding our boundaries

Before I started doing my inner work, I had always struggled with setting boundaries and making self-care a priority in my life. Being super driven to succeed, I wanted to do everything perfectly and I wanted people to like me. As a result, there wasn't a lot of time or space for boundaries or self-care.

When I sat on the leadership team of that very successful and fast-growing wealth management company, leading a large team of people to whom I felt deeply committed, I felt as though, as the organisation grew, it needed more and more from me. I found it difficult to say 'no' to requests and demands from my boss, colleagues, team members and clients. I was always willing to take on more, believing it was my responsibility as a leader to set an example for others, and in a way, trying to prove my value. So what if I was working late most nights? So what if I was on-call seven days a week, twenty-four hours a day for a staff or media 'crisis' year after year after year? So what if I was getting sick more often? So what if I woke up anxious most mornings with my to-do list running my life? So what if joy and spontaneity were a dim memory?

I ignored my own care, and I ignored the other things that were important in my life. Until that one night I arrived home from an event, feeling empty and exhausted, and burst into tears. In that moment I had a sense that something inside of me was trying to reach me, a quiet whisper that something needed to change. Interestingly, rather than listening to that whisper and perhaps trying to put some boundaries in place in my work and life, I walked away from my career instead.

But then I moved to that large, publicly listed communications and advertising group and repeated the same pattern, continuing to ignore that quiet whisper inside. In my need to prove my worth and value again, I tried even harder to take on everything I could, a lot of which was outside of my scope and way outside of my areas of expertise. No matter how hard I worked or how hard I tried, or whom I tried to get close to, it just did not work.

Rather than stopping and facing the truth of what was going on in this very toxic environment, I tried to push through. Looking back, it is apparent now that it was a complete mirror of my own internal state and personal relationships at the time. A mirror of my own lack of self-worth, lack of self-respect and lack of boundaries. Yet, I tried to push through. Once again, I learnt the hard way that our greatest strengths, when overplayed, become our greatest limitations. I didn't know where my off button was, and I couldn't see the impact this was having on all areas of my life.

I repeated the same pattern yet again when I started my own coaching company. One of the goals of starting my own business was to have more choice, flexibility and control over my time. But unconsciously, I was so scared I would fail that I worked even harder than I had in my corporate roles. I said 'yes' to work that I didn't really want to do, 'just in case' the work I did want to do didn't materialise. Even on days when I wasn't with clients and knew I needed to rest, I would get busy as a way of not having to feel my fear, doubts and insecurities. Trying to *make* things happen rather than letting things unfold at their own pace.

But what I found was that my business did not start to grow until I got very clear on what I did and didn't do, was able to articulate this to my clients, and stay in integrity by holding my boundaries.

Conscious reflection

As you reflect on the different areas of your life, where might you be trying to push through and not listening to your authentic yes or no? What would it be like for you to listen to yourself and stop pushing through?

The need for compassionate boundaries

One of the most important insights I've had about my life is simple, yet profound, and I use it every single day: My life and my relationships are shaped by what I say 'yes' and 'no' to.

My 'yes' and my 'no' decisions are what my boundaries are made of. Brené Brown defines boundaries as, 'A clear understanding of what's okay and what's not okay for you'. Our boundaries are the inner guidance system we use to make every single decision in our lives. They are the way we navigate every relationship in our lives.

It can be hard to see all the invisible ways that boundaries — or often the lack thereof — impact our work and our lives. In my experience, our lack of boundaries is equivalent to our lack of self-worth.

Boundaries are what we say 'yes' and 'no' to in the physical, emotional and mental realms. When we honour our boundaries and others', we take responsibility for our perceptions and interactions. We allow others to have their own feelings and needs, without needing to change them or take responsibility for them. When our boundaries are defined and held, we are living in a place of choice, rather than obligation and blame. We're living and connecting authentically and compassionately.

It is important to become aware of when we don't hold our own boundaries and when we may cross another's boundaries. If we take the example of the workplace, some of these boundary violations would include unwanted touching, invading someone's personal space, making inappropriate comments, bullying, belittling people, using offensive language, discrimination and harassment. Others are more subtle, yet equally significant, such as micromanaging, not allowing people to make decisions or taking ownership of their work, ignoring or dismissing someone's complaints or concerns, making someone feel guilty or responsible for your emotions, using emotional manipulation to get what we want, overworking employees, etc.

Three types of boundaries

1. *Physical boundaries* signify how much space we like between ourselves and others. What kinds of physical touch and affection we want and don't want.

2. *Emotional boundaries* are our capacity to allow others to feel their own strong emotions without needing to fix them. This applies to ourselves as well. Are we able to feel our whole range of emotions without blaming them on anyone or anything else? Emotional boundaries are also about how we allow ourselves to be treated by others. What feels okay and what doesn't, and most importantly, expressing this boundary aloud.

3. *Intellectual or mental boundaries* are how we respect both our own and other people's perspectives, no matter how strongly we disagree. Can we respect that other people see and do things differently than us, and is it okay for us to be different as well?

In her research, Brené Brown found that the most compassionate people are also the most boundary-conscious people. Healthy boundaries are not walls between us and others; they are respect and love for ourselves and others.

Unfortunately, many of us are not comfortable setting and holding boundaries because we too often care more about what people will think than what we need. We don't want to disappoint anyone. We want everyone to like us. We may even hold the belief that it's generous and selfless to put others' needs before our own. There exists a misconception (especially for women) that we're expected to handle everything flawlessly. Declining an opportunity can sometimes trigger a cacophony of inner self-criticism: 'What gives you the right?' 'You're not displaying enough care as a mother/spouse/friend/co-worker.'

My journey with boundaries has taken me from often being resentful, blaming, angry and exhausted to more deeply trusting myself, to assuming others are doing the best they can, and to making self-care primary in my life. It started by consciously and courageously working with my 'yes' and 'no' responses. Two key areas of my life had to shift. The first was making self-care a priority, which meant taking back time for myself and saying 'no'. The second was being able to have the uncomfortable conversations, and then bear the discomfort and the afterburn and guilt of saying 'no'.

It was another profound insight for me to learn that when I say 'yes' to something, I am always either, consciously or unconsciously, saying 'no' to something else. When I say 'yes' to that extra project, I am really saying 'no' to that extra free time I was hoping to spend with my son. Or when I say 'yes' to helping a colleague with a problem, I am saying 'no' to getting the work done that I committed to doing for myself today. I often feel very passionate about my work, so it can be very easy for me to override and justify why I was working too hard.

However, I finally understood that when I said 'yes' to yet another work 'need', I was usually also saying 'no' to my son's or family's needs, or my friendship and connection needs, or my own health and self-care needs. This made it much easier for me to assess my boundaries and my yes and no decisions. This has been an important reframe for me in finding the freedom to say 'no'.

Boundaries are important because they help define and establish healthy relationships with ourselves and others. They create a sense of safety, respect and dignity for everyone involved.

Benefits of healthy boundaries

◆ *They protect our physical and emotional wellbeing.* Boundaries help us set limits on what we are willing to tolerate or accept from others. This can help protect us from harm, abuse and toxic behaviour in the workplace and in our relationships.

◆ *They improve our self-esteem.* When we establish boundaries and stick to them, we send a message to ourselves and others

(continued)

that our needs, feelings and opinions matter. This is the cornerstone to self-respect and can improve our self-esteem and inner confidence.

♦ *They enhance communication.* Clear boundaries can help improve communication by establishing expectations and creating mutual understanding. They can help avoid misunderstandings, conflicts and hurt feelings.

♦ *They foster healthy relationships.* Healthy relationships are built on mutual respect, trust and support. Boundaries help create a framework for healthy relationships by establishing expectations and limits.

♦ *They promote personal growth.* Setting boundaries and sticking to them can help us learn more about ourselves and our needs. It can help us grow and develop as individuals and improve our relationships with others.

A big part of how I went from overworking to finding boundaries and finally myself, was learning how to bear the discomfort of saying 'no'. In the beginning, I was becoming aware of the boundaries I needed to have, but often still struggled to put them in place. I struggled with saying 'no', or speaking up about what I needed, or allowing others to feel their own disappointment.

I recently heard Brené Brown talk about her boundary mantra: 'Choose discomfort over resentment.' This is exactly what I've now learnt to do. In those moments where I have had to say, 'No, I can't' or 'I'm sorry, I'm not available' or 'I am completely at capacity on other priorities at the moment', I still feel the discomfort rise. The familiar tug in my belly from the fear of how I may be seen and judged. But I breathe and I say it anyway. I sit in my uncomfortable feelings in the now, rather than possibly feeling resentful and resorting to being passive aggressive later.

For example, I remember when, upon going quite out of my way to pick a friend up to go to yoga for the tenth time, I quite passive-aggressively said, 'Maybe one time you could drive yourself'. What I could have said instead was, 'Sorry, I can't take you this time'.

I don't want to feel resentment, frustration or anger toward my friends, colleagues and loved ones, yet, this is how it feels when I say 'yes' and I really want or need to say 'no'. I also often end up not feeling valued, mostly because I am over-giving. I have learnt that I'd rather be loving and generous and direct about what's okay and what's not okay. It is far more compassionate to others and me to freely and willingly say 'yes' than to pretend. In the same way we want to develop more gentle self-compassion toward ourselves, we also want to grow fierce self-compassion that empowers us to stick up for ourselves and hold our boundaries.

In my experience, as women, we are often discouraged from being in touch with our anger. Yet, quite often, our healthy anger is what tells us someone has crossed a boundary or that we haven't held a boundary. Next time your frustration or anger begin to rise, check-in with yourself and see if a boundary issue is involved. Often, the positive energy of healthy anger is what propels us to feel strong and empowered, to say or do what we need to for ourselves. When I began to set new boundaries, I got more in touch with my anger, which helped me to see and then let go of my need to please, perform and perfect. I also got more in touch with my vulnerability.

Setting boundaries is something we may not typically think of as vulnerability. But saying 'no' and taking time for ourselves (whether it's family time, creative time or other self-care time) is a huge act of vulnerability in a culture where productivity and, for women especially, being nice and accommodating is expected. I was talking to a client who was sharing how hard she finds it to ask her assistant to schedule decent breaks for her during her very busy days. It is just so foreign, and often uncomfortable, for her to focus on and ask for what she needs.

While setting boundaries is ultimately a compassionate act for us and others, we also need a number of self-compassionate strategies to support us, especially when we are first practising. The first strategy is to give ourselves some time before we respond to any request. Try saying, 'Can I get back to you?'

When someone asks us to do something, it's a vulnerable moment. We're caught between honouring our own needs and the desire to help others. It's often easy to answer with a quick 'yes' to avoid the discomfort. But by asking, 'Can I get back to you on this?', you give yourself breathing space to consciously check-in to consider if it's a genuine 'yes'.

While you are giving yourself this space, try this: envision your future self following through with the request and see what arises. How do you feel? Saying 'yes' can be easy right now because we think we'll be able to handle it. But, eventually, all the things we say 'yes' to now catch up to us in the future, creating overwhelming obligations for ourselves.

Imagining what our 'yes' will realistically involve in the future is important because it might not sound like much. 'Sure, I can have a quick look at that report for you.' But that might mean there is a lot of feedback you need to give. Or it might mean having another meeting, or going back and forward several times.

I coached a wonderful woman named Fiona who said 'yes' to everything at work, and she loved it. She loved being involved in multiple projects, she loved all she got to learn and all the people she got to meet. All her clients and stakeholders knew they could come to her and she would say 'yes' to helping and sort out any problems. She was incredibly capable, dependable and reliable, and it became an important part of her identity and brand. In addition to that, in her family, she was the person who everybody came to with their problems. In her 'spare time', she also spent a lot of time helping her husband with his business.

We teach people how to treat us, and Fiona was teaching practically every person in her life that, no matter what was going on in her work or life, she would still do whatever they needed. The problem was that, eventually, Fiona completely burnt herself out. When we met, she was exhausted but did not know how to do life any differently. She had been performing this way since she was a young girl when she took care of her mum who had mental health issues. She had grown up way too young and become overly responsible. It was what her self-worth and her identity were built around.

When I first started working with Fiona, she was quite defensive and resistant to the idea of practising more boundaries. She felt like I didn't understand how much pressure she was under and how much she cared about her work. However, as we explored it, she realised that her poor boundaries were not only hurting her, but also her team, her clients and the company. Over time, very gently, she realised she was doing many people around her a disservice. When we jump in and sort things out for people, they often don't have to work things out for themselves. She found many of her colleagues at work had just become lazy, so it was quick and easy for them to go to Fiona and let her sort things out, rather than having to work it out for themselves.

Fiona learnt to set boundaries in a way that was firm and respectful. She started saying, 'Sorry, I have a lot on my plate at the moment and can't help with that right now'. She started to delegate tasks to her team members and trust them to do their jobs well, and hold them accountable when they didn't. She learnt to say 'no' to unrealistic demands and negotiate deadlines that were achievable. She also started to prioritise her own wellbeing by taking breaks, exercising and spending time with her family and friends.

As Fiona's boundaries improved, so did the consistency of her performance and the performance of her team. They became more efficient, organised and effective in delivering high-quality work to their clients. Fiona's colleagues and clients started to respect her more, not less, for her ability to set boundaries and prioritise her work and her wellbeing. In the end, Fiona learnt that setting boundaries was not a sign of weakness, but a sign of strength. It allowed her to be more effective, productive and happy in her work and her life. She also realised that setting boundaries was not a one-time event, but an ongoing process that required mindfulness, communication and self-care. She realised most people just found someone else to ask or worked it out themselves.

At first, it felt super hard and brought up a lot of anxiety and made her feel very vulnerable: What if people didn't value her anymore? But over time, she found that people actually respected and valued her more.

Get clear on your priorities

Before we can set boundaries, we need to know what our priorities are. We do this by taking some time to reflect on what is most important to us, both professionally and personally. Once we have a clear understanding of our priorities, we can set boundaries that align with them. For example, if family time is a top priority for you, you may choose to set a boundary around not working on weekends or taking phone calls after a certain time in the evening.

One of the many gifts of learning to set more boundaries is you will have more time to focus on what is important and meaningful to you, both at and outside of work. Many of the women I have worked with have realised that they can be a lot more successful and accomplish what is important for their role when they get clear on what they need to focus on and stay in integrity with that.

Secondly, communicate your boundaries clearly. Once you have established your boundaries, it is essential to communicate them clearly to your colleagues and clients. You can do this by setting expectations up front, such as letting them know when you are available or what types of requests you can and cannot accommodate. Be firm and polite in your communication, and don't be afraid to say 'no' if a request does not align with your boundaries.

When you have given yourself the time to consider your 'yes' and 'no' and you've honoured yourself with a 'no', it's then time to practise self-compassion, because this is when the uncomfortable feelings, like afterburn, guilt or anxiety may arise. The interesting thing about guilt is that while it's certainly uncomfortable, it's helpful. I notice that sometimes when I say 'no' and I feel guilt, the guilt has shown up either out of habit or an old belief that hasn't quite shifted. I may feel guilty for not going for a coffee with a friend because of the belief that protecting time for myself is selfish, but when I'm aware of this belief, I can question if it's still resonating or not. Then I can soften into myself, acknowledging how challenging it is to shift this belief, and I can remind myself I'm doing the best I can right now.

I've learnt that if I struggle to hold boundaries at work, I am very likely to struggle to hold boundaries in my home life as a wife, friend and parent. Although, interestingly, some women I have worked with have been great at holding boundaries at work, but really struggle in their personal life, or vice versa.

As parents, understanding what healthy boundaries are with children is equally important. At home, parental boundary violations can be:

- physical, such as hitting or physically restraining a child

- verbal, such as yelling, using harsh language or making hurtful comments

- emotional, such as guilt-tripping or manipulating a child to get what you want

- invading a child's privacy, such as reading their diary or texts without permission

- not respecting a child's personal space or physical boundaries, such as forcing them to hug or kiss someone they don't want to

- ignoring a child's emotional needs or dismissing their feelings

- disrespecting a child's cultural or religious beliefs and practices

- using fear or intimidation to control a child's behaviour

- making a child responsible for adult problems or conflicts

- neglecting a child's basic needs, such as not providing adequate food, shelter or medical care.

Again, some of these seem obvious, but for many of us, we grew up in cultures or families that didn't know better and we may parent in a similar way. Now, as parents, it is up to us to establish clear boundaries with our children and our partners to create a safe and nurturing home environment. We need to communicate with our children in a respectful and empathetic manner, and seek professional help if we need support in maintaining healthy boundaries.

Setting boundaries is not just about saying 'no' to requests, it's also about taking care of ourselves: making sure we are taking breaks throughout the day, getting enough sleep and engaging in activities that help us recharge. When we prioritise our wellbeing, we will be better equipped to handle the demands of our job and maintain the boundaries we have set. Remember, setting boundaries is not a one-time event, but an ongoing process that requires practise and persistence. With time and effort, you can establish healthy boundaries that support your professional and personal growth.

CHAPTER 7

Tuning into our needs

I have seen in myself, and in many of the women I work with, how often we either don't really know what our needs are or, if we do, we neglect them. It takes conscious practice to, firstly, tune into our needs, and then make small commitments to honour these needs in our life. In this chapter we begin by exploring our relational needs, why we need to honour and prioritise them, including creating space to self-care.

I spent over ten years as a single mum and sometimes I felt deeply lonely. I had a core group of very good friends, a precious son, a dog, a home, a business. But I didn't have a romantic relationship. I didn't have another adult to share my life with day-to-day. I didn't have someone who had my back or could be there to help and support me. While I was okay being on my own and loved much about my life during that period, I also missed not being in a relationship. In fact, at times, I longed for it so deeply, it hurt. I missed the companionship, the emotional closeness, the touch, the laughter and the mutual care. I could be open to meeting people, I could go on dates, I could spend time with the people I loved and do things I loved, but I couldn't seem to meet what can be a very basic human need for a loving, intimate relationship.

Because of my history, I am not sure I believed I deserved to be loved. And it is hard to be with someone or meet a need if you don't feel you deserve it.

Back then, and sometimes even still now, my tendency was often to try to ignore my needs, including my need for love, connection and support. I typically got busy over my loneliness, or I over-worked, ate junk food, drank too much alcohol, or used social media to try to cover up and avoid my underlying needs. I noticed I would often make my loneliness and my need for connection wrong. I had a lot of shame attached to this need in me. I think it is because I had experienced a lot of rejection of these needs as a child, and as an adult it is a need that had often taken me off track.

I am definitely one of those people who have looked for love in all the wrong places. Many times, I had unconsciously looked to men in power or authority, or men who seemed important, in the hope of getting some sense of safety and validation for myself. I have kissed and been kissed by men who were not mine to kiss. I have abandoned myself in my longing to feel loved, wanted and important.

While hard and painful at times, this time on my own was such an incredible experience of deep healing in my life. Exceedingly slowly, I learnt how to love myself a little more. I learnt how to *be with* these feelings that were as much about my past as they were about my present. Instead of running away from my feelings and my needs, I learnt it was okay to feel this way and be kind and loving and compassionate to my loneliness and longing. To allow it to be as it was. To accept where I was in my life at that moment and to consider activities that deeply nurtured me. I began to learn the essence of my own self-care. Perhaps a massage for some touch, asking a friend for a long hug, having a cup of tea with one of my girlfriends and telling her how I was feeling, a warm bath with candles or a good chick flick. The important part was that I started to take action around my needs.

Tuning into your unmet needs

When I can't meet a need and neither can anyone else, my self-care may simply mean *being with* that unmet need with kindness and compassion. Self-care doesn't mean that we don't ask for other people's support. Many of our needs are met in connection with others, and this is an important part of meeting our needs. The self-care element here is often about asking, 'How do I be with my unmet needs?' Those needs that no one else can meet for us, even when we ask them.

As an example, you may really need a break from your young children. When you explain this to your partner, they may not have the physical or emotional space to meet that need. How do you be with that disappointment? How do you find a way to still nurture yourself? Do you perhaps book childcare or ask a girlfriend or family member for help? Or do you encourage your children to watch their favourite movie so you can find some space for yourself?

One of the hardest things I have found about embracing self-care is putting my needs ahead of others' needs. Even while writing that sentence, I still have a little voice in my head that says, *Oh my goodness, I can't believe you just wrote that! That sounds so selfish.* But I really have learnt the hard way that if I don't take care of my needs, I am not the best version of myself. I am not as present as a mum, partner, friend, colleague, leader. I end up in resentment and then either subtly, or often not so subtly, take it out on others.

Taking care of our needs is not selfish — it is responsible. It is how we become the best version of ourselves in order to best serve the people in our lives.

If you are anything like me, you won't necessarily always know what it is that you need. The first thing to do when we're feeling stressed, overwhelmed, anxious, afraid, angry or jealous is to practice identifying our underlying needs. This can be the hardest part for me, especially when I am stressed. What exactly do I need? Do I need some time to myself? Do I need company? Do I need something to eat? Do I need to sleep? Do I need a good cry? A holiday? Some time in nature? To do my taxes, which I have been putting off and feeling anxious about? Do I need a hug? Or do I just need some fun? Is it an emotional need, mental need, physical need, spiritual need or a financial need?

For me, the best way to work this out is to take some time out with this conscious practice.

Conscious practice

◆ *Conscious pause:* Stop what you are doing and take one minute to sit and breathe deeply into your belly.

◆ *Body scan:* Check-in with what is going on in your body. Where are you holding stress in your body? What does it feel like? What shape is it? What colour might it be?

◆ *Name and soothe your feelings:* Name and soothe those parts of you that is feeling stressed or anxious. Perhaps gently put your hand on your heart, acknowledge your difficult feelings and provide some kind reassurance that they are understandable and okay. Gently change your self-talk to be more supportive of honouring your own needs. Allow your nervous system to settle and some stillness to arise.

◆ *Reflect:* Ask yourself, 'What do I most need in this moment to support me?' If you are still struggling to work out your needs, you can journal or call a friend and work out what you need.

◆ *Respond:* Now you act on whatever that need is: have a rest, say 'no' to something, have a conversation you need to have. Or if you can't take action straight away, make an agreement with yourself that you will create space in the next twenty-four hours to meet that need and prioritise your own self-care.

Chloe and I had been working together for a couple of months, and every time we met, she would explain in great detail why she had not been able to do any of the self-care commitments she had made to herself. Her reasons were always consistent and predominantly revolved around having two children who needed her attention when she was not at work. Between work and her kids, she did not feel she had any additional time or capacity to even consider her needs.

I hear this a lot and I understand this struggle. Yet, as we explored further, Chloe got very clear within herself that she was also avoiding self-care because she did not know what her needs were. She also did not know how to slow down and prioritise herself and her needs, as she had never been taught how. It felt hard, awkward and selfish for her to prioritise herself. Her mother had been 'needless and wantless' her whole life, and in role modelling this, Chloe believed she was meant to do the same.

I took her through the process on page 140 on identifying our needs, and Chloe started to get clear on what her needs were. What she also noticed when she first started this practice was how hard it was for her to name and soothe her anxiety and guilt, and her often harsh self-talk, which made these feelings worse. An important part of this practice for her was to notice, name and acknowledge the feelings she was having, welcome them as completely understandable feelings given her history, and slowly change her self-talk to support the importance of acknowledging her own needs. This allowed her to identify the things that would support her to show up the way she wanted to at work and at home, and that would help her to feel more fulfilled and less overwhelmed and resentful.

She recognised she needed to create time and space to connect with her partner, who she realised she was missing even though they saw each other every day. She wanted to make time to nurture this relationship, for herself and for their kids. She needed to talk to her partner and agree to a time each day that she could spend thirty minutes doing *her* thing: a bath, a walk, a meditation, listening to a podcast — just time for herself. She needed to schedule a catch-up with one of her girlfriends every couple of weeks, as she was feeling lonely around her friendships. These catch-ups helped her feel more part of the world outside of work and kids.

As Chloe started to practise meeting her relational needs, she noticed a shift in how she felt about herself and her life. She was a happier and more present mum. After connecting more with her partner, they started having more fun together as a family. A lightness arrived at home, and at work she felt calmer and more confident in handling challenges that arose.

Not only does self-care just make common sense, but its benefits are overwhelmingly proven by science.

Metta meditation

One self-care practice found in mindfulness is *metta meditation*. 'Metta' is an ancient Pali word (the language spoken by the Buddha) meaning 'loving-kindness', or a strong wish for the welfare and happiness for yourself and others. In metta meditation, we project benevolent feelings and wishes to ourselves, loved ones, friends and even strangers and enemies.

One study at Stanford University showed that a regular seven-minute practice of metta meditation can increase social connectedness.[28] Researcher Barbara Fredrickson at the University of North Carolina found that metta meditation can help boost positive emotions and wellbeing in life, which then strengthens our inner resources to deal with challenges.[29] A study by Richard J. Davidson showed that metta meditation literally changes the structure of the brain, including increasing subjects' ability to see things from another's perspective and moderating the amygdala, which is responsible for fight, flight or freeze responses.[30] Metta meditation has also been shown to lower reactions to inflammation and distress, both of which are associated with depression, heart disease and diabetes.[31] If you're interested in trying metta meditation, go to jowagstaff.com/bookresources and download a seven-minute guided metta meditation.

Simply pausing to accurately identify our feelings in stressful moments can be enough to put us in a calmer state. When we don't accurately identify our true feelings, the stress we feel around them is amplified. With no clarity, the feelings are intensified by unconscious confusion. Research shows, however, that when we name our feelings, we tend to move out of amygdala-based responses and into our prefrontal cortex, where we can act more rationally.[32]

Tend and befriend

Self-care is particularly hard when we are under stress, which of course is when we need it most. Not only is this self-evident from personal experience, it's also backed by science. As we previously explored, when our brain registers a threat, adrenaline and cortisol are released and our body responds with fight, flight or freeze. Scientists have also distinguished a fourth reaction that impedes our ability to self-care during stressful times when we need it most. This reaction is referred to as *fawn* or *tend and befriend*.

Like fight, flight and freeze, tend and befriend aims to protect us. It does this by turning our attention away from our own stress and putting our attention on someone else. When we are stressed, or triggered emotionally, the tend-and-befriend reaction can fire what is called *caring stress*. This is where we funnel our stress into a focus on others.

I was recently waiting for one of my major corporate clients to sign off on a very significant scope of work for my business. When they had originally asked for the proposal, it had been positioned as a mere formality and we had already agreed on the timing and logistics for rolling out our leadership program across their organisation.

Then, out of the blue, I received a call from the chief operating officer, saying all external costs had been put on hold. While they were still going to try to get the proposal across the line, they would not know for sure for another four weeks. This was a make-or-break deal for my business, so for the next four weeks I had to sit in enormous anxiety, financial fear and uncertainty of what it would mean for me and my team. Would I have to make members of my team redundant? Would I have to scale back the business and the investments I had planned to make in the coming year? Would all my other clients do the same given the economic climate we were in? I had not felt this stressed in a long time.

A day later I got a call from a girlfriend who was having problems in her marriage. Without her asking me to, I started to get very involved in helping her. I also found myself making and dropping off meals to another friend who was sick, as well as getting caught up in a family issue that had nothing to do with me. In isolation, all these acts may just be compassionate gestures. However, I know myself well enough now to know that I had slipped into caring stress. Rather than sitting with my own fears and anxieties and getting clear on my own needs and what would support me through this difficult time, I got super busy focusing on others.

Self-care is about valuing and respecting ourselves

When we neglect our own needs, we often become more stressed, unhappy and dissatisfied, which can drive feelings of low self-esteem. Even though my wiring, upbringing and culture may tell me it's selfish to put my needs first, the reality is that if I don't, my stress levels will affect how I treat others. This helps me to see that perhaps it's more selfish to *not* take care of my own needs, which causes me to go into overdrive to look after others and likely take my anxiety or resentment out on the people around me.

The cliché about putting your oxygen mask on first in case of an emergency in an airplane is spot on. Caring for yourself is one of the most important things you can do for yourself and for the others in your life. When you fill your own cup up, you can use the overflow to nurture others. It can feel selfish. It can feel uncomfortable and even hard. That feeling of afterburn, which we discussed in Chapter 2, can come up, just like when we first practise any new behaviour. However, as we practise these new behaviours and prioritise our self-care, we will start to experience a deep sense of inner self-respect and radical resiliency.

When I look back over my life, I know now that what I wanted most was to feel understood and respected. But I went about it in all the wrong ways. And that's okay. I understand why I thought pleasing others and driving myself excessively hard would earn people's respect. But what I really understand now is we must start by focusing on our own self-respect. We often want others to value and respect us, but first we must value and respect ourselves. We teach people how to treat us, by how we treat them, how we allow them to treat us and by how we treat ourselves. We also teach others how to care for themselves when we role model it ourselves.

It doesn't mean we stop nurturing others. It means we start deeply nurturing ourselves. It means we refuel our tank before it gets too empty. Ideally, well before it gets empty!

It's important to find equilibrium between the demands and hustle of daily life and engaging in activities that nurture a feeling of tranquillity and overall wellness for both our minds and bodies. That said, I have two pieces of potentially bad news for you on self-care:

1. Not every self-care activity feels good

Some self-care practices feel amazing immediately, like going back to bed for more sleep when our body is telling us we are tired, choosing to stop, having a rest or afternoon nap, calling a friend or sitting in the sun with a cup of tea. But not all of them feel good immediately — some bring up resistance or anxiety!

The best examples of these for me are life administration things, such as doing my taxes, renewing my insurance, asking people for money they owe me, and getting my will in place. Many of these fall under financial self-care. Also, the inner work we continue to explore (and is at the core of this book) can often feel hard — facing our shadow selves, our histories, acknowledging and feeling our feelings, holding new boundaries and practising new behaviours are never easy to begin with, and yet they are what allow us to establish a foundation of authentic self-care. There are also physical self-care activities that I can avoid, such as eating well when I am stressed and all I want to eat is something high in sugar or fat.

I have noticed that, after I take the actions that I don't enjoy in the moment, I feel a lot better overall: more calm, connected, confident and empowered.

2. *Self-care isn't a one-time thing*

Oh, how I wish it was. In fact, my go-to pattern is often to over-extend my capacity to give to others and to focus on other people's needs — tend and befriend in overdrive. Or alternatively, I get caught in overdrive and empty my tank fully. Then, when I am completely stressed and exhausted, I finally remember that it is time to self-care to fill my tank again.

For me, and many women I have worked with and talked to, this cycle simply does not work. If my tank gets completely empty, it takes quite a lot of energy to fill it up again. Ideally, self-care is a consistent repetition of many different habits and actions, sometimes big, sometimes small, which together soothe us and make sure we are consistently at our optimum: emotionally, mentally, physically and spiritually.

Prioritising self-care

In recent years, because of evidence-based research and brain science, I've noticed many professionals starting to take the need to invest in their own wellbeing seriously; in particular, sleep, diet, exercise and mindfulness. If you're anything like me, you might have thought of this as downtime to be squeezed in when we can find the time, which is rarely available. Now, thanks to the research, we understand that investing in our own self-care and wellbeing daily dramatically enhances our productivity, clarity, calmness and how we show up both at work and at home. It is the foundation of being sustainably successful in all areas of our life in this incredibly demanding world we now live and work in.

There are three important reasons why we really need to make self-care and wellbeing a priority in our life.

The first is because self-care *gives us energy*, and we need all the energy we can get. Here's the hard truth: Time is fixed. It can't flex. We get 160 hours per week, that's it. But our energy can flex and make us sharper and more energised in the time we have available. Productivity is less about managing time and more about managing energy. As counterintuitive as it sounds, the more we slow down and prioritise what we need to, the more effective and productive we can be at work.

Secondly, self-care can give us a competitive edge by *boosting our creativity and confidence*. Our mind is more creative and innovative when we have had enough sleep. Research shows that sleep-deprived people come up with fewer original ideas and fall back into old habits. In addition, people who have a regular exercise routine have lower levels of stress and anxiety, and at the same time, have higher levels of self-efficiency, which is our belief and confidence in our own capabilities to manage situations. Increased levels of creativity and confidence translate into better performance at work.

Thirdly, self-care *increases our endurance* over the long haul. In other words, self-care allows us to have sustainable success. Long-term success requires consistent self-care habits. We can put in long hours and achieve great things, but only for a short while. This is not sustainable. Marriages suffer, families suffer, our health eventually begins to fail. There is a price we will eventually pay for not taking care of ourselves. The women I know who prioritise self-care are the ones who are successful in the long-term and in all areas of their life: with their families, their health and their work.

Conscious reflection

Get clear on your needs

Take a moment to reflect on the following questions as foundations for understanding what you need:

♦ What makes me feel happy and relaxed?

♦ What are the things that give me energy?

(continued)

◆ What are the things that deplete my energy?

◆ What is my favourite way to spend a day?

◆ What is a list of things I would like to say 'no' to in my life?

◆ What is a list of things I would like to say 'yes' to in my life?

Off the back of these reflections, what one thing would you like to do this coming week to honour yourself and your needs? I also encourage you to keep coming back to this list of questions and answers regularly so you can continue to build on the clarity you have gained.

CHAPTER 8

Getting practical with self-care

Having explored our relational needs, now we can focus on our physical self-care, including the impact of hustling to prove our worth, managing our gut health and lifestyle choices, prioritising our executive wellbeing and how this can empower us to elevate our careers and lives. For me, physical self-care can often feel like an almighty chore. Is it just me?

The way this has become easier for me is to change my attitude in how I look at it. Once again, this is where self-compassion comes in. When I bring an attitude of self-compassion and self-care to my need to look after myself physically, something shifts within me. I begin to see what I put into my body, how I rest and sleep, and what exercise I perform as an opportunity to nourish and nurture myself. It changes from a feeling of, 'I *should* do that', which I often resent and feel irritated about, to a sense of, 'That feels like a really lovely thing to do for myself' or 'I *get to* do this'.

I have found my ability to practise and continue with physical self-care has needed to come from self-respect, self-acceptance and self-love, not self-punishment and judgement. As I have learnt about and put self-care into practise (very imperfectly, I might add), I have grown to value and love myself more through the process.

Another important insight was when I discovered that anxiety, depression and fatigue can all be symptoms of an unhealthy stomach lining and gut flora. Our gut flora (the health of the bacteria in our gut) affects our brain function. Scientists have now discovered that there are over 100 million neurons (or nerve endings) in our gut, which is why they are now referring to it as our 'second brain'. While it talks to our brain, it can also act completely independently and influence behaviours in our body.

This was truly profound for me to learn, as I had never realised there was a relationship between our gut and our brain — until I was forced to.

Gut health, stress and burnout

I woke up one day and could not get out of bed. My body felt like lead. Every muscle was tired. My eyes were so heavy I could barely open them. We all have those days where we would rather crawl back under the blanket, but this felt different. I had zero energy. I felt physically, mentally and emotionally exhausted.

Yet, at the same time, my mind was racing and I felt super anxious. The idea of falling back to sleep was equally impossible. Luckily, my son was with his dad, so I cancelled all my appointments that day and moved to the couch. I was so tired, but I didn't know how to rest, and there was so much I needed to do. It was a confusing feeling — totally exhausted but unable to be still. My first thought was that my Graves' disease had returned, which is basically an overactive thyroid, but I'd had my bloods checked and my thyroid was all okay.

Night after night, I struggled to get to sleep, but woke up quite suddenly around 4am day after day, with my brain racing. While I sometimes drifted back into a light sleep, I would wake to the same impossibility of having to get out of bed and go to work. Some days I pushed through, got Hugo ready for school, saw clients, ran a workshop, came home totally exhausted, got dinner ready and fell into bed as soon as Hugo was asleep, only to repeat the cycle the next day. I felt much more irritable, easily angered and more cynical than I usually am. I often had a sense of overwhelm, like doing life in any form felt totally impossible.

While my mum already picked Hugo up after school some days, after a few weeks of this pattern, I finally asked my mum for extra help with Hugo, and asked Troy to take Hugo so I could try to rest. Nobody seemed to be able to tell me what was wrong with me. Some suggested I was depressed, which I probably was; others suggested I had some kind of flu. All I knew was I was feeling increasingly scared by my inability to get up off the couch. There were days that I literally struggled to get myself to the toilet. Other days I could do a few things, but then had to collapse soon after. It was scary and I felt increasingly powerless around my health.

Eventually, someone suggested I go and visit an integrative doctor. She ran a lot of tests (blood, urine, faeces) and diagnosed me with adrenal fatigue and stomach issues. In short, she basically diagnosed me with severe burnout. I understand now that I was finding it so hard to rest because my adrenal glands were in overdrive. While I was completely exhausted, I had large amounts of cortisol flooding my body. My nervous system was over-activated and did not know how to physically switch off and rest, which was adding to my fatigue. My adrenal system was completely burnt out from chronic stress thanks to me constantly living in survival mode.

Hustling to prove my worth

My burnout didn't just arrive suddenly out of nowhere. It had come about through years and years of not taking care of myself, of not learning to slow down and rest when I needed to, of not learning how to self-care, of saying 'yes' when I needed to say 'no'. Ultimately, the root cause of my burnout was my lack of boundaries and constant hustle to prove my worth. I needed to start setting some limits on my work to protect my health and wellbeing.

Why I always seem to need to learn my lessons the hard way, through experience, rather than listening to others' experiences is beyond me. But that has been the story of my life. I hope it will be different for you, that you can learn from my experience rather than having to experience it yourself. I hope you choose to learn how to look after yourself and nourish your needs before your body must give way.

I remember hearing an analogy once that the universe will first gently tap us on the shoulder to try to get us to pay attention to what is important (e.g., someone might share their experience like I am now and we resonate, but we completely ignore it). Then the universe will less gently 'hit us over the head', and we might get the flu twice in one month, or we might sprain our ankle multiple times. And again, instead of thinking, *Perhaps I need to slow down a little and take better care of myself*, we ignore it until eventually the universe abruptly 'drops a house on us' and completely stops us in our tracks. We can no longer ignore what our body, heart, soul or spirit has been trying to tell us for some time.

This real physical rock bottom forced me to re-examine my attitude toward my physical self-care and its connection to my mental and emotional wellbeing. The couple of years leading up to my rock bottom had been very busy for me. I had been doing a lot of new and wonderful things and the newness meant that, at times, it was also very challenging and stressful. Looking back, I was just too busy and trying too hard and doing too much. Too busy for my own self-care. Too busy to be conscious of the food I was putting into my body. Too busy to exercise regularly. Too busy to get the sleep, and in particular, the rest that my body desperately needed. Too busy to meditate. Too busy to notice my thinking and the impact anxiety and stress and staying busy, including in my head, was having on my body and mind. Too busy until my body literally stopped working and I was diagnosed with adrenal fatigue, intestinal parasites, and leaky gut syndrome.

The gift in it all, though, is that I had no choice but to slow down. No choice but to rest my body and my mind. No choice but to get very clear on what nourished and nurtured my body and soul, and what did quite the opposite. I also got to experience firsthand how not looking after my physical self-care affected my mental and emotional state, as well as the other way around — how not looking after my emotional and mental wellbeing took its toll on my physical wellbeing.

It was difficult on all levels, and yet it was also a wonderful awakening for me. The gift of slowing down, finding my boundaries and practising self-care led to a whole new way of learning how to respect myself and my needs. The gift of learning to live in the ebb and flow of life rather than the dramatic peaks and troughs that came through a lack of self-care.

Managing gut health with lifestyle choices

Research tells us that the health of our brain is partly dependent on our gut health. Therefore, performing at our best requires maintaining our gut health with lifestyle choices. According to research, these include, in particular, reducing excess sugar and refined carbohydrates and increasing our probiotic intake.

I have cut out coffee, as it increased my anxiety. I have cut back to almost no processed sugar, as I recognised how it negatively affected my mood. I now start every day with a glass of warm water and lemon to get my digestive system moving and naturally boost my immune system, and I follow this up with a daily intake of highly nutritious greens, which have many benefits, including supporting my gut health. These small changes have made a massive difference to my life, including having much more energy, clearer thinking and less anxiety.

One of the best descriptions of this is in a documentary called *The Connection: Mind your body*. As the documentary explains, research that confirms ...

> ... *a healthy gut encourages, and perhaps directly maintains, a healthy mind. By healthy mind we are talking about our mental state. So with a healthy gut, we are less stressed, less negative, and have fewer obsessive thoughts, which can lead to increased anxiety, moodiness, and depression.*[33]

As we have already learnt in Chapter 4, when we are stressed, our threat system gets triggered, and we go into fight, flight or freeze. And these days, 99 per cent of our stresses or perceived threats are created in our minds. Every time our threat system is triggered, it can create serious wear and tear on our body, including our gut! Therefore, learning to turn on our relaxation response in our soothing system is a very important part of our self-care. As Dr Herbert Benson, professor of medicine at Harvard Medical School, explains, the two basic features in evoking the soothing response are: 1) repetition and 2) disregarding other thoughts when they come to mind. Or in other words, finding ways of breaking the train track of everyday thinking that has us stressing ourselves out.

This is exactly what our daily mindfulness practices do, whether that be a breath meditation, self-compassion meditation, repeating a mantra over and over, saying a prayer or simply being fully present to whatever it is you are doing — even just brushing your teeth. All these practices allow us, through repetition and disregarding other thoughts, to switch on our soothing system.

Essential practices

Essential for our physical self-care is the need for sleep, rest, good nutrition and regular exercise to maintain our wellbeing. Let me be clear, none of what we are talking about here is related to body image. Although, like so many women, I have grappled with body image issues throughout my life. With these body image issues have come food issues, including emotional eating; eating sugar or fatty foods, as a way of not staying with what is really going on for me; and feelings of loneliness, unworthiness, sadness or anxiety. Or I will withhold nourishment and under-eat as a way of controlling how I feel about myself and look to the outside world for my esteem.

May we all have compassion for what we do to ourselves to try to feel like we are enough in a world and culture that idealises physical perfection and bombards us with images of unrealistic body shapes. I find it heartbreaking that society places such a high priority on our externals, perpetuating the myth that having a specific body shape somehow goes hand in hand with happiness and fulfilment.

I encourage you to look at food as a way of nurturing and nourishing yourself and providing you with the energy you need to live out a truly meaningful life. If we are putting lots of unhealthy fats, processed foods, refined sugars and chemicals into our bodies, it will create unhealthy gut flora and unquestionably affect our mental, emotional and physical wellbeing.

If you struggle with looking after your nutrition, one thing that has really worked for me is seeing a naturopath or the equivalent in your community. I have also found an incredible integrative doctor, who draws upon conventional as well as complementary and alternative medicine. They look at the symptoms and treat the underlying causes. I have found it to be a very holistic approach as well as having a strong focus on my gut health.

That said, this has not been easy for me. I watched both my grandmother and mum be very focused on food and how they looked and never feeling enough, even though my mum was very thin and beautiful. It is hard to separate our relationship with ourselves and our relationship to food. It has been hard for me to navigate my emotional relationship with food, where my insecurities around my body can play out, or I use food to numb out from my feelings, as opposed to food being an action of self-care with good nutrition and regular exercise.

Start slowly

Remember to start slowly. As I have practised more self-acceptance, self-respect, and most importantly, self-compassion, it has become easier for me to really care about the food I put into my body and create consistent space for rest and exercise. The most challenging areas of my life to commit to creating change in have been nutrition, rest, exercise and my regular meditation practice. I often wonder why it is so hard for me to do the things that are so good for me, until I remember that when you have a history of caring for others more than you do yourself, then it is a long journey home to learn deep self-care and self-love. In addition, as women, we all live in cultures that tell us that taking care of others is more important than taking care of ourselves.

You might like to reflect on where you sit on that physical self-care spectrum. On one end, you might be high on self-neglect and/or self-abuse. Or on the opposite end of the spectrum, you might be very aware and self-nurturing around consistent sleep and rest, good nutrition and regular exercise. As always, let's have some compassion for ourselves as we stumble and learn to practise and move along the spectrum of physical self-care.

I would encourage you to slowly, with the support of a friend, commit to small acts of nurturing physical self-care. I find small changes work for me because I'm more likely to try them and keep them going. If you are currently not doing any exercise, perhaps just one walk a week is a great place to start. For me it is Reformer Pilates, which I found after trying many different types of exercise, most of which I just didn't enjoy. I have really enjoyed feeling into my body, getting out of my head and being stronger in my core and arms.

Sleep and rest are also vital components of self-care. We now have solid research that tells us that we need at least seven to eight hours of sleep a night or our mental health and wellbeing will be affected in the long-term. When I can, I also take the opportunity for an afternoon nap. My therapist has taught me that whenever I feel tired, I need to stop and rest. That can mean sitting in a chair or lying down on the couch for even just five to ten minutes. Most importantly, it is not just about resting my body, it is also about resting my busy mind.

When I stop to rest, even if it is just for a one-minute conscious pause, I practise bringing my attention to my breath, to stop the flow of my day-to-day thinking, to turn on my soothing system. Really, to find some peace and quiet from my mind and my day. Some days it can feel hard to do this, especially when there are just too many other demands. But I have learnt over time that the more I slow down, the more I take time for rest, the more productive and creative I actually am.

Whether it be food, exercise, sleep or rest, physical self-care is ultimately about becoming truly conscious of what our body needs, by listening to it, and most importantly, practising whatever it is we need.

Ten wellbeing practices

I would like to offer you ten practices that will empower your work and life. Notice what calls to you.

1. Consistent sleep for at least seven to eight hours each night

There are now many conclusive studies that show that being sleep-deprived negatively impacts our cognitive functioning and emotional resilience. These studies show that we are depriving the more sophisticated part of our brain, making it difficult for it to do its job. Having a minimum of seven to eight hours of sleep consistently is a mandatory practice for a high level of wellbeing and sustainable success.

2. Regular exercise and physical movement

Regular exercise and movement throughout the day improves executive functioning, lowers absenteeism, and helps us manage our mental and emotional wellbeing. Find an exercise that feels good for you, whether it's walking your dog, running, Pilates, yoga, going to the gym, etc. Also, if you sit at a desk, make sure you get up and walk around regularly. Do walking meetings, or just take time to stretch and move your body throughout your day.

3. Nutrition

We really are what we eat. Reaching for sugar, salt, fat or alcohol in the hope that it will make us feel better has the opposite effect. It may numb our tiredness, anxiety or stress in the short-term; however, research now tells us that our gut health is strongly correlated to our mental and emotional wellbeing, and vice versa. It is critical, especially at times of high stress, that we be mindful of what we are putting into our bodies and what we need to function at our best, mentally, emotionally and physically. Consider, what is your vice? What's your go-to food or substance under stress? Make a commitment to cut it out of your life for a month and notice the difference it has on you. After the initial detox (that first week can feel hard), you will be amazed at the energy that returns.

4. Meditation

Neuroscience now tells us that a daily meditation practice, in addition to having multiple long-term health benefits, decreases our stress levels and improves our ability to stay focused, the speed of our decision-making and our resiliency. Make a commitment to download a guided meditation and sit for a minimum of five minutes each day for thirty days. You will see the evidence for yourself after you've experienced the difference this makes in your life.

5. Reflective journaling

Daily journaling helps us to know ourselves, our feelings, our self-talk, our beliefs. Research shows that many successful executives have a daily reflection practice that enables them to better manage themselves and their relationships. Just journaling for as little as five minutes a day can support your mental and emotional wellbeing, and help you gain clarity on what is important and what you need to be focusing on.

6. Write a gratitude list

This has had a profound change on my life. Spending just a few minutes a day listing out what you are grateful for in your life is shown to increase positive emotions, optimism, empathy and lower depression. When Hugo was younger, we had a wonderful family practice that we did around the dining room table at night, where we each said out loud three things we were grateful for in our day. We typically also talked about our struggles as well, because gratitude is not about denying reality, but really bringing focus and attention to what you are grateful for in your life. By doing this, it increases positive emotions and really supports us to thrive in our life.

7. Digital detox

It is very difficult for us to fully switch off and deeply rest from our work. Being constantly attached to our phones, email and social media does not help! It's important to set boundaries and purposefully create space for the other important areas in our lives. Set a goal to not check your email or phone for at least an hour after you get up, and perhaps two hours before you go to bed. On Sundays, you could even do the challenge of going digital-free for the day.

So many people I've worked with have created boundaries around the time they put their phone or their emails away so that they really are able to be fully present to their life outside of work. At first, it can feel stressful, because we all have such a habit of checking our phones or checking our emails or feeling like we're missing out on something. But it's the only way to really switch off and deeply rest and be present to the rest of our lives.

8. Stop, rest, relax and nourish your soul

Many of us can easily put our hands up as busy addicts who are suffering from *rushing woman's syndrome*. Some of us even wear it as a badge of honour. Those who have been busy for so long often don't know how to slow down. But slowing down is crucial to a sustainable and enriching life. Research done by Bronnie Ware, for her book *The Top Five Regrets of the Dying*, found that the top five regrets of the dying were:

- *not having the courage to live a life true to oneself instead of to others' expectations*

- *working so hard*

- *not having the courage to express feelings*

- *not staying in touch with friends*

- *not letting oneself be happier.*

Let's learn from these regrets, let's learn to stop and create space in our life for what is important, including laughter and play, inviting people and activities into our life that bring us joy, and nourishing our hearts and souls.

9. Daily self-compassion practice

There are very few of us who don't have a nagging inner critic. Many of us would never speak to another person the way we sometimes speak to ourselves. Being compassionate toward ourselves has been shown to produce much better results than being hard on ourselves. Becoming aware of how we talk to ourselves and learning to be our own best friend also enables us to be more empathetic, compassionate and kind to others. I suggest you download a daily self-compassion practice and do it every day for thirty days. Notice the difference for yourself, especially in difficult times.

10. Human connection

Human beings have always lived in groups and depended on one another for protection, sharing resources and reproducing. This social connection is biological, as it triggers the release of the hormone oxytocin, which helps to strengthen social bonds and creates feelings of trust and attachment. Studies have also shown that social isolation and loneliness can have detrimental effects on our physical and mental health. Without regular human connection, people may experience feelings of loneliness, depression and anxiety, which can lead to a range of negative health outcomes, such as cardiovascular disease, decreased immune function and even a shortened lifespan. Yet, when we are busy or are struggling, many of us have a tendency to withdraw into ourselves, and not make space for a coffee or lunch with the friends who nurture and support us. By consciously creating space to nurture important relationships in our lives, we will enhance our wellbeing.

To start with, just pick one thing that you feel would really support you in your life and commit to it for thirty days. If you miss a day, don't give yourself a hard time, start again the next day. Making and keeping small commitments to ourselves not only helps us with our wellbeing, it also helps us to build our inner confidence, our trust in ourselves.

Create daily rituals

Self-care does not happen unless we create space for it. So how do we do that? One of the ways I have learnt to overcome my old go-to 'boom-bust' pattern is through creating a daily ritual that allows me to check-in with my needs. My daily ritual is how I make sure I look after my mental, emotional and physical self-care needs. I have a note on the side of my computer at home that reminds me to check-in with these each day, especially as I build new habits. The title is, *How can I love and care for myself today?* I have learnt that, when I start each day with this same ritual, I stay more confident, calm and connected.

How we start and end our day can either set us up for a good day filled with much ease and *success*, or can have us on the back foot from the start. Committing to a *consistent* morning ritual, if you haven't already, can change how you experience your day and your life.

Having worked with hundreds of high-performing executives over the years, one common trait that has always stood out to me is they create daily habits that support them in both their career and their life. They have also re-framed the idea that these daily habits are about adding more to their to-do list. In fact, just the opposite, they are focused on how they can keep their battery fully charged and ensure they are able to show up with passion and purpose in their organisations and lives.

Creating new habits is not easy. Most attempts fail because we stop at insight and don't build habits. Sustained change requires laying down neural pathways to form new habits through consistent daily practice.

Leadership Circle, which I work closely with, undertook specific research to better understand the daily habits of exceptional leaders (as defined by their roles combined with their Leadership Circle

Profile 360° assessment results). They found that each of these leaders consistently created space for three important things every day.

◆ a morning ritual for setting intentions and priorities for their day

◆ daily exercise, which they increased on more stressful days

◆ evening reflections and unwinding from the daily grind.

I'm going to share a few examples of my daily rituals. I suggest these as a starting place to the women I work with in our coaching program, to support them to get in the habit of self-care by setting them up for success each day. I invite you to try these rituals for the next ninety days and see what you notice.

I have given you the rituals and exercises that work for me. Obviously, you can customise whatever works best for you.

Morning ritual

Start each morning with a daily meditation practice. When I first started, I practised for a minimum of five minutes, with my focus on creating consistency and establishing a new habit—even just a couple of minutes of practice will help with this. I then slowly built up to fifteen, then twenty minutes.

You may like to try a guided meditation as you get started. You will find a selection with different timeframes to choose from on my website (jowagstaff.com/bookresources). There is so much science and research now available about the benefits of meditation. For me, it has been nothing short of life changing, as it supports my self-awareness and my ability to manage my thoughts and emotions, and find a new, deeper level of calmness and inner confidence.

Meditation is not about stopping our thoughts. Rather, it is about observing our thoughts. It is about being with ourself, being with our breath, noticing how busy our thoughts may or may not be, and noticing what is going on in our body. It invites us to be gentle and kind with ourself, as over and over again, we notice our mind wanders and we bring our attention back to our breath. Through this practice we develop our muscle to be present, to ourself and others.

Once you have completed your meditation, grab a journal and do the following exercises:

◆ *List your priorities*. What are your three most important priorities for the day?

◆ *Plan your meetings and set your intentions*. What is your main intention for today and how do you want to show up in your meetings today?

◆ *Set boundaries*. What do you need to say 'no' to today so you can say 'yes' to what is important?

◆ *Identify your behaviour of the day*. The behaviour you want to practise doing more of today is_____. The behaviour you want to do less of today is_____.

You can build many of these practices into your morning routine, for example, reflecting over a coffee, when brushing your teeth, getting to the office, or before you jump on your first online meeting. Then, commit to creating space for the following:

◆ *Building executive presence.* Commit to practising a one-minute conscious pause four times throughout your day. Put reminders in your diary, especially before important meetings, to slow you down. Simply sit and focus on your breath for one minute, allowing you to come back to yourself and your nervous system to settle.

◆ *Manage stress through movement.* Commit to thirty minutes of physical exercise or movement every day. Tip: This may be an early morning walk or run, or perhaps two fifteen-minute stretches during the day, or a walking meeting.

Evening ritual

Keep a journal beside your bed and do a quick check-in before you switch off your light, or on your desk so you can do it before you close your computer for the day. Remember to do your evening reflections with gentle awareness, not harsh self-judgement.

◆ *Gratitude list*. List three things you are most grateful for in your life today. If you have children, you may like to invite them to share three things they feel grateful for today and perhaps one thing they found difficult today. This helps build an attitude of gratitude, as well as honesty about their struggles. Tip: Don't try to fix what they found difficult, just listen, acknowledge and empathise. And of course, lead off with your own first.

◆ *Build inner confidence*. Acknowledge three things you are happy with/proud of today (something you did or liked about yourself, or how you showed up). The practice of self-compassion and building your self-esteem is life changing. If you become aware your inner critic is activated, you may like to do a five-minute self-compassion meditation to support you to rewire how you speak to yourself and learn to become your own supportive inner coach.

◆ *Priorities reflection*. How did you go with your three priorities today?

◆ *Presence check-in*. How did it go with your one-minute conscious pause today?

◆ *Rest and connect*. What have you done to switch off, slow down, disengage from work and nourish your soul today? What will you commit to doing tomorrow?

◆ *Behaviour of the day check-in*. How did you go with the behaviour you wanted to do more of, and the behaviour you wanted to do less of?

- *Movement check-in.* Did you help manage your stress through movement today? If not, how can you create space for it tomorrow?

- *Simple daily health check-in (sleep, food and water).* Did you get seven to eight hours sleep last night? What do you need to do tonight to support your sleep? How did you go with fuelling your body regularly and with good food today? What can you do to support yourself with this tomorrow? Did you drink at least 2 litres today to keep yourself hydrated and support your energy levels?

These simple rituals provide me with the opportunity to check-in with myself and my needs, with my breath and body, and with all I am grateful for daily. It's an opportunity to turn on my soothing system and practise kindness with myself and set my day up for *success.*

I also have some non-negotiables I give myself on a weekly basis. In addition to my daily meditation and movement, these include weekly therapy as a form of support, growth and self-reflection; Pilates, yoga or strength training two to three times a week; and I ensure I plan space for time in nature, fun and friendship. There is not a week that goes by that I don't give myself these gifts. Although, to be honest, the one I struggle most with is the fun — just allowing myself room to play. I am still working on that one!

You may want to create a daily ritual that looks similar to this, or it may be quite different. It may be something you only do at night if mornings just don't work for you. Or later in the morning once children are taken care of. Whatever or whenever, as long as it's a daily gift of time just for you.

CHAPTER 9

Financial self-care

I don't know about you, but for me, and many of the women I know and have worked with over the years, money can be a very confronting and uncomfortable topic. During our upbringing and within our cultures, there can be unspoken rules around not talking about money. We often like to bury our heads in the sand about it. When the issue of money is raised, we may feel shame, regret, powerless, undervalued, denial, guilt or perhaps a range of other emotions.

I don't believe there is one woman on the planet who has not faced issues around money at some point in their lives — whether that be about overspending or underspending, under-earning, managing success and wealth, etc. Whether you carry the responsibility of being the primary breadwinner or the primary caregiver at home, you are not alone. If this topic challenges or confronts you in any way, please know it's okay and together we will explore this topic with enormous self-compassion.

In fact, if this is a sensitive subject for you, before we dive into it, I would invite you to place your hand on your chest with me now and take two deep, long breaths in and out. Say the following mantra out loud:

I am willing to become aware of and learn whatever will support me to truly value myself, deeply respect myself and care for myself financially. Whatever I become aware of today, I will hold within me with great gentleness and kindness for myself.

To look at our relationship with money, just like physical self-care, we need to start with our relationship with ourselves. The more we learn to value ourselves, love ourselves, and feel worthy, the more likely we are to act around our financial self-care. In fact, our level of self-worth and our beliefs directly affect how we handle money.

We also need to look at our past. The Schachter-Singer Theory of Emotions, based on the work of psychologists Drs Stanley Schachter and Jerome E. Singer, posits that we perceive the world through the thoughts that we develop as a child. For example, if we were sent the message as children that we are capable and competent, then as adults, we will see ourselves the same way. The perspectives we carry into adulthood from childhood affect all aspects of our lives, including, of course, our relationship with money. Children who felt competent and capable can more confidently take on money matters as adults. Those of us who felt incapable and incompetent as children will often struggle with self-worth as adults, and struggle to confidently take on money matters.

Confronting my financial demons

An example of this for me was when I started my first business after a seventeen-year corporate career. At the time, I was feeling quite insecure about my capabilities in this new environment, and ultimately, my own worth. I still remember the visceral sensations in my body of both anxiety and excitement when I finally understood the magnitude of what I had done. It is often my experience that anxiety and excitement are the *same feeling*. It is our self-talk that decides which one we feel it as. When I went into self-talk that fed my doubts and insecurities, my fear and anxiety would go through the roof. When I focused on my new vision and purpose and my self-talk was one of encouragement and support, these same initial butterflies in my stomach turned into feelings of great excitement and joy, and knowing that I was choosing to walk a path that had been calling to me for some time.

I am not sure there is anything more terrifying than starting your own business. Perhaps because it triggers almost every limiting belief we have about ourselves, and creates a lot of instability as we lean into constant uncertainty and (often) financial fear. It's a great recipe for inviting our nervous system to work overtime — either in fight, flight or freeze.

I had built my previous identity on the brand and identity of the businesses I had worked for, on the title that the businesses had given me, and the kudos and power that came with those brands and titles. I was good at selling and marketing other people, businesses and products. Now, suddenly, all I had to sell and market was myself. I had to find a new identity, and at the same time, build a solid business plan and take action. While I was far from financially destitute, I only had enough money put aside to support me and my new business for six months. That put a lot of pressure on me and my poor nervous system, as I had no cornerstone client to support me.

Off the back of this financial fear and my own deep insecurities was a lack of clarity and self-belief of what I was good at. So, I went hunting for any kind of consulting work I could find, even though it went against everything I wanted to do. After about three months, this turned into a desperation that I tried to hide, although in hindsight, I have no doubt that my potential clients felt the desperation I felt in myself. When I am in fear, my natural tendency is to work harder, to try harder, to be better, to try to work everything out in my head. Yet, counterintuitively, that often leads me in the wrong direction, and it meant I was often saying 'yes' when I needed to say 'no' and stay my course. It also meant I was running on nervous energy and not slowing down and taking care of my physical, emotional and mental wellbeing so I could show up as my best.

Not trusting I had any value to bring on my own, I joined another leadership and training consultant in her business and worked for her three days a week at a quarter of what is now my daily rate. It was a wonderful experience, and I am very grateful to her for the opportunity she gave me, as it helped me to understand just how valuable my skills are. Over time, I noticed I was starting to feel resentful at how much I was being paid versus the feedback I was receiving and what I felt I was contributing. This resentment was not about the other consultant — she was paying me what was appropriate for what she needed. My resentment was a really healthy sign for me that I needed to back myself more and step up into my own leadership.

Once I stopped working for her, I then decided to join another consulting business as a partner. While I was more senior in this business, again, my decision came from a place of not feeling I could do it myself, thinking I needed something else or someone else to give me permission to value myself. Over time, I realised our values were not aligned in terms of the type of work I wanted to do. However, the gift again was that they had set fees around what I charged myself out at, which were twice the daily rate I would ever consider charging myself — and people paid it. I slowly realised that I was paying away a significant portion of my earnings to them for little value. So, again, I made the decision that it was time to try it on my own.

Throughout this time, I was very focused on increasing my skills, taking courses and getting accredited in different tools. These were all very beneficial and interesting. However, in hindsight, this was also coming from a place of, *I am not enough as I am. Hopefully, if I get just one more 'piece of paper' or accreditation, I will finally feel confident that I know what I am doing.*

But, eventually, I had to stop and say to myself, *no more training right now. There is nothing more to prove. You can't keep putting this off. You must start putting yourself out there.*

I was finally left with having to focus on marketing and selling myself. The first place I started was building my website. I was introduced to the amazing Ruby Blessing, who is a brand and web designer and digital guru, and she sent me a brand brief to fill out. It asked me to get very clear on my values and purpose and describe my brand (which was pretty much me) in words, colours and pictures. It was honestly excruciating at the time, trying to get clear on what I wanted to stand for, to find the right words to describe myself, worried I would seem too egotistical, or at the other extreme, not credentialed enough. I wanted to be safe and have a very broad offering that would capture the potential of lots of business. However, I have learnt since that narrowing and focusing my proposition brings clarity and flow.

As part of this, I had to develop a rate card. I have learnt that the only pushback I ever get around my rates is when I am not clear on my own value. In other words, pushback is a direct mirror of my own internal insecurities and doubts. I still vividly remember, when I was very busy one month in my early years, and someone wanted me to coach them one-on-one. I wasn't sure I wanted to work with them from a values perspective. Rather than exploring that and potentially saying no (which I would now), I increased my prices by 40 per cent, thinking they would then say no. They didn't, and that became my new pricing.

My business started with me struggling to know how to focus and gain some consistency in the work I wanted to do, and for many years having no idea where my next month's or quarter's work was going to come from, with no financial buffer to support me if something didn't arrive. I finished the year prior to writing this book with nine coaches and a wonderful support team working for me and my clients, in a seven-figure business, with over a year's salary and business expenses put aside as a buffer. None of this was a linear trajectory — it was all iterative. I made many mistakes and experienced many failures and disappointments. But these mistakes and disappointments led me to exactly where I was meant to be, like a re-correction I didn't even know I needed. And each year I learnt to value myself a little more.

Conscious reflection

Taking a moment to pause. Perhaps put your hand on your heart if it feels soothing. Breathing deeply into your belly, ask yourself:

◆ In what areas of your life is your self-worth high and you find it easy to value yourself and ask for what you feel you need and deserve?

◆ In what areas of your life might your self-worth be holding you back from valuing yourself and having the career and life you truly want?

Learning to respect and value ourselves

As mentioned, in the early years of my business, I found myself undercharging my clients, or in other words, not valuing myself. I have seen the same thing happen with the many women I have worked with after they take a career break, either after having a child or taking some time out. When they go back to their old role, or start applying for jobs, after maternity leave, they often struggle to ask for the job or salary they deserve and are qualified for, as their sense of worth is more fragile. They often feel less confident than they once did. As an upside, despite what we may feel, what I often see and have experienced myself is how the unique challenge of motherhood enhances our impact in the workplace. We are still just as good (if not better) than we were before we took time out.

Part of the problem, though, is we, and the society we live in, often tie what we do to our self-worth. We build a belief that our sense of worth comes from the *outside in*, rather than from the *inside out*. This whole book is all about challenging that belief, for us to build our worth from the inside out. In addition, we need to be aware of our strengths, talents, passions and values, as well as our limitations, and learn to deeply believe in ourselves. It often surprises me how many women struggle to tell me their strengths when I initially ask them, or underestimate these strengths. When we are able to play to our strengths and value ourselves, as well as our skills and talents, it is much easier to ask for what we are worth.

Exploring our beliefs and assumptions about money

Our underlying beliefs about money, and ourselves, drive our thoughts, feelings and, ultimately, our behaviours around money. Many of our beliefs come out of our childhoods, how we watched our parents, grandparents, friends, other significant people, our culture and communities deal with money.

Here are some of the beliefs and assumptions about money that I picked up in childhood, as well as some that others have shared with me over the years:

◆ Money doesn't grow on trees.

◆ You must work hard to survive and be successful, which means valuing work over family.

◆ Half of all marriages end in divorce. You can't trust a man to look after you, so you must learn to look after yourself.

◆ We judge people on what they do and how much money they make.

◆ When I have 'enough' money, life will finally get easier and I can relax.

◆ Money equals control and power.

◆ Being a mum is undervalued and not respected.

◆ Money is how we show love or withhold it.

◆ Spending money and buying stuff makes you feel better.

◆ My worth and value are built on my wealth.

Conscious reflection

Do any of these thoughts resonate for you, or are other ones coming back to you from your own childhood? Take a minute to jot down a list of beliefs that you have around money from your childhood. A belief can be a thought, an opinion or an expectation that you now have around money because of what you heard or behaviours that you witnessed in your childhood. For example, you may have had a

(continued)

single mother who had to work very hard just to make ends meet, or a father who gambled, or one who was super tight with money, or a parent who spent with no regard for the future. Consider how those behaviours may have affected your beliefs.

The more we become aware of our beliefs, the more we can become aware of the behaviours they drive in us. Some of our beliefs may be outdated or illogical. Once you identify your beliefs around money, I would invite you to answer five questions for each of them:

1. Is this belief logical/rational, or is it a belief I made up through the lens of a child?

2. Do I have evidence that this belief is true or rational?

3. How might this belief be harmful or limiting me?

4. Is this belief supportive? How does it support me to create the life I truly desire?

5. Given all the above, what do I need to be most mindful of in terms of how this belief is affecting my life and how can I support myself to shift this belief?

Becoming compassionately aware of our beliefs and where they come from is the first step in re-creating our relationship with money. Once we know our unseen beliefs and assumptions, we can use our ongoing mindfulness practice when an issue or decision around money arises. For example, when I start to go into financial fear, I can pause, breathe, check-in with my body, soothe any anxiety that my thoughts and beliefs about money may be creating within me, and reflect on my beliefs and thoughts around this money issue. Then, I can respond with a different attitude or behaviour, if appropriate.

While our beliefs, thoughts and expectations toward money are set up by what we experienced in our childhoods, as adults we can become aware of these thoughts and expectations. More importantly, we start to take full responsibility for the role they play in our lives and how they may be sabotaging us. This is incredibly empowering.

Valuing ourselves at work

I once read a story about a financial services organisation that did some research to figure out why so few women were responding to their advertisement for financial planners. In that advertisement, they listed the five key skills and competencies they were looking for from potential candidates. The research suggested that when men looked at the list of skills and competencies, they would generally say to themselves something like, 'No problem, I have three out of these five skills and *could* do the other two, so I will apply'.

In contrast, women tended to say to themselves, 'I only have three out of the five skills, so I will not apply'. Is this about women devaluing themselves, or is it simply that women are more honest than men? What I have noticed is that many of the women I have worked with have underestimated their capabilities and sometimes not put their hands up for roles and missed out on potential opportunities.

For example, Janice really wanted another job, but never felt she had quite the right experience for the jobs she was seeing advertised internally or externally to her organisation. Instead of going through the process of applying (and potentially learning and growing through the process, even if she were not successful), she sat back feeling powerless.

To counter this powerlessness, she worked even harder to get somebody to notice her. Eventually, as we worked together, she got up the courage to apply for her dream job, even though she felt it was out of her league. With careful preparation, a focus on her strengths, and confidently articulating how she would take care of the areas in which she was not as experienced, she got the job. But she would never have even applied without encouragement and support.

Tracy was recently offered a new role as a first-time manager. She accepted a very small pay rise without question, given she felt she did not really have the experience and simply felt grateful to get the opportunity. I was coaching her manager at the time, and while he was surprised Tracy had not pushed back and asked for more, he was very happy that he had saved the business some money in a difficult financial climate. However, within weeks, Tracy was running rings around the previous manager (who they had paid significantly more), the team was performing better and the financial results had improved significantly — which is why they had offered Tracy the role in the first place.

The organisation valued her, but she did not value herself enough to ask for what she deserved to be paid, or at least have a conversation about what might be possible. Of course, wouldn't it have been good if the organisation valued her enough to offer her the money she should have been paid? Sure. Was there likely some unconscious bias going on? Absolutely, which is why I did end up coaching her boss on that very topic. Gender bias is not okay, *and* we must take responsibility for ensuring we speak up and ask for what we deserve. We can't wait for others to value us first; we must start by valuing ourselves before anyone else.

Another way not valuing ourselves can show up is almost the complete opposite of the previous example. In my corporate career, I was forever asking for pay raises, big bonuses and promotions. And most often, I got them. However, upon getting the job or pay rise, I would often then overwork and over-perform, totally exhausting myself to try to prove they had made the right decision.

Find your value in the workplace

To value ourselves more financially in the workplace, we need to ensure that we:

- ◆ *Negotiate for higher pay.* As women, we tend to be less likely to negotiate our salaries compared with men. However, it's important to negotiate for higher pay when starting a new job or when discussing raises. Do your research on industry standards and be confident in your worth.

- *Seek out leadership roles.* Taking on leadership roles can help women increase their visibility and demonstrate their value to their employers. Seek out opportunities to lead projects or teams or consider asking for a promotion.

- *Network with colleagues and industry peers.* Building a strong professional network can help women learn about job opportunities and increase their chances of getting promoted. Attend industry events and connect with colleagues on LinkedIn to expand your network.

- *Advocate for ourselves.* As women, we can often face unconscious bias in the workplace, which can lead to us being overlooked for promotions or opportunities. It's important to advocate for yourself and make your accomplishments and contributions known to your employer. Keep a record of your successes, and be sure to highlight them during performance evaluations or when discussing career advancement.

- *Know and believe in our own value.* All of the above points are wonderful actions to take, but at the core, to empower ourselves, we need to do the inner work to understand where and why we may be limiting ourselves and slowly build our deep inner confidence and belief in ourselves.

Three financial self-care practices

My mum was a financial planner, and while I did not always listen as a teenager and young adult, she taught me a lot about the principles of how to look after myself financially, which was a great gift. These principles include learning to empower ourselves by taking responsibility for living within our means and not burdening our future self, providing our future self with a cushion and taking time to do a financial hygiene checklist. Let's explore these in detail.

1. *Live within your means and do not burden your future self*

While I am generalising, I would suggest that some of us are spenders and some of us are savers. If you are a saver, this can often land you in good stead and you automatically live within your means and set your future self up for a financially rewarding future.

However, there are still some potential challenges to consider for savers. Some savers can end up with regrets as they spend all their time saving and miss out on some of the joys and experiences money can offer them. At the extreme end, savers may also go without important things they need, like good medical care, a warm coat or a visit to the dentist.

When I talk about living within your means and not burdening your future self, I am talking more to those of us who sit in the spenders camp. Interestingly, while there are some areas where I can be a big spender, like on overseas holidays and food, there are other self-care areas that I used to have difficulty bringing myself to spend money on, such as going to the dentist, getting glasses or having a doctor's check-up.

In a 1960s experiment, often referred to as the marshmallow experiment, a team of researchers at Stanford University devised a scenario involving pre-schoolers. They presented these young children with a selection of treats, including marshmallows, pretzels and cookies. The researchers instructed the children to choose just one treat, explaining that if they could resist temptation for a short period and not eat the treat, they would be given an additional treat. Essentially, by postponing their instant gratification, they had the chance to double their treat. The researchers followed these children into adulthood and discovered that those who delayed their gratification experienced significantly greater success in life compared with those who sought immediate satisfaction.

For us spenders, it is hard to delay the gratification. When we have access to money, it can be hard to resist the urge to buy what we want right away. While it may seem like we can afford it in the moment, we often don't consider the long-term consequences of our day-to-day actions and choices, and may end up burdening our future self.

I, personally, have a pattern of spending money before I earn it and then feeling the enormous pressure of needing to then go out and create more income. I noticed this play out for me for many years. In my business I could have a super strong quarter, and off the back of that go out and buy things, assuming I will have another strong quarter. Instead, work might dry up, and all of a sudden, I am struggling to cover my day-to-day expenses. There was even a period when I was constantly re-drawing on my mortgage to manage this.

In the end, the money always came. That was not the problem. The problem was that I wasn't allowing my nervous system to rest or putting enough money aside for a rainy day. I was always in financial fear, which triggered deep and old feelings of instability for me: the same instabilities I felt as a little girl when my dad left us with nothing, and my mum had to go to work.

What I learnt over time is that my internal financial stability comes from me not committing to discretionary expenses, like holidays, clothes, new furniture or a new car, before I have earnt the income and set enough aside to ride the ups and downs of life. It is only then that I got relief from the fear, anxiety and pressure, which I was ultimately creating within myself. It sounds so obvious; however, it is easy for us to repeat old patterns unconsciously. Thankfully, after recognising this pattern in myself, I was able to make a commitment to stop doing this. I now have at least a year's buffer in my accounts. Yet, what I find very interesting is that I can still feel panic and insecurity when I don't know where my next client is going to come from. It shows me how easy it is to drop back into beliefs and feelings of *It's never enough* or *I will never feel safe*, even when that is not true anymore.

Our future self, either next month, next year, or ten or twenty years down the track, will need to deal with the consequences of us not taking responsibility for our financial self-care now.

Six practices your future self will thank you for

1. Get clear around the beliefs that are driving your spending behaviours, including when you may be shopping just to numb out for a while.

2. Set a budget. Whether it be for your family and household or just for yourself, it is very important to have a clear picture of your weekly or monthly income and expenses. Personally, I find it a pretty confronting process and it always surprises me how the little things really add up. But it sure brings me into reality around my spending habits! And, as incredibly uncomfortable as it can be, it is very empowering to get clear and have something to refer to when I need to tighten my belt a little.

3. Track your expenses. If, as part of creating your budget, you are not clear on all your ongoing expenses, one thing I have found that really works is to download a highly rated, reviewed and safe app and spend a few months tracking everything you spend. If you are like me, you'll be thinking, *No way, I don't have time for that*. But I was pleasantly surprised that the budget app I used automatically tracked all my money. I just had to link it to my bank accounts and create the relevant spending categories. It also alerts me if I'm overspending, and I can set up savings targets. It was very powerful for me to get clear on what categories I was spending my money in. It was a real eye-opener to see just how much money I spend on food alone!

4. If you struggle with impulse spending or overspending, I really encourage you to cut up your credit cards. I know some people who just keep a credit card at home safely tucked away for the times they really need one, but these days, most of the time you can use an eftpos or debit card for purchases. If you do use a credit card, it is great financial self-care to pay the full amount owing each month, not just the minimum payment, as soon as it is due. Find a credit card with no fees.

And make the most of any loyalty programs attached to your card. I was recently able to hand back my points and receive $1600 cash from my bank.

5. Differentiate between good debt and bad debt. Good debt is when you borrow money to help grow your assets, such as for an investment property, buying a house that forces you to pay off your mortgage (an asset). Bad debt includes borrowing money for things that do not increase in value, such as credit card spending or a personal loan for a car (a depreciating asset). If you have any outstanding bad debt, it is important to get this paid off ASAP. And if you have multiple credit card debts, you may also want to consider consolidating it into one personal loan to be able to get a cheaper interest rate and then focus on getting that debt paid off first.

6. And finally, it is so important to practise mindful spending boundaries. Know the difference between your needs and your wants. Stop and ask yourself before each purchase, *Do I need this? Can I afford this? Is it getting me closer to my vision for my life, or taking me further away?*

Becoming aware and mindful of what we are spending our money on supports us to live within our means. Not burdening our future self with poor financial decisions now is an important part of respecting ourselves and practising financial self-care. Once we have this in place, and we know we are not burdening our future self, we can go one step further and start to provide a cushion for our future self.

2. Provide your future self with a financial cushion

While in our mindfulness practices we talk about learning to live in the present, rather than the past or future, money is one area, no matter how uncomfortable, where we need to take time out to consider our future. It can be so easy to bury our heads in the sand

and avoid the consequences of today's choices on our future self. I do believe, as with most things in life, we need to find a level of balance between saving and spending, enjoying the life we are currently living, and providing a cushion for our future self.

Four habits to prepare for the future

1. If you are not already doing so, *start a savings habit*. Even if things are tight for you now, practise putting a little aside each week for your future self. Ideally, we want to get into the habit of saving 10 per cent of our income, with the aim of eventually having six months of basic living expenses in the bank. This will provide you with more choice and freedom as to how you live your life. I know one of the things that can most debilitate me is financial fear. By creating this cushion, I have been able to explore a new and more fulfilling career.

2. Consider putting in place a *regular savings plan* feeding directly into a managed investment fund, or what is known in the US as a mutual fund. My son's dad and I did this when our son was born. It is a small monthly amount that has been accumulating for the twenty-two years he has been alive. With compounding interest and the growth of the underlying portfolio, it is now a substantial amount of money for his education or his first mortgage. It not only provides a cushion for my future self, as I don't have to pay more money for his education, it is a cushion for his future self as well.

3. I can't stress strongly enough the importance of making the most of the *compounding effect*. Einstein famously said, 'Compounding is the eighth wonder of the world'. Compound interest is when money is invested and earns a return year on year, like interest on a savings account or dividends on shares. Every year, the interest is recalculated based on the previous year's base amount, plus that year's interest, so you are earning a return on a growing amount every year.

4. And lastly, it's wise to *invest our savings*, so they are growing and working for us, literally while we are sleeping. Whether that is investing in domestic or international shares, property or other assets, I would really encourage you to educate yourself around the benefits of investing. I, personally, am a very big fan of getting professional financial advice, but I say that with a few warnings. Firstly, make sure you are getting the best advice possible from someone who is licensed to do so and, ideally, get someone who comes personally recommended. Secondly, getting advice doesn't mean we get to abdicate our responsibility for what we are investing in: do your own due diligence. And thirdly, always diversify your investments—never put all your eggs in one investment basket.

3. Financial hygiene checklist

My final recommended financial self-care habit is to reflect on the following financial hygiene list periodically and make adjustments as needed.

- What are my beliefs around money?

- Do I value and respect myself: my skills, talents and passions, as well as my limitations?

- Am I living within my means and not burdening my future self?

- Am I clear on my income and expenses?

- Do I have, or am I in the process of, paying off all my bad debt?

- Am I developing a cushion for my future self through saving and investing and getting support and professional advice where needed?

- If I am over 45 years of age, have I put some time, thought and gained some professional advice to plan for my retirement?

◆ Do I have a Will in place? This is critical if you have any assets, and if you are in partnership, it's important that your partner has a will too. Get professional advice or buy a will kit online.

◆ Do my partner and I have death cover in place, should something happen to either of us? This is particularly important if either of you have any debts that may affect each other, or you rely on each other's incomes to maintain the life you are accustomed to.

◆ Do I have income protection cover in place? Income protection covers you if you have an accident or get seriously sick and are unable to work. This is also important for your partner if they work.

◆ Do I read and take full responsibility for any forms I am asked to sign, including if my partner asks me to sign something for them? I can't tell you how many women I know who signed forms without being aware of the liabilities they were taking on, and got themselves into trouble when investments or businesses went bad. You may still choose to sign it, but please always read it, and be aware of what is being asked of you and the potential consequences.

◆ Am I fully self-supporting? Do you know how you will take care of yourself should anything happen to your partner? This may include ensuring you have the right insurances in place, and are having the conversations you need to with your partner.

◆ Am I clear on our financial situation as a couple and do I communicate around everything I need to? This is a tricky one and I do deeply respect that this is not easy, and that couples work money out in many different ways. However, the important thing is that you talk about it. I recently watched someone who had been married for eleven years and has two young children lose her husband suddenly. He had not updated his Will in those eleven years, and all his money was left to his adult children from a previous marriage. She will go to court, which is likely to find in her favour; however, that will take quite some time and it is already putting a great strain on her and on the great relationship she has with his adult children.

Communication is such an important part of working through our money issues. I have one friend who is a stay-at-home mum and never talks about money with her spouse. She often complains about how hard it is to ask her partner for money. Yet, I have another friend who regularly explores concerns with her partner and together they come up with a mutually satisfactory setup. For example, both receive a 'salary' from their paid work, and have equal access to the money coming in and stick to an agreed-upon budget.

Of course, the solutions are as varied as the couples. My suggestion is just that it's an issue that should be talked about and agreed upon. Money is one of the top three things that couples fight most about; however, it is never about the money — it is what the money represents for them and in their relationship: power, freedom, control.

In Chapter 15, we will explore authentic communicating and suggest ways that can really support you to have the often vulnerable and challenging conversations that money can represent. No matter our situation, it is up to us to ask the difficult questions, to value ourselves and, ultimately, to empower ourselves by taking responsibility for our financial self-care.

While always a little confronting, even as I write this, it has been a gift to reflect yet again on the areas I need to go back and refocus on. May this financial self-care checklist provide you with a great overview of where you may still need to take care of yourself more financially, or provide you with the comfort that you have solid foundations in place. May you gain a sense of deep self-respect, empowerment, enormous self-compassion, and kindness as you take responsibility for your financial self-care and the meaningful life you are creating for yourself.

PART III
Be yourself

CHAPTER 10

Finding our authentic selves

In 2015, I had the gift of training as a Search Inside Yourself certified teacher. Search Inside Yourself was born at Google when one of Google's earliest engineers put together a team of leading experts in mindfulness techniques, neuroscience and leadership. They developed an internal course for fellow Google employees, lovingly called Search Inside Yourself, before they left Google to set up as an independent, non-profit leadership institute. I was selected along with three other Australians and seventy-six people from all around the world to fly back and forth between Sydney and San Francisco to learn how to embody and facilitate their two-day emotional intelligence and mindfulness leadership program.

One of the many things I loved about this training was its experiential nature. It was perfect timing for me, as I was still very much in the process of trying to work out what I was doing with my life. If I am honest with myself, I probably did the training because I was still looking for a product or brand that would make it easier for me to sell what I do, because I still didn't really value my own capabilities and reputation at the time. Whatever the reasons were, I received many gifts from doing it.

In addition to meeting some truly inspiring, compassionate and like-minded people, one of the benefits was that they invited us to explore our own values and vision for our lives and our leadership. I had not imagined getting clear on my values would be a hard thing to do — until I tried to do it. I am not sure I had ever really stopped and asked myself what my values were before this.

They took us through a couple of exercises I'll share with you in Chapter 11. After going through them, I vividly remember my surprise when I eventually landed on my top five values. One of them was *beauty*, which on one level didn't surprise me, as I am a great lover of nature, colour, textures, comfort, design, etc. But what did surprise me was what a relief it finally felt to write that down, acknowledge it, own it and allow it to start to guide my life. At first, beauty felt trivial and not serious enough to be a guiding value for my life. However, over time it helped me to better understand myself and why creativity, nature and aesthetics are so important and nurturing to me. Beauty is an expression of goodness, harmony and balance. Even the most left-brained logical thinker sees the beauty in a well-designed system. As someone once said to me, 'Beauty, well understood, is everything!'

The other two values I uncovered, which were significant components of what unfolded next in my life, were *courage* and *authenticity*. I don't think there is anything I admire more than seeing people have the courage to truly be themselves. Yet, for all the reasons I have previously shared with you about my history and learnt patterns, showing up authentically has presented many challenges for me. When I finally wrote down *authenticity* as one of my five core values and asked myself if I had been living in congruence with this value, I realised the answer was no. I was forever trying to be someone else, thinking I was not good enough as I am, and was totally out of integrity with myself.

This exercise was both enlightening and confronting, as it revealed how difficult it is to be in tune with our most authentic selves, and to show up as such in our daily lives.

What is authenticity and how do we become truly authentic?

After I realised that one of my top five values was authenticity, I went on quite a journey to try to understand for myself what authenticity meant in practice. ChatGPT (for whatever it's worth) told me:

Authenticity refers to being genuine, true to oneself and honest in one's actions, words, behaviours and interactions. It involves embracing and expressing one's identity, values and beliefs without pretending or conforming to societal expectations or pressures.

Did being honest in one's actions, words and behaviours mean I should let everybody know when I was feeling sad or angry or upset? Did it mean I should wear my heart on my sleeve at work? That if I didn't like someone, I should just tell them? That I should never do anything I didn't want to do and could say whatever I wanted, whenever I wanted, if I was being honest?

I have seen some very inappropriate behaviours from people that they then described as 'being authentic'. This often looked like managers losing their tempers at team members, speaking rudely, ignoring someone because they didn't rate them well, or calling people out and criticising them in a public place — because they were just being 'honest'. I don't believe any of this is true authenticity.

There is a difference between our emotions and our feelings. It is an important difference, especially when we are talking about being authentic. I loved it when I heard the simple concept that emotions are universal to us all. In fact, in their simplest form, there are six primary human emotions: happiness, sadness, fear, disgust, anger and surprise. They arise within us as brief physiological and psychological responses to a specific event or stimulus.

Feelings, however, are highly subjective experiences that arise from our interpretations and thoughts about emotions. They are more nuanced and can be influenced by our experiences, beliefs and context. For example, when we are asked to speak to an audience of 1000 people, we may automatically have an initial emotion that arises within us. For some, perhaps this emotion is happiness because they would love that opportunity. For another, it may be fear because they don't want to do it. The longer-lasting feeling will depend on our previous experiences of speaking to large groups, or the stories we tell ourselves, which may create a feeling of excitement or a feeling of high anxiety. Feelings are our emotions plus the story going on in our head about that emotion.

I share this because we don't have to justify our emotions. Our emotions are what's real for us at any given moment, there is no running dialogue attached. Emotions are not destructive, and they change often and quickly. We never have to justify our emotions — these are authentic. In our practice of authenticity, it is important to own and express our emotions, such as *I am feeling sad* or *I am feeling angry*. But in doing this, we also have to be very conscious of when our *feelings* are running away with us due to the stories we are telling ourselves or the assumptions we are making. If we're not conscious of these, we will then dump these personal feelings onto others or allow these feelings to hijack our relationships at work and in our personal lives.

This doesn't mean we don't have big feelings! I saw a beautiful example of a female leader who, very sadly, lost her mother suddenly, and fully owned her emotions at work. She told people she was feeling incredibly sad and, at times, very angry. When she didn't feel able to contain her feelings, she took time off or excused herself from a meeting rather than try to pretend nothing was going on in her life or potentially take her feelings out on people around her. We can be authentic, contained and have boundaries that are respectful and compassionate toward others and ourselves.

For me, authenticity at work means being true to yourself and embracing your unique qualities, experiences, values and strengths while navigating the professional environments we work in. It involves presenting and expressing ourselves genuinely and respectfully without compromising our values and purpose, or conforming to societal or gendered expectations.

When we practise showing up authentically, we can also acknowledge the challenges many women face in male-dominated industries or organisational cultures that may have biases or expectations that differ from our own. We want to create and be part of cultures that encourage women (and men) to be authentic without fear of being judged or penalised based on gender stereotypes.

Here are six ways to become more authentic in the workplace.

1. Self-awareness and personal growth

Authenticity starts with self-awareness: understanding our values, purpose, vision, strengths and weaknesses. We need to recognise our unique qualities and what we bring to the table as professionals. This also encourages us to pursue opportunities for development, take risks and challenge ourselves to grow as we stay true to our values and aspirations. When I became clear on my values, purpose and vision, it was much easier for me to practise living and leading in integrity with myself, while watching the limiting beliefs I told myself and not allowing them to take me off track. It also supported me to take risks and challenge myself in ways that moved me toward my vision.

2. Embracing our individuality

Authenticity encourages us to embrace our individuality and express our thoughts, ideas and perspectives without conforming to societal norms or stereotypes. It involves being true to ourselves and not suppressing our authentic voice or identity.

Trisha struggled to speak up and offer her views and perspectives in meetings. Her inner critic had numerous reasons why she should stay quiet, just as she had done growing up as the youngest child with five older and much louder siblings. As she committed to taking more risks and offering her opinions, even if she was not sure they would be valued, she found her visibility started to grow, and over time, she was seen as a real expert in her field. More importantly, her inner confidence also grew as she started to recognise what others already saw in her.

3. Overcoming stereotypes and biases

Women often face stereotypes and biases in the workplace. Authenticity involves challenging and breaking through these stereotypes, refusing to conform to traditional gender roles, and showcasing our skills and abilities based on merit.

I worked with Priyana in India at a time when she was working with a very traditional older male Indian leader who constantly overlooked her for opportunities or his time and support, and instead, focused on the older males in his team. This was the same experience Priyana had grown up with in her family, so she was used to feeling invisible and staying quiet. Although, now she could really see the impact it was having on her sense of self and her career.

As we worked together, she started to showcase her accomplishments in team meetings, she started reaching out and networking with other parts of the organisation, particularly with other female leaders for mentorship, and she started asking her manager for specific opportunities, respectfully calling out biases she saw. Over time, her manager started to take more notice of her and he became aware of his biases. But even better than that, Priyana got herself a new job in a very different, more nurturing environment and felt proud of how she had shown up and respectfully advocated for herself, growing her inner confidence.

4. Building genuine connections

Authenticity fosters the development of genuine connections with colleagues, managers and subordinates. By being authentic, we can establish trust, foster inclusivity and create a supportive work environment where diversity of thought and expression are valued.

I recently worked with a group of twenty young aspiring female leaders across multiple countries. One of the gifts of the process I took them through was coming together regularly as a group to authentically share struggles, strengths and aspirations. At the end of the program, they collectively decided to keep the group sessions running. They understood that what each of them needed most was a place to show up, be authentic, foster inclusivity and support each other in managing their wellbeing and in their career aspirations.

5. Honesty and transparency

Authenticity entails being honest and transparent in communication and interactions with others. It involves expressing one's thoughts and emotions openly, while also actively listening and respecting others' viewpoints.

Jenny was having a lot of difficulties with an internal stakeholder named Lisa. Lisa never did what she said she was going to do. She would often put her hand up for something and then pull out at the last minute because she was 'just too busy'. It felt like the last straw for Jenny when Lisa had said she would write and present half of a customer presentation with Jenny, and then the night before said she was sick and would not be able to do it.

Jenny had known this would happen and yet she had agreed to let Lisa do it. Jenny had avoided addressing any of the previous times she had felt let down and now was in a very difficult situation. This time she agreed to address it. Together, we talked through her approach and then she sat down with Lisa and explained the impact her behaviour was having on her. She asked Lisa if there was anything going on that she should be aware of, or if she had any suggestions of how they solve this together for the future.

Then she sat and listened as Lisa told her she was currently going through a divorce. Her daughter was suffering severe anxiety because of it, and she herself was feeling completely overwhelmed but didn't know how to say no to the demands she felt Jenny was always making of her.

While this didn't make it okay for her to be always letting Jenny down, as they better understood what was going on for each other, they were able to agree how they could work better together going forward. Lisa agreed to stop and think about what she said 'yes' to and what she said 'no' to, and to let Jenny know well in advance if there would be a problem completing her requests. Jenny agreed to be more conscious of what were reasonable and unreasonable requests. Through honest and transparent communication, they became closer, acknowledging that their fear of conflict had caused them to avoid these perceived difficult conversations.

6. Balancing vulnerability and strength

Authenticity recognises that vulnerability can be a strength. We learn to (and hopefully feel empowered to) share our experiences, challenges and successes without fear of judgement, thus creating an environment that embraces vulnerability as a path to growth and understanding.

Stacey, a senior leader in her organisation, came across as a very strong female leader. She always had an opinion and view on everything. She showed up and spoke in such a way that gave other people the impression she had everything under control. This behaviour stemmed from Stacey's childhood in a very chaotic home with a father who drank too much and a mother who was always trying to cover her father's behaviour.

But as part of our 360° feedback process that Stacey undertook, she heard that she did not seem very authentic, real or vulnerable, and that people didn't really trust her. Stacey was shattered by this feedback. She truly saw herself as authentic and did not realise that the front she put on to manage her own feelings and show the team that she was in control and a very capable leader, was having the opposite effect.

After receiving this feedback, she started to recognise that, even as a senior leader, she did not need to be responsible for everything on her own. She still set a strong direction and held others accountable, but she started to open up more about some of the struggles the business was having. She started to ask for more help. She let people know if she was going through difficulties that were relevant and affecting how she was showing up as a leader. As a result, her team blossomed, and the culture of her large team improved almost overnight. Being both soft and strong is a combination few of us have mastered, but it is one of the most powerful and effective places to live and lead from.

My hope is we can all work in companies that emphasise the importance of breaking through gender biases, embracing individuality and building genuine connections to foster a diverse and vibrant workplace culture. Through this, we can create inclusive and empowering environments where women can fully express themselves, contribute our unique perspectives and thrive professionally. It is also my hope that, as women, we do our inner work, including getting clear on our values, purpose and vision for our work and our lives so we can show up more fully to being our authentic selves in the workplace.

CHAPTER 11

Finding our authentic values and purpose

Stopping to get clear on my values and purpose changed everything for me. I had always felt incredibly passionate about supporting women to live a life true to themselves, in hindsight probably because I wanted that so deeply for myself. They say we teach what we need to learn! But as I got clearer on my values and my sense of purpose, I felt a stronger call within me to start living in more alignment with myself. It makes so much sense in hindsight. I had been living my life true to other people's values. I had been looking outside of myself for my purpose, success and validation.

Our values drive a lot of our decisions in life. We don't receive a list of values at birth, we pick them up as we move through our life learning social norms and noticing which behaviours are acceptable and which are not. In our homes and families, at school, from the media and other environments, we learn what others think is important, which often then becomes the source of our beliefs and rules, and we attribute them to our values.

But are these values true to who we are today? Do they reflect what we hold as important and meaningful in our life now?

These are questions many of us don't stop to ask — and rarely answer. It can be difficult to figure out what we believe independent of everything we've been taught, what really matters to us and who we want to be.

To live and lead true to ourselves, it's important to reflect on and clarify our values throughout our life. We all have the potential to grow and change through our different experiences. Therefore, our values can and must grow with us. As I shared earlier, one of my core values is authenticity and I practise it daily. But just a decade ago I would have ascribed little importance to authenticity, as it was not something I witnessed a lot of in my upbringing.

Sometimes we can feel a bit lost in life, or our career, or we can go through major transitions in life, like becoming a parent, going through a divorce or midlife crisis, experiencing burnout or a global pandemic. In those times, it can be a good opportunity to check-in with our values. Are we clear on our values? Are we living in alignment with them? Or are we living outdated values? Or living values that we did not consciously choose? If you feel you've veered away from your authentic self, don't be disheartened — your true and authentic self is always waiting for your return.

Our values are the general expression of what is most important for us. They help us make decisions, choose what's right and wrong, and know how to act in various situations. Our values can serve as reminders about what we cherish, particularly in tricky situations where we might be pressured to act according to someone else's values. In this way, knowing our values helps us stay true to ourselves as we move through life.

Our self-awareness practices allow us to acknowledge what's in our hearts and stay in touch with what's meaningful to us. Our ongoing self-awareness allows us to question and redefine the values we want in our lives today. Some cultures and religions tell people what they should value and how they should act, but that's not what we're talking about here. Authentic values are consciously chosen by us. They come from listening to our heart and tuning in to what matters most to us, even if they are different to our family's and community's values.

Whether we have clarity around our values or not, they exist and are driving our decisions and actions. They are always operating in the background, influencing and motivating us, which is why it's so important to get clear and conscious about our values, and to keep them up-to-date to ensure they are truly our values and not someone else's.

When the way we think, speak and behave matches our values, life feels on track. We feel whole, confident, connected, aligned and empowered, with a greater understanding and clarity about our deepest nature. This provides us with our own personal compass that points to our true north, our authentic self.

A reflection for discovering your core values

How do we even start to answer the question, 'What are my core values?' Let's do a reflection that I did during my Search Inside Yourself training that I found very valuable.

Who do you admire?

Bring to mind three people whom you deeply admire. They may be real people in your day-to-day life, they may be famous people or even fictional people. You may know them well or not at all. These will be three people who have inspired you. Who are they? Write their names down.

Then, under each name, list what qualities and characteristics each of these people have that you greatly respect and admire. Allow whatever it is to just bubble up. There's no way to get this wrong.

Usually, the attributes we choose in people we admire point to core values that we hold in high esteem for ourselves. Those key characteristics that you most admire in the three people you chose are likely core values you hold for yourself.

You may like to go to my website (jowagstaff.com/bookresources) where you will find a beautiful PDF values workbook, which includes a list of values that you can also reflect on.

Now write a list of values that came up for you. Spend a few minutes reflecting on this list. Do these feel like your personal core values? You can make some adjustments, add, remove or change them until you come up with the final list of your top five values.

Once you are clear on your top five, which may take a few hours or a few days, put the list somewhere you look frequently, such as your computer monitor or on the fridge. I also encourage you to share them with people, including how they come alive for you in your day-to-day life.

Now comes the challenging and exciting part: aligning our daily lives and behaviours with our core values. People ask me, 'How do I know if I'm living my core values?'

It can be answered with one question: 'Are you fulfilled?'

You may be looking at your list of core values and thinking, 'Oh, wow, that's why I'm feeling so dissatisfied. I'm not living many of these.' If so, take a gentle breath and support yourself in this realisation, perhaps feeling some gratitude for these new insights.

I remember taking a client named Patricia through this process. At the end, she had five very clear core values, which she had never articulated to herself: authenticity, connection, family, tenacity and achievement. When we started to explore if and how she was living in alignment with these five values, she realised that all her time and energy was going into tenacity and achievement, which gave her a lot of satisfaction. However, she was completely out of integrity with authenticity, connection and family. This was a simple and yet profound turning point in her life.

Once we're aware of our core values, it's easier to identify what's getting in the way of living a life true to ourselves. Living our values means placing greater emphasis on and making a greater commitment to people, activities and experiences that really express those values. Once Patricia recognised where she was out of alignment, it was easier for her to start holding boundaries around what she needed to do more and less of. It helped her find her voice and express herself more authentically, both at home and at work.

I have noticed many times that, once we are truly living in alignment with our core values, life shifts in the most beautiful ways. Our values are who we are, not who we think we should be, which is why our values serve as a compass to ensure we are moving ever closer to our most authentic and meaningful life. Our values serve as the light that illuminates our genuine path in life and supports our purpose.

Purpose makes our lives meaningful

We humans are complex creatures, with a deep-rooted need for meaning and significance in our lives. Having a sense of purpose gives us direction, motivation and fulfillment. When we have a clear sense of purpose, we tend to feel more agency over our lives, more resilient in the face of challenges and more satisfied with our accomplishments.

Purpose also gives us a reason to get up in the morning, to work toward a goal and to move toward something greater than ourselves. Having a sense of purpose has been linked to numerous health benefits, including lower levels of stress, improved mental health and increased longevity. Furthermore, not having purpose can lead to us experiencing serious psychological difficulties. Having a strong sense of purpose can also help us develop stronger relationships, both with ourselves and others, as we work toward a shared goal.

After working with thousands of women and men from many diverse cultures, I have come to see that the pursuit of purpose is a very personal journey that varies from person to person. There can also be certain societal and cultural factors that contribute to women feeling like they need to find their purpose more strongly than men. For example, women have historically been expected to prioritise their roles as caregivers and homemakers over pursuing their own individual goals and ambitions. This has led to a cultural narrative that suggests that a woman's primary purpose is to take care of others, rather than to pursue her own interests and passions. If we have felt this pressure, especially as part of our upbringing, learning to balance our personal pursuits with our responsibilities to our families and communities can make the search for purpose sometimes feel more challenging.

The ongoing exploration of a higher purpose, like getting clear on our values, is a very important and personal journey that supports us to gain further clarity on who we are and how we can be of service to others. In my experience, it is a creative process of discovering the sweet spot of what is truly important to us and what the world needs.

Seven steps for discovering your purpose

I believe our purpose is already inside of us and becomes clearer as we set an intention to fully explore it with ongoing self-enquiry. However, the quest for purpose can be guided with frameworks. One of the best I've ever experienced was given to me by Michelle Duvall, founder of Fingerprint for Success, where she offers seven essential steps to finding your purpose. If you go to jowagstaff.com/bookresources, you can download a PDF version of this next practice to write in and keep.

Step 1: List ten things you want most out of your life

Start by imagining yourself at the end of your life happily sitting in a rocking chair in your favourite place and thinking to yourself, *I am ready, I am complete, I have fulfilled all that I ever wanted to.* As you think back over your life and all the things that you feel most grateful for and most fulfilled by, make a list of the top ten key personal experiences or achievements that you would like to have in your lifetime.

A couple of examples of mine include having had the gift of:

♦ being a mum and being able to give the gift of being a loving, present, conscious mum to the best of my abilities

- creating a loving, self-compassionate and peaceful relationship with myself where I feel the freedom to truly be myself — I am at peace with who I am and my life

- being of service to others and making a positive difference in the world, while feeling free to be myself.

Step 2: List ten things that you most want to see happen on the planet

If you had a magic wand and could solve any problem in the world, what changes would you make? What do you care the most about? What gets you frustrated and annoyed when you watch or read the news? If you were at a dinner party, what topic would get you fired up?

List the top ten problems you would like to solve in the world. Don't worry if you could never achieve them on your own, or in your lifetime, add them anyway.

My examples included:

- Every human being is raising their level of consciousness and becoming more self-aware and compassionate to themselves and to each other.

- An end to child and human trafficking and slavery.

- An end to inequity and bias, particularly toward women.

Step 3: List ten characteristics/traits that best describe you

What qualities best describe you? If you were being introduced to others, how might they describe you? What would your parents, partner, children, co-workers and friends think best describes your personality, approach to life and style? List your top ten.

My examples include:

- tenacious

- warm

- courageous

- caring

- authentic.

Step 4: List ten skills or abilities that you can do and love to do now

What do you *love* to do that you can do now? It can be any part of your life, and any ability that seems insignificant or amazing to you or others. The key here is to identify things that you love to do and can do now. List your top ten.

My examples include:

- coaching

- speaking

- communicating.

Step 5: Identify your top priority from each group

Review all your entries for steps one through four. Identify if there is a theme that runs through each step or a clear top one that best describes you for each step. Highlight or circle your number one priority for each step before moving on to step 6.

My examples include:

- Step 1: Being of service to others and making a positive difference in the world, while feeling free to be myself.

- Step 2: Every human being is raising their level of consciousness and becoming more self-aware and compassionate to themselves and to each other. (This would fundamentally change how we treat ourselves and each other and change the world we live in.)

◆ Step 3: Authentic

◆ Step 4: Communicating

Step 6: Write a first draft of a personal mission statement

Using these top priorities from the first four steps, now use the template provided to create a first draft of your personal mission statement. Do not evaluate or judge the statement. Complete the following sentence:

I [full name] will [top priority from step four] using my [top priority from step three] to accomplish [top priority from step two], and also achieve [top priority from step 1].

My example is:

I, Jo Wagstaff, will communicate using my authenticity, to accomplish every human being raising their level of consciousness and becoming more self-aware and compassionate to themselves and to each other, and also achieve being of service to others and making a difference in the world, while being free to be myself.

Step 7: Rewrite, finesse and share

Sometimes, it feels spot on the first time. Other times, the statement will feel clunky and awkward. As you read it out, observe how you feel in your body and how the words resonate with you. Then, identify the words that do not yet fully resonate and make any changes.

As mentioned, this is an unfolding journey that provides a wonderful opportunity for lots of self-enquiry. Put your statement down for a few days, then pick it up again and allow it to become clear to you.

Many women I have worked with have struggled even answering the first four questions (as I did the first time I did it). Yet, these questions help us to better understand ourselves.

My rewrite example:

I will coach and communicate with others, using my authenticity to support myself and others to raise our consciousness, become more self-aware and compassionate both to ourselves and to each other, and through simply being myself make a difference to all who I connect with in my work and life.

This resonates deeply with me, and at the very least, expresses the essence of what brings purpose and meaning to me and helps guide my life choices. At its core, it is simply about learning to be myself, and through showing up that way, supporting others to do the same. No pressure!

Forget the grandiose purpose

I have worked with so many women struggling to define or articulate their purpose. What I often notice is a pressure to find some grandiose purpose — a feeling that they need to do something very important. But that pressure can stop us from ever getting clear.

I have also experienced this pressure within myself. I spent many years struggling to work out my own purpose. But the truth was that most of the time I was unconsciously feeling like I had to justify my existence. I took the anger and rage I felt about what had happened to me out into the world and wrapped it up as my purpose. I felt an often-overwhelming responsibility to 'fix' the world, in the same way I would have liked to have fixed my family and those around me who hurt me. I took my longing as a little girl to feel seen and important out into the world wrapped up as my purpose in the hope of finally getting this need met. I took my unconscious fears of never feeling safe in my own life out into the world wrapped up as my purpose to try and change the world so that I, and everyone else, could finally feel safe.

I have often found that our greatest purpose comes out of our greatest pain. You may notice in my own Step 2 example that some of the things I want to see changed on the planet are things I didn't want to experience myself or heal in my own life. I have worked with many women whose list is strongly based around equity. Often, when we explore their history, it becomes obvious that this is the main thing they would have liked to experience in their own life.

Janet was from a family who migrated from Greece, and as a little girl, she always felt like an outsider. Now her driver is to not have other people experience this in the workplace and in her community, with her value of inclusiveness.

Petra was incredibly passionate about climate change. When we explored her past, she recognised that this came from a place of not feeling safe and in control as a little girl. The impact of climate change was triggering her deepest fears; the planet no longer felt safe for her and her family.

I see many evangelists doing the same — and don't get me wrong, we need to change a lot in our world. I also deeply believe we need to start with our own inner evolution. We must heal our wounds and pain so then, when we follow our purpose, we do so from a place of self-awareness, embodiment and groundedness. This is a very powerful place from which to bring about real and sustainable change.

What I have come to believe is our purpose may simply be to show up in the world as ourselves. Here is what I know now: We do not need a purpose to justify our existence. I believe our purpose comes from within us, from what is deeply meaningful to us. We cultivate it and then we take this into our vision for ourselves and our lives. One of my favourite quotes is from the co-founder of Leadership Circle, Bob Anderson. He writes:

While one part of us is working to stay safe, win approval, and move up, another part of us is longing to live a purposeful life and to make a significant contribution through our work. Most of us harbour a vision for work about which we are passionate. The dilemma is that the freedom, vision, and passion (that are both the foundations and the benefits of leadership) are incompatible with organisational safety, approval seeking, and advancement. We cannot pursue both safety and freedom simultaneously. Caution and courage are mutually exclusive. There is no safe way to be great. We need to make a choice, and the choice we make determines the nature and extent of our leadership and our lives, as well as the culture we contribute to creating.

How do we optimise the tension within us between purpose and safety, between passion and fear? How do we overcome the internal fears and anxieties that want to keep us safe, and therefore limit us? We do this by translating our values and purpose into a clear vision, committing 100 per cent to this vision, and practice showing up each day in alignment with these.

CHAPTER 12

Translating our values and purpose into vision

In Chapter 10, I mentioned going through the Search Inside Yourself training. After they took us through the values exercise, they then took us through one to gain clarity on our vision for the future. After these exercises came the scary part: sharing our vision with the group.

I still remember sitting on the cream, carpeted floor in a large room in San Francisco with a group of four other people. The space was filled with natural light as inspiring music played in the background. We had gotten clear on our top five values and had explored whether we were living in alignment with each of them. Next, they had invited us to get clear on the vision we had for our life and work. The concept of admitting my dreams and aspirations to myself, writing them down on paper, and then reading them out aloud to this group felt quite intimidating. I felt my perfectionist arrive, *What if it is not quite right?* I felt my shame arrive, *Who do you think you are to have such dreams? You can't admit them out aloud; people will laugh at you.*

At the time, I was a single mum, living in a small cottage in an inner-city suburb. I worked alone, with only Australian clients, and my business was very reactive, in the sense that I still took whatever was offered and was lucky to be making $100 000 a year. As I reflected on this, I took a deep breath, called on my values of courage and authenticity that I had just identified, grabbed my pen, and gave myself full permission to write from my heart, with no limitations.

With their guidance, I started with my vision for my life overall. Here is a bit of what I wrote at the time:

I am married to a truly beautiful, kind, strong man. We travel the world together and support and share in each other's lives. Our relationship with ourselves and with each other is a priority for us both. I have a wonderful and healthy relationship with my son Hugo. I am a present parent who supports him to step into his own life and sense of self. We live by the beach in a beautiful, earthy, graceful home. We regularly have close friends visiting, as does Hugo. Our home is filled with warmth, sunshine, beauty, nature, grace and love.

Within this home I have an incredible space where I write and create. I am considered an expert in my field. I am involved in inspiring women to truly be ourselves, to feel confident, calm and connected. I stand fully in my truth. I am a widely read published author and speaker. I co-create and collaborate with an inspiring, aware, authentic, grounded, embodied group of human beings. I support and mentor women in all areas of life and in many countries and communities to step fully into their embodied strong feminine, healing from their past and opening to love of all parts of themselves. My life is one of love and service.

Our life is deeply nourishing, filled with much play, laughter, nature, nurture, deep and important friendships, warmth, love and abundance.

I then went on to write my specific career vision:

I am a sought-after public speaker, facilitator, coach and published author in the areas of self-awareness and living life with courageous authenticity. I work in my own business consistently earning over $300 000 a year. I work part-time, with flexible hours, giving me plenty of time for myself, my son, my partner, my friends and much fun and adventure in my life.

I collaborate with people whom I respect, care about, and really enjoy working with, and with whom I feel respected, cared about, and that they enjoy working with me in return. I am part of a like-minded community with a sense of belonging, mutual values, mutual respect and mutual support.

My personal purpose is to inspire myself and others to develop an authentic and fulfilling relationship with themselves, with others, with their work and with life. I do this through more awareness, acceptance, respect, compassion, connection, authenticity, fulfilment, and love in our relationships and community.

I live in service and gratitude.

I trembled as I read this out aloud to my group, noticing the parts that felt most unlikely and, therefore, embarrassing that I thought I was worthy of that. At the time, the things that felt embarrassing and unlikely included being happily married, living by the beach in a beautiful home, consistently earning over $300 000 a year while working part-time, collaborating with others, being a published author, being a public speaker, empowering women and working across multiple countries. These all felt so far out of my grasp at that moment in time, and perhaps I was scared of what it meant if I really claimed this life and career vision. I sometimes wonder if it feels easier not to claim our dreams, as then we don't have to feel disappointed if they don't work out!

When I got back from San Francisco, I shared this with my closest girlfriends when we were away together for a long weekend. It was a way of *officially* offering my vision up to the universe. It was a powerful experience as I received so much support and encouragement from my friends. I then picked it up and read it out loud every single week for a few months to keep it alive. It also helped me make decisions that aligned with my vision, rather than making decisions that would take me away from this vision.

Over the next couple of years, I took purposeful action toward my vision, even though, at times, it felt like the vision had a life of its own. I found a female business partner and together we created a business and online learning program called Authentic Woman, where we quickly attracted over 70 000 followers across our social platforms, with lots of great engagement. I also started coaching more women within corporate organisations and was invited to do numerous keynotes, locally and globally.

A year later I started a new romantic relationship, and we got married in 2019. Whilst perfectly imperfect, at the core he and our relationship are as my vision describes. Together we bought a 'beautiful, earthy, graceful home' on the beach, one we arguably should not have been able to buy for the money we could afford. But for whatever reason, the owner and real estate agent agreed to our price, which many people told us was well under the market rate at the time. I met like-minded people I still collaborate with today and who are also dear friends. I met and often exceeded my income targets year on year, and last year my business' revenue far exceeded what I put in my original vision, and I had nine coaches working in my business with two support staff.

As simple as it sounds, I kid you not when I say that every single thing I wrote down came into being in the following few years — except this book. This book has been one of the hardest for me to commit my time and energy to, probably because it is the most authentic and vulnerable thing I imagine I will ever do.

While bringing my vision into being might sound very simple, I am not saying it was easy. We cannot manifest what we don't truly believe or if we do not believe we are worthy, and I have definitely come face-to-face with all of my limiting beliefs, self-doubts, insecurities and fears. They all got louder before they settled. Doors closed and others opened. It was not a linear path. After investing enormous time, energy, love and money into Authentic Woman, it never made it off the ground commercially. And while we remain friends, my business partnership ended in a way that was heartbreaking for me at the time.

I suspect one of the reasons Authentic Woman never succeeded is because I still had more inner work to do: more healing around my experience of feeling abandoned and let down by the women in my life, and in particular, my own self-abandonment and lack of self-belief in my own capabilities. On reflection, I can see I was always looking to someone else to give me the courage to follow my own dreams.

However, Authentic Woman morphed into a large community of like-minded women, and my signature virtual group coaching leadership program for women all over the world who want support to elevate their leadership and life. I also work with many large local and global organisations where I have the gift of working with both women and men.

This is when I realised I could be of even more service to equality and unity by also supporting men to become more self-aware and conscious of their patriarchal work environments and unconscious biases that still play out in many workplaces. For all genders, the path to know ourselves, care for ourselves and be ourselves leads to us all feeling more confident, calm and connected from a place of authenticity and freedom.

In my experience it is never a linear path to bring our vision into being.

Create your life vision

To help you create your own life vision, I would like to take you through the same process I went through. If you go to jowagstaff.com/bookresources you can download a beautiful PDF version of this next practice to write in and keep.

The basic idea of this exercise is to envision your ideal future in your mind by writing about it as if it were already true. Envisioning is based on a very simple idea: it's much easier to achieve something if you can visualise yourself already achieving it. It's a necessary, although insufficient, condition for achieving it, as we must also take purposeful action to move toward it.

As I have previously mentioned, in her book *The Predictive Brain*, psychiatrist Regina Pally describes it this way:

> *According to neuroscience, even before events happen the brain has already made a prediction about what is most likely to happen, and sets in motion the perception, behaviours, emotions, physiological responses and interpersonal ways of relating that best fit with what is predicted. In a sense, we learn from the past what to predict for the future and then live the future we expect.*

In other words, we're already telling ourselves stories about how our life is going to be, but it's largely unconscious. We have already spent a lot of time exploring our past and the often limiting beliefs we may unconsciously have that are holding us back. You can think of this exercise as a kind of corrective one. Now we have a chance to expand our sense of possibility, to bring some creativity and greater consciousness to the process and to our future.

Let's do this in two stages, the first with a focus on your life overall and the second stage with a focus purely on your work and career.

Stage 1: Your life vision

Consider the following question, thinking about all aspects of your life: If everything in my life, starting from today, meets or exceeds my most optimistic expectations, what will my life be like in five years?

Questions to consider before you start writing. How would you describe your 'perfect' life if you were describing it to someone five years down the track? In this future:

- How are you spending your time and energy?

- Where and how are you living?

- How do you feel about yourself and your life?

- How would the people who are important to you be describing you? How would your kids, husband, family, friends, colleagues and anyone who is important to you describe you and your life? How would you and your life appear through their experience?

Sit in silence for a few minutes, with your eyes closed, reflecting on these questions, perhaps visualising this life of yours in five years' time. Also, reflect on the values and personal purpose exercise you did previously and what you know is truly important and meaningful to you. Don't let your mind put any limitations on your vision, otherwise you will never really know what you most deeply desire. Your mind will often automatically look for all the reasons why your dreams are unreasonable, unlikely or impossible. This is a wonderful mirror of the limiting beliefs that are running your life and limiting your potential.

This exercise is about shrugging those off. Think big and bold — if that is what you desire. Or think 'small' if you really just want a very simple and quiet life. Most importantly, listen to yourself and your heart, not what you think other people might want you to write or be.

Then, grab your journal and write:

> If everything in my life, starting from today, meets or exceeds my most optimistic expectations, what will my life be in five years?

Allow yourself to fully explore this as you write. I would encourage you to free-write rather than type, as this allows us to access our right brain more easily. You don't have to do this perfectly. You may want to spend ten or fifteen minutes journaling on it and then come back to it numerous times over the next few days or weeks. Importantly, write it as though it has already happened (e.g., 'I am', 'I live', 'I own').

Once you are satisfied it covers everything important to you, write it up again and share it with the important people in your life. There is as much power in sharing this as there is in sitting down and honouring yourself enough to do it.

Stage 2: Your career and leadership vision

Now that you are clearer on your overall life vision, let's focus on your career and leadership vision. I like to do this separately because I find that, if we do them together, our career can take up way too much of our vision. I believe it is important to get clear on our overall life vision, and then within that, the role our career plays.

Firstly, take some time to consider the following questions, thinking about all aspects of your career. Suppose you are living your greatest desires and being the most authentic and empowered version of yourself in five years' time. You are talking to a friend about your work/career/business/leadership.

◆ Describe the ideal role you are in (the company, culture, responsibilities, purpose, and team)?

◆ Describe yourself as an executive or leader (your values, purpose, behaviours, actions and characteristics)?

◆ How are you feeling about yourself and within yourself?

◆ What have you achieved?

◆ What has your team achieved?

◆ How have you grown and developed?

◆ What are you earning?

◆ What are your key strengths, which you love to lean into?

◆ What does your team say about their experience of working with you? How do they describe you as a leader?

◆ What does your boss, peers, stakeholders/customers say about you? How do they describe you as an executive or leader?

◆ Why is this important to you?

Sit in silence for a few minutes, with your eyes closed, reflecting on these questions, perhaps visualising this career, business, leadership and success of yours in five years' time. Then, grab your journal and write:

> If everything in my leadership, business and career, starting from today, meets or exceeds my most optimistic expectations, what will my leadership and career be in five years?

Start describing this vision for yourself and your career. Again, importantly, write as though it has already happened (e.g., 'I am', 'I live', 'I own', 'I have travelled'). And, remember, you can pick it up and put it down over the next few days to finesse it and allow it to become clear to you.

Once you are happy that your career and leadership vision covers everything that is important to you, remember to share it with the important people in your life, and especially those who can support you with it, perhaps your boss, peers and/or team.

I also then put my life and career visions together as one, so those parts of my life are fully integrated and supporting each other in my final vision.

In addition to this, I have a routine of writing a new vision for my life every three or four years, or whenever anything significant changes in my life. Sometimes I may make only subtle changes to one area of my life that needs some special attention. Other times, I may completely rewrite it, as new opportunities have come my way and I have started to recognise some changes I want to make or a direction I want to take.

I am regularly moved by what my clients write as they explore both their life and leadership visions. I often notice a deeply grounded and contented state when they read them to me, usually with a beautiful smile on their face, and often a little shyness as it is a vulnerable process to share our dreams with another person. With her permission, I would like to share part of Tess's leadership vision with you.

At the time Tessa wrote her leadership vision, I had just taken her through her 360° feedback process. She used this and her coaching to get very clear on how she wanted to show up in her new role. She began by writing:

I am a value-driven, ethical leader who shares my thoughts and purpose with my team and builds trusted relationships with each person in my team and in the organisation. I value everyone, not only the extroverts, but also the introverts, the people who often go unseen and are not recognised for their contribution because they don't call it out loud.

My team members see me as a person of integrity and what I say I mean, and that is also shown in my actions. I am a leader who empowers people and makes them believe in themselves and that they can do amazing things. As a leader, I bring out the best in every person and still allow them to be the person they are or want to be — it is okay to be YOU. I encourage people to speak up without fear. I listen deeply, show accountability for what I am committing to, and I make things happen.

Ignite new possibilities

Often it is simply creating the space to reflect and honour my life that ignites a new level of creativity and desire. I am also very aware of the part of me that thinks my life is 'never enough' can try to *make* my vision happen rather than *let* my vision happen. For me, this process is quite a spiritual one. It is about setting a very clear intention that comes from my deepest longings and desires, and then I practise letting go of the outcome. What I have noticed over the years is my vision has become less about my material needs and more about how I feel and show up in the world.

Becoming more conscious of who we are today takes space and courage. Space and courage to get honest with ourselves. To spend time both honouring our dreams and aspirations, as well as understanding (with great self-compassion) the templates, behavioural patterns, beliefs and assumptions that have come from our past.

To believe in ourselves, first, we must listen to ourselves. We must ask ourselves, 'What do you most yearn for?' and truly listen for the answer. As we gain a deeper understanding of how to know ourselves, care for ourselves and be ourselves, we can also show up more fully in our own life and in our relationships with others, with all the joys and challenges these brings.

Let's explore this now.

CHAPTER 13

Being ourselves
in relationships

Life is all about relationships: the relationship we have with ourselves, the relationship we have with others, the relationship we have with money and material things, with our career, with nature, with life itself. Yet, for most of us, relationships are rarely simple. In this chapter, we will explore why they are important, why they can be filled with complexity and how we can show up more consciously and authentically in all of our relationships.

We are social creatures, and our need for connection and belonging is deeply ingrained in our nature. Connection supports our emotional wellbeing by fulfilling our emotional needs. It provides a sense of support, validation and understanding, which can help alleviate feelings of loneliness, anxiety and depression. Positive social interactions and relationships have been linked to greater life satisfaction and happiness.

Connection helps form our identity, as our identity is shaped, in part, by our relationships with others. Belonging to a group or community helps us establish a sense of who we are and provides a framework for our values, beliefs and behaviours — as long as we do so authentically and don't abandon ourselves to try to belong. We need to belong to ourselves first and foremost. Connection fulfils many of our inherent social needs, such as the need for companionship, intimacy and a sense of belonging. We seek out connections and relationships to satisfy these needs, as they provide us with social support, love and a sense of purpose. Being part of a like-minded community or social network allows us to share experiences, celebrate achievements and provide mutual assistance during challenging times.

Interacting with others and forming connections also stimulates our cognitive development. Our social interactions expose us to different perspectives, ideas and knowledge, fostering learning, problem-solving and critical thinking skills. Collaborative efforts and discussions with others enhance creativity and innovation.

Studies have shown that social connections and a sense of belonging can also have positive effects on our physical health. Strong social ties are associated with a lower risk of developing chronic diseases, improved immune function, and increased longevity. Having supportive relationships can also help in coping with stress and reducing the risk of mental health disorders.

From an evolutionary perspective, the need for connection and belonging is believed to have played a crucial role in our survival as a species. Early humans relied on group cooperation and social bonds for protection, hunting, gathering and raising offspring. These social connections facilitated the exchange of knowledge, skills and resources, leading to improved survival and adaptation to the environment.

Overall, the need for connection and belonging is deeply rooted in our biology, psychology and social nature. It is an essential aspect of human existence, contributing to our wellbeing, personal growth, and overall quality of life.

Why are relationships so difficult?

Given this, learning how to be ourselves in relationships feels like a core competency to having a meaningful and fulfilling life. And it sounds pretty simple; after all, who else are you going to be if you are not being yourself in a relationship, right? It may be simple as a concept, but in my experience, in practice, it is one of the most challenging aspects of life.

I have heard many of the people I have worked with say, 'Work would be very easy if I didn't have to worry about people'. While said slightly facetiously, there is always a grain of truth in that comment. Relationships are complex. We don't just bring our adult selves into our relationships; we bring all our histories with us.

After my painful relationship with Tim ended, I spent almost ten years without a meaningful romantic relationship. This was a good decision for me for the first few years. I had never *not* been in a relationship, and I wanted to find out who I was on my own before exploring who I was in a relationship again. Plus, my time, energy and focus all went into building a new life for Hugo and me, being a present and available mum, building my own values-aligned business, and importantly, doing a lot of deep healing.

This allowed me to become more self-aware of the impact of my history, and the beliefs and patterns that were stopping me from thriving, as well as getting clear on my strengths, values, purpose and the vision for my life. That was more than enough to keep me busy! However, in the following years I became increasingly aware that I was still single because I was in a lot of fear and avoidance of losing myself in a relationship again.

I had found a level of happiness, and at times contentedness, that I was worried I may have to give up. And, if I am honest with myself, the control I had over my life also felt comfortable. But, at other times, I felt a deep longing, an ache to be in relationship. So, I started to dip my toe back in the water. It felt unfamiliar and very uncomfortable and hard. Was I being too fussy? Was I not being fussy enough? I had a good life, and I told myself I only wanted a relationship if it was going to add something meaningful to my life. I only wanted to be with someone who was doing their own inner emotional work. In hindsight, I realise this was important to me because that would mean they were more self-aware and less likely to hurt me.

In truth, I think I was just terrified. Terrified of getting it wrong again, of hurting someone or being hurt. At times I wondered if perhaps I was not meant to be in a romantic relationship again — perhaps I had been too hurt by my past experiences. Loving someone deeply makes us vulnerable, and for many of us, that can feel like too much of a risk to ask of ourselves.

But, eventually, I met Marco. Actually, we had been friends for the ten years I had been out of a romantic relationship. We had a lot of mutual friends and often hung out and travelled together as a group, and were all on our own healing journeys. We probably knew more about each other than you would ever want someone to know about you when you first start dating! Our friends still joke that Marco had a crush on me for many of these years, but I had put him in the friend category. Once again, I think that I was just scared. The most challenging part of my life has always been (and I suspect will always be) relationships. I feel sad writing this, and yet it is the truth for me.

But, finally, I said yes to a date, and I found many things to fall in love with. Marco makes me laugh; he is committed to his own growth; he loves being in the ocean as much as I do; he loves animals; the simple things in life make him happy; he has a huge heart; he gave Hugo his first surfboard, which became a mutual passion, and they became friends; he respects and supports me.

Three years later, we stood on a cliff overlooking a giant ocean swell in Uluwatu, Bali, with forty of our closest family and friends, and were married. Other than the joy of becoming a mum, I am not sure I had ever felt more happiness than I did that day.

However, the honeymoon phase soon ended, and Marco and I were left to work through our differences, the same as all couples.

Marco had not had an easy childhood either. His father was a chef and ran a very popular restaurant in Sydney's Kings Cross district. He was super critical of Marco and would rage a lot. He was always working, drinking and gambling with his crew, and was very unavailable as a father. Ironically, while unavailable, he also had super high expectations of Marco. No matter what Marco did, he never felt he could get it right or get his dad's positive attention or approval.

His mum, sadly, lost her mother at a young age and was separated from her siblings and placed in a convent. In Marco's early childhood years, she was very absent as she had tried to numb her pain with alcohol, before eventually and courageously finding sobriety. Because his dad was never around (and possibly because it was the only safe connection she may have known), his mum looked to Marco to get her connection needs met. Within that, she often smothered him with her needs, leaving little space for his own.

On that clifftop in Bali, Marco and I declared our deep love and respect for each other in our vows.

> I, Jo, take you, Marco, to be my husband. I give you my heart, my respect and my faith in our love. Through life's joys and greatest challenges; through periods of abundance and of apparent lack; in times of health and in sickness, I will support and encourage you in fulfilling your dreams and purpose. I will listen to you, be a shoulder to cry on, and hold and comfort you when you are upset. I will make time for us to connect and have fun together. I commit to growing with you as a partner, a friend and as a human being. I will try to own my own imperfections and accept yours. I give you my heart and my soul and I am so grateful to be marrying you. These are my promises to you, until my last breath.

While our vows sounded romantic, we were also unconsciously invoking both of our histories, our patterns and the insecurities that were set up in our childhoods, which were in complete polarity to each other. Like me wanting the closeness, appreciation and attention that my dad never gave me, at precisely the same time as Marco wanting the freedom and space that his mum never gave him.

Our couple's therapist once said to us, 'Until you heal these wounds, your partner will not be able to emotionally be there for you at that exact moment you need them most'. Ouch! That is what I most longed for. Oh, the fun of relationships.

I only began to understand the depths of the complexity of relationships when Marco and I went to a powerful, albeit confronting couple's constellation workshop, run by a wonderful gestalt psychotherapist, Maria Dolenc. Maria opened the workshop by saying, 'Relationships are not here for your enjoyment; they are here to wake you up'.

At first, I had an enormous amount of resistance to this. Aren't relationships meant to make us happy? If that wasn't the case, what's the point of being in them? But I now appreciate that this belief puts a lot of pressure on our relationships. If our happiness is tied to our relationship, then we are in for one hell of a rollercoaster. Relationships trigger every sensitive area and blind spot we have in ourselves. I have come to believe that it is not an either/or. I like to think relationships can bring both: a place where we can learn to nurture, hold each other, and experience fun and joy, and yes, most definitely, the place where we get to see ourselves, warts and all.

I remember Maria inviting the ten couples who were in the workshop to do an exercise using Byron Katie's Judge Your Neighbour Worksheet.[34] In the second-to-last question, it invites you to make a complaint against your partner — it even invites you to be petty and judgemental! For me, at the time, even admitting that I had a complaint felt hard, let alone writing it down and sharing it with Marco and the group.

I wrote, 'Marco is so passive'.

The next question was, 'What about this do you never want to experience again?'

I wrote, 'I never want to feel like Marco is passive, as then I feel like I must plan everything, think of everything and organise everything. I don't want to feel like his mother!'

We were then asked to turn that final statement around. Maria invited me to swap out mine and Marco's names, so I wrote, 'I never want to feel like I am passive; I want Marco to plan everything, think of everything, organise everything'.

I could really feel the truth in that, especially the part about me not wanting to feel like I am passive. I used to find it very hard to relax. I can resent what I can sometimes perceive as Marco's passiveness because I find it so hard to not take over and organise everything; to just relax, trust and let things unfold. I tend to go into over-responsibility and over-functioning, and that doesn't leave any space for others to step in. In fact, it often encourages others to go into under-functioning.

I remember saying to Maria, 'But I don't want to feel like I am his mother!'

She pointed out the obvious, 'Then stop behaving like his mother'.

That's not about Marco, that's about my own need to be in control. Marco can show up as passive to me, and I can feel triggered by this, because I am such the extreme opposite. I am always on the go, always doing, always achieving. As I have learnt to see this about myself and accept this within myself, Marco's passiveness, which most of the time is not that at all, has been a role model and reminder for me to slow down, to rest, to let go. That judgement, that projection, has become a gift of understanding myself better.

The past is intimately connected with the present

To create authentic and fulfilling relationships, it helps to become aware of the role our past can often play in our relationships with others. We've already discussed in Chapter 3 the role our attachment style plays in our relationships. Now, let's explore other relationship dynamics created by our personal histories, starting with *transference*.

I remember reading a quote by Nobel Prize–writer William Faulkner, 'The past is never ended; It isn't even past'. This perhaps best sums up transference and the impact it has on our day-to-day relationships. To help us really understand this concept, I draw on the work of psychotherapist Dr David Richo. If you want to explore this in greater depth, you may want to read his book *How to Be an Adult in Relationships*.

As Dr Richo explains, human beings are hardwired to grow and evolve. As part of this, often quite unconsciously, when choosing our relationships, we look for two primary things: a level of comfort and some challenge. A level of comfort is a relationship that feels both comfortable and where we will receive comfort. We also seek out some level of challenge. Even though this may sound contradictory, consciously or unconsciously, we all want to be stretched a little. There is something built into us that wants to grow. It is the nature of evolution, and transference is one of the processes that enables this growth.

As part of our innate desire to grow and evolve, we hold onto things that have happened in our past that we have not fully dealt with or that haven't been put to rest. This is especially true of any emotional pain or disappointment. We then unconsciously go looking for other relationships in which some of our original unmet needs might get their chance to be fulfilled. This is a very normal way of looking for what we missed out on before. This means that the past is intimately joined to what is happening in the present — and in fact, sometimes it can be hard to tell the difference!

The five core human needs

In his book *How to Be an Adult in Relationships*, Dr Richo provides a beautiful summation of the core human needs we all have from birth, beginning with our relationship with our parents, that's become the 'essential ingredients of love, respect, security and support'. He refers to them as the Five A's:

1. *Attention:* As a child, we need our parents to pay attention to us, look after us, feed us, change us and meet our basic needs.

2. *Acceptance:* We need to be accepted as we really are, rather than people trying to make us what they want us to be.

3. *Appreciation:* We need to feel valued and cherished and believe we are worthwhile.

4. *Affection:* We need to be shown non-sexual, age-appropriate physical affection.

5. *Allowing:* At the same time as the first four, we need to be allowed our independence to make whatever choices fit with our deepest needs and desires as we evolve over the course of our lives.

He suggests this is also a beautiful working definition of love, whether it's love for our child, partner or friend. This is how we know we are loved: when we experience feeling someone's attention, acceptance, appreciation, affection and, within all this, they allow us to be our own person. This is how you know you love someone; when you can offer them the same. True intimacy can be seen as the ability to give and receive these at the same time, with the same person.

Transference

According to Dr Richo, the parts of our original needs that were not fulfilled by our parents are carried forward — in other words, we *transfer* them into our present relationships. It is very rare for anyone to get all their childhood needs met; after all, our parents are imperfect human beings, just like we are ourselves.

Where transference shows up in our present-day relationships and how strongly depends on which needs weren't met for us, and to what extent. Most of us want to move on from the past and create authentic relationships where we can be ourselves and allow others to do the same. Unfortunately, we often tend to go through our lives simply casting new people in the roles of our parents, siblings or other significant people with whom we still have unfinished business.

How this plays out is that feelings and beliefs from our past re-emerge in our present relationships. This happens in our lives every day. We unconsciously glimpse important people from our past in our partners, children, friends, work associates, enemies and even strangers. Then we transfer feelings, needs, expectations, biases, fantasies, beliefs and attitudes onto them.

We are hardwired to replay the past until we stop and grieve our unmet needs as a child and learn to meet and internalise our own basic needs. We must learn to offer *ourselves* attention, acceptance, appreciation, affection, and allowing independence. The more we do so, the more we are able to consciously choose relationships that can provide a healthy adult level of these needs.

In Chapter 1, I shared how my dad was quite absent in my life, both emotionally and physically. I didn't receive much attention or appreciation from him. I never really felt valued or cherished by him. My needs for attention and appreciation were not fully met. In my relationships now, not just with my husband or son, but with friends and in the workplace, I can very easily transfer the belief that nobody sees, values or appreciates me, or wants to give me attention. Sadly, I often have a belief come up that nobody really wants to spend time with me, that they would rather be somewhere else doing something else with someone else, as this is how it felt with my dad.

In another example, when my younger brother, Rob, and I were in our teens, my dad re-married and I never felt like our dad or our step-mum wanted us. I felt like we were a nuisance to them. This was exacerbated when they had two more children when I was in my twenties who I love dearly. At the same time, I felt like Dad had created a whole new family and he told me he was a much better father the second time — family dynamics are so complex!

For many years, I found I was unconsciously transferring these complex feelings onto my ex-husband and his wife, especially when they also had more children, literally casting them as my dad and step-mum and my son as my little brother. I could sometimes unconsciously transfer these feelings of my son not being wanted compared with his stepbrothers, or me being a nuisance and a bother to them, when in reality, they love my son dearly and I have a legitimate need for communication with them around my son.

It is important to remember that transference is a deeply unconscious process, not a deliberate or chosen one.

Slowly, over time, as I have become aware of these wounds, I am increasingly able to notice this transference in me and the stories that come with it. I have also learnt to check it out with the other person, so I am able to get a clearer perceptive on what's my transference and what isn't.

This happened just recently with my husband. He was behaving quite distant, mentally absent and restless. When he's like this, I automatically start to feel like there is something going on. Then I start feeling anxious and notice myself wanting to withdraw. Instead of doing that this time, I simply asked him if anything was going on and explained what was coming up in me. He explained that he was feeling pressure at work. I have slowly, with deep self-compassion, learnt that often an old story, belief or feeling of mine is being unconsciously transferred onto the current situation, even though, at times, it can feel so real. It is also a good opportunity for me to be with these old feelings and gently give them the attention and appreciation I am craving deep within myself.

Transference in the workplace

Transference can play out both positively and negatively in the workplace. For example, suppose you had a supportive and inspiring mentor early in your career who provided guidance and believed in your potential. In that case, in your current workplace, you may unconsciously transfer the positive feelings of support, trust and motivation onto your new manager. As a result, you may develop a strong sense of loyalty, work diligently and actively seek opportunities for growth and development.

Equally, we may do the opposite and transfer our unresolved issues or emotions onto a co-worker, boss or even the organisation as a whole. This can result in distorted perceptions and reactions that are not based on the present reality, but on past experiences.

Cathy shared her experience of this with me. She had a very difficult relationship with a previous manager who was overly critical and dismissive, not unlike her father had been. Then, when she started her new job, she realised over time that she was starting to unconsciously transfer her previous experience and negative feelings and mistrust onto her current manager, assuming he would also be critical and dismissive. As a result, she became more defensive, resistant to feedback and overly sensitive to perceived criticism, creating tension and affecting her work performance.

This kind of negative transference can impact our work environment by leading to misunderstandings, strained relationships and decreased collaboration. It may also hinder professional growth and development, as we can feel reluctant to seek guidance or take risks due to our transferred fears and anxieties.

Another example was Jema, who had a difficult relationship with a micromanaging boss in a previous job. She also grew up feeling like her mum didn't trust her and was always trying to control her. In her current workplace, she very unconsciously transferred these negative feelings of being controlled and mistrusted onto her new manager. As a result, she started to resist authority, become overly defensive, or was constantly seeking reassurance, even when her current manager was not exhibiting the same micromanaging behaviour. This started to create a very strained relationship with her manager and others around her, and was hindering effective communication and disrupting teamwork.

Addressing transference in the workplace is not simple. It always starts with becoming curious about what could be playing out for us, to foster our awareness and seek to differentiate between past experiences and present reality. Then, through open and honest communication, to resolve what may or may not be happening.

We can also re-create our family dynamics in the workplace or our community. Look around your workplace and with your growing self-awareness you will see those people who trigger you in the same way your parents or a brother or sister may have, or a significant aunt or uncle. My dad was quite an angry man and I know as soon as someone gets really frustrated or angry in the workplace, I can get triggered into old feelings and into either my fight, flight or freeze response. In that, I am transferring my belief that that person will hurt me with their anger in the same way my dad did, when they may have just been expressing their anger, and it doesn't threaten my safety at all. Or I attribute certain mum-like qualities onto my boss and then go about trying to please them in the same way I did with my mum.

Alternatively, you could find yourself hesitant to fully trust an individual who exhibits characteristics or physical traits reminiscent of a former spouse. Or you might also discover a tendency to be excessively accommodating toward someone who bears a resemblance to a friend from your early years.

I recently explored this with my client Adele, who grew up with two very competitive older brothers who always got her father's attention and praise for their accomplishments. She now found herself working in a small team of older men. Although she was starting to recognise that her peers where not competing with her, she was certainly competing with them. She was often left feeling as though she could not get her manager's attention, and nothing she accomplished was ever good enough, just like she had felt in her family.

So how can we know what is from the past versus what is real? How do we stop this transference from happening? Unfortunately, there is no quick fix.

For many years, both in my friendships and intimate relationships I kept replaying out the same unsatisfying patterns. Not only was I transferring my history and unmet needs and beliefs onto these relationships, I also unconsciously picked people who played these old roles and just repeated the same pain over and over. Have you ever changed jobs because you don't like your current manager or teammate, and then in your new job, there they are, another person with a different face but the same traits that you were trying to get away from?

Following these suggestions from Dr Richo, I took four key actions that began to give me more awareness and allow me to experience more freedom around my transference:

1. I explored my transference patterns through a combination of my ongoing mindfulness practice, reflective journaling, coaching and deep relational psychotherapy, and became increasingly conscious of my main patterns.

2. On a daily basis I practised giving myself more attention, acceptance, appreciation, affection and allowing myself more freedom to truly be myself.

3. I felt the feelings I had never allowed myself to have, which were sitting under these patterns: the disappointment, anger, fear and hurt. Finally starting to acknowledge and grieve my unmet childhood needs has been critical to healing this transference. This was vital (and something I would have preferred to have skipped), but even though it's been very painful at times, this is where the healing is. We ultimately need to do our emotional inner work if we are going to have any chance of not playing out the same patterns over and over again in our relationships.

4. I started to check-in more with people (friends, colleagues, family) to help me get clear on what was real versus what I was transferring from my past.

All this helped me gain enough awareness and, ultimately, choice around my relationships — both what I want in my relationships and how I show up in them. Getting to know ourselves and being able to show up as ourselves in relationships with others is an ongoing, lifelong journey of getting to know the deepest parts of ourselves, including our strengths and the parts of ourselves we may want to avoid and project onto others.

Over time, this inner work is where the freedom is — freedom from our past so we can live in the present. Through deepening our self-awareness, with compassion, we can truly begin to create the relationships we ultimately desire.

The shadow mirror of our triggers

I remember when someone first said to me, 'Whenever you point your finger at someone, notice there are three fingers pointing back at yourself'. This was a very confronting game-changer for me in relationships, as I had always been pretty good at blaming others. This is what I think of as the shadow mirror: what we see in others is often a reflection of ourselves — the good and not so good.

Another way of thinking about this is becoming aware of how we can *project* ourselves onto others. We have explored transference as being the unconscious redirection of feelings, attitudes and expectations from past relationships or experiences onto a present person or situation, so now let's explore *projection*.

Projection is a psychological defence mechanism where we attribute our own unacceptable or unwanted thoughts, feelings or characteristics onto others, usually without our awareness. It involves unconsciously disowning certain aspects of ourselves and perceiving them in others instead, and this can happen in both our personal and our professional relationships.

Examples of projection for reflection

◆ *Mind-reading:* Expecting others to read our minds and know what is going on for us, or thinking we can read someone else's mind and know what is going on for them without asking them are forms of projection.

◆ *Anger:* If we struggle with acknowledging or expressing our own anger, we may disown our own anger, considering it unacceptable or inappropriate, and instead, perceive others as constantly angry or easily provoked. For instance, we may interpret a colleague's assertiveness as aggression or assume that someone is always in a bad mood, even if there is no evidence to support these perceptions. By projecting our

(continued)

own disowned anger onto others, we avoid confronting and addressing our own emotional state.

◆ *Incompetence:* If we struggle with feelings of incompetence, we may perceive colleagues as inept or unskilled, even without objective evidence. By projecting our own disowned incompetence, we protect our self-esteem and avoid confronting our own limitations.

◆ *Arrogance:* If we have difficulty acknowledging our own arrogance or overconfidence, we may project those qualities onto others. We may perceive colleagues or superiors as excessively self-assured or boastful, even if their behaviour does not align with those assumptions. By projecting our own disowned arrogance, we avoid confronting our own inflated sense of self-importance, which may just be in our heads, or at the other extreme, our own deep insecurities.

◆ *Untrustworthiness:* If we struggle with trusting others, we may assume that people around us are untrustworthy, constantly questioning their motives or loyalty. By projecting our own disowned untrustworthiness, we protect ourselves from potential betrayal or disappointment.

◆ *Giving advice:* Often when we give advice to someone, we are talking to our current or younger self, rather than the other person. In general, I prefer not to give people advice unless they specifically ask for it, and even then, I typically only share my experience or ask them questions to support them to explore it for themselves. On the rare occasion I find myself giving advice, I have learnt to always stop and listen to my own advice and take it on for myself.

◆ *Neediness:* This is one of my key ones, as I have a big reaction and repulsion to super needy people. I have learnt this is because it is a part of me that I have previously hated: my need for connection, support and love. It felt so unsafe for me that I pushed these needs away. I learnt to be anti-dependent (as opposed to independent or, even better, interdependent), to look after myself and to push down and numb out all those parts of me that needed others. When I first started this inner work, I could not have told you what my needs were. I was very practiced at being needless and I projected this onto others rather than leaning into exploring this within myself.

Just writing that, I was reminded of all the parts of myself I don't like to own, that are hard to be with. If you feel the same, put your hand on your heart and take a deep breath and offer yourself some self-compassion.

I have learnt that the more vehemently we deny the parts we most dislike in others, the more we need to get curious and gently come to terms with that part in ourselves. There are individuals on political platforms now who I absolutely detest — and the word and feeling 'detest' is a dead giveaway that I see something in them that I do not want to see or allow in me. Some of their language and behaviours also trigger a deep feeling in me of not being safe, a powerlessness that is hard for me to be with. Yet, I notice that my projection is around the polarisation of views. I am equally polarised in my negative views of these people as others are in their positive views of these political figures. I am equally self-righteous; I just feel more justified because my opinion is 'right'.

To be ourselves in our relationships means committing to ongoing self-awareness, vulnerability, humility and boundaries. It means being aware of our past and how it can play out in the present for us, at work and at home. It means having the courage to be vulnerable, to ask for feedback, to share with others what is coming up for us, which begins by being honest and vulnerable with ourselves. This takes great humility and an understanding that we are all imperfect human beings doing the best we know how.

We also need to continue to develop good boundaries, because just as we can transfer and project our past onto others, others will transfer and project their past onto us. Our practice is to understand and own our part in relationship dynamics, while having compassion for, but not taking on, other people's parts, including not accepting unacceptable behaviour. By owning our transference and projection, we increasingly become more authentic in how we feel and show up in our relationships.

CHAPTER 14

The art of being both soft and strong

I remember asking my therapist, 'How do I look after myself and all that is important to me and still be gentle, soft, open and vulnerable?'

It seemed so inconceivable to me, especially as I had experienced abuse at the hands of men as a child, when I *was* gentle, soft and vulnerable. Soft hadn't felt like a safe place for me to live from. In fact, I spent my whole life trying to protect myself. And yet many of the ways I had found simply separated me from people: my judgement, money, work and busyness to name a few. And it's exhausting! I am so tired of trying to protect myself, when really what I want to do is simply surrender and trust others.

My therapist suggested that there is a difference between surrender and collapse. Surrendering to what life offers is about letting love in, letting myself love, being open and honest and vulnerable with those people I trust. It also includes respectfully speaking up, holding boundaries, letting people know when I feel hurt by their behaviour, while also accepting when life and love don't go my way. She suggested that I sounded more worried about going into collapse, which is where we allow or justify unacceptable behaviours, don't hold boundaries, don't speak up or respect ourselves, don't take responsibility for our own needs and actions, or are inauthentic. I think she was right.

Over time, slowly, gently, I have learnt to feel safe on the inside. To hold compassionate boundaries instead of walls. To become clear on my needs and wants. To find my voice, without being defensive or aggressive. To ask for support. To embrace my femininity. To self-care. Within this, learning to both soften and stand in my strong feminine, to trust myself, others and the flow of life.

In my experience, there is both an art and a science to learning how to be both soft and strong in our relationships. It's a delicate balance that can greatly impact our professional success and overall wellbeing.

Being soft in our relationships means demonstrating empathy, understanding and compassion toward others and ourselves. It involves active listening, being open-minded and considering the perspectives and feelings of our co-workers. Softness allows us to be open, curious, build trust, create harmonious working environments and foster meaningful connections. It enables us to resolve conflicts constructively, provide support and inspire collaboration.

On the other hand, being strong means setting boundaries, asserting ourselves, holding people accountable, advocating for our needs and goals, and taking purposeful action. It requires an inner confidence, self-respect and the ability to make difficult decisions, trusting ourselves and our capabilities as well as trusting others and their capabilities. Strength enables us to navigate challenges, handle conflicts assertively and appropriately, and take charge of our professional growth. It ensures we take responsibility for when we make mistakes and for our part in conflicts and issues, and that we don't take responsibility for another's mistakes or responsibilities. It ensures that our voice is heard, that we value our contributions, and we pursue our vision.

The *art* lies in finding the right balance between softness and strength in different situations. It requires adaptability, emotional intelligence and the ability to gauge the needs and dynamics of each interaction. By being both soft and strong, we can build resilient relationships that foster trust, encourage growth and drive positive outcomes.

The *science* of this balance lies in understanding the principles of effective communication, conflict resolution and interpersonal dynamics. It involves learning about different personality types, communication styles and cultural nuances. By applying evidence-based strategies and techniques, we can enhance our ability to navigate relationships with finesse.

Five practices for cultivating the art of soft and strong

Ultimately, cultivating the art and science of being both soft and strong in our relationships empowers us to build fulfilling connections, promote collaboration and achieve personal and professional success while maintaining our emotional wellbeing. It is a lifelong journey of self-awareness, skills development and continuous growth. In my experience, it includes the following five key areas.

1. Deep listening

Deep listening is a crucial skill for effective communication and building strong relationships. And listening is hard. It is why good therapists and coaches do so much training and their own inner work, so they can learn how to get out of their own way, see their own 'stuff' and be fully present for someone else. We can learn not to interrupt or control the conversation, give advice or try to 'fix it' just because we are feeling uncomfortable within ourselves.

We all know what it is like when someone starts talking and straight away, rather than listening, we start thinking about what we will say when they stop. In that moment, we miss the essence of what they are sharing. We listen to respond rather than listen to understand.

Deeply listening involves being genuinely curious and fully focusing on and understanding what the other person is saying, without interrupting or pre-judging. We engage in deep listening by being fully present, maintaining soft eye contact, using verbal and non-verbal cues to show interest, being aware of their body language and their subconscious meaning, asking clarifying questions, and paraphrasing or summarising to ensure understanding. I think of it as listening with your whole body.

I remember when I first started working with Abigail. She had recently stepped into a first-time leadership role, and she had received feedback from her boss that her team did not like working for her and a couple were considering leaving. She felt pretty devastated as she had been hugely successful in her previous roles and did not want to, in her words, 'fail'. Her team's biggest complaint was that she never listened to their point of view or asked questions. She went too quickly into action, telling them what to do, often talking over people, and they did not feel valued or motivated.

Abigail thought she was trying to teach them what do to, to help them be successful. Her intention was genuinely coming from a good place, but she was disempowering them. It sounded like a simple fix: stop and listen and ask questions, but it was not natural for Abigail. Her anxiety around them missing things, not doing it as well as she could, or it all taking too long, meant she would often jump in and take over. Learning to regulate her anxiety and see success as empowering the team to get the result, rather than her getting it, were key components of her learning how to deeply listen.

As a coach, people are often amazed at how much I remember weeks or months after they have shared something with me. But I have learnt that when I am fully present to someone, listening deeply to their words, their emotions, their body language and what is running underneath what they are saying, then it is almost impossible not to remember. There is no greater gift we can give our children, our relationships or our work colleagues than deeply listening to them, without judging or fixing or changing anything. Perhaps not surprisingly, research shows that deep listening promotes trust, understanding and mutual respect in workplace interactions.[35]

2. Emotional intelligence

Emotional intelligence refers to the ability to recognise, understand and manage emotions in oneself, and to recognise and understand them in others. Developing our emotional intelligence enhances our relationships by improving empathy, self-awareness and interpersonal skills. It involves being attuned to others' emotions, regulating our own emotions effectively, and adapting our communication style accordingly.

Numerous studies have demonstrated the positive impact of emotional intelligence on teamwork, leadership effectiveness and overall workplace relationships. This is why all successful relationships start with the relationship we have with ourselves. If we are avoiding our own emotions, struggles, limitations and needs, it will be almost impossible for us to be with someone else's. Our awareness of our emotions, or sometimes lack of it, dictates so much of how we show up and react or respond in our day, in our relationships, in our lives.

A really good example of a complete lack of emotional awareness in my life recently was an argument I had with my son Hugo. As I walked into the house on Friday afternoon, Hugo came flying down the stairs, talking excitedly at 100 miles an hour, asking if I would please, please drive him to his mate's place, which happened to be across the other side of town in what was now Friday afternoon, peak hour traffic, because his car was in the garage. I snapped a very strong 'no' back at him, quite angrily, and I really dismissed him. And as I did so, I watched that big smile and his face drop and his shoulders slump as he just turned and walked away from me.

In that moment, I had set our evening up to be disconnected and disappointing. What I'd not been conscious of was the level of frustration and anger that I already had in my body before I walked into the house. I had had a disagreement with a work colleague earlier that day, and I was still holding onto my frustration around that. Under my frustration was fear of the consequences of our disagreement. And under that fear was a great deal of disappointment as to how I'd handled myself. And I literally dumped all that disappointment, frustration and anger onto Hugo.

Hugo had been excited because his mate had just won an award. Understandably, they wanted to celebrate together, which I'd not even listened to. He had also been happy to see me, as typically I came home happy on Friday afternoon ready for the weekend ahead.

In the past, we would have just both stayed grumpy at each other for the rest of the evening. Thanks to my ongoing compassionate self-awareness practice, once Hugo walked away, I took a one-minute conscious pause to breathe deeply into my belly. I dropped out of my head, and I checked in with my body and what was going on for me. I was able to notice the anger, the frustration and the disappointment that was already in my body. And then I soothed this anger and frustration by talking to myself in a gentle self-compassionate way. I reflected on my day and realised that it was not Hugo that I was upset with.

Then I could respond. I could go and apologise for my behaviour and the way I'd spoken to him and explain that I had taken my earlier disappointment and frustration out on him. I could repair the situation. It was a great lesson for both of us. And if you only ever remember to pause and breathe whenever you get upset, it can seriously change your entire life.

Had I been more emotionally aware in the moment before I walked in the door, or as soon as I saw Hugo and felt myself getting angry, I could have stopped, breathed and checked in with myself, acknowledging what was going on for me, and I would have stopped the whole encounter from happening. But here's the self-compassionate awareness part: I'm human. To be human is to be flawed. This is a practice, and we are not always going to get it right — especially as parents. So when we don't, it's okay. And the really great and important thing is we can go back and repair and reconnect.

Our bodies are constantly giving us valuable information about what's going on for us, well before our mind knows. And yet we spend so much time living in our heads, listening to our thoughts, cut off from our bodies. The more aware we are, the more attuned we are to the sensations in our body, then the more we can take advantage of the wisdom in our bodies and the wisdom in our emotions. Through embracing our inner work, we learn to respond rather than react, and show up more consistently in our relationships at home and at work. Such a gift for ourselves and all of those around us!

3. Courage

To build strong authentic relationships, we need to take risks. We need to genuinely care. And when we genuinely care, we can get hurt or feel disappointed or rejected — and that happens. There are four very valuable foundational pieces of wisdom that I've learnt over many years about building authentic relationships, and they all take courage.

The first is understanding that *rupture and repair* is a normal part of all healthy relationships, and it actually builds trust and deepens our relationships. It's how we get to know and understand each other. When we avoid conflict, it does not support anyone (neither you nor them) to grow. Yet, many of us avoid conversations that may lead to conflict as we are scared of what that will mean. Will we lose our job? Will we not be liked? Will it lead to the complete breakdown in this relationship, which we can't afford to have happen?

Yet, relationships are all about rupture and repair — it's what we do. We make mistakes, we disappoint people and people disappoint us, both in our personal and professional relationships. And we can learn how to repair. We can go back and give a genuine apology. Or we take a lot of curiosity into a conversation that needs to be repaired and rebuilt, and strengthen the trust and the honesty within the relationship. With curiosity, and an intention to have an authentic dialogue, we suspend judgement and do our best to not take things personally. Easier said than done! When we can become deeply curious about what is going on for us and what is going on for someone else, it creates the space for repair. It is the avoidance of these conversations that often causes more ongoing rupture.

The second thing I've learnt about courage in relationships is that you can be as direct as you need to be if the other person *knows you genuinely care about them*. So, you need to show people you care regularly. John Gottman, a relationship counsellor with years of research in this space, shares that we need to have five positive feelings/interactions to every one negative feeling/interaction to create a healthy and stable relationship. This is good to remember for all our relationships! Once people know you care, it is very important that you learn how to be direct and clear in both your expectations and needs. I have watched so many people get frustrated with others for not doing what they want them to do, only to realise that they were very vague in the way they asked for what they needed.

The third insight is, to have meaningful and authentic relationships, we need to practice being *real and vulnerable*, whilst also discerning. We don't have to share everything with everyone. Trust is earnt, starting with trusting ourselves, and we also need to give people the opportunity to earn our trust. Trusting another makes us feel vulnerable: what if they let us down? Or perhaps a better question is: how will I handle it when someone lets me down, or they don't meet my expectations of them? Vulnerability takes courage, the courage to be with what arises in us when others are human, and when we are human too.

The fourth piece of wisdom is that *we co-create every situation*. It's never just our fault or just their fault. This is not a blame game. Some of us, especially when we are triggered, have a tendency to either blame ourselves 100 per cent and berate ourselves, or we blame the other person 100 per cent and can punish or be unforgiving. Or, if you are anything like me, you may oscillate between the two extremes. Once we have settled our nervous systems, and have come out of fight, flight or freeze, our growth comes from getting curious about what we have contributed to the situation. With a great deal of self-compassion, we can ask ourselves what we could have done differently; what beliefs, assumptions, and insecurities drove us to behave the way we behaved. With just as much compassion, we can also get curious about what is going on for the other person, without taking responsibility for their reaction. And we can speak up and put a boundary in place if someone speaks to us or behaves in a manner that is unacceptable. Boundaries take great courage when we first start practising them and yet they sit at the heart or all healthy relationships and at the heart of us being able to be both soft and strong.

All these foundation blocks take courage.

Let's go back to Abigail's story on page 244. After receiving what was obviously some very hard feedback and deeply reflecting on her history and reactive tendencies, she called her team together. She shared the feedback she had been given directly with her team, as well as some of her upbringing and where her overdrive came from. She shared the pressure she had been feeling in all areas of her life over the last six months, and told the team she understood why they were feeling the way they were, whilst at the same time having compassion and understanding for herself. She apologised for the impact her overdrive and perfectionism had had on them, and importantly, as I truly believe there is no point in apologising unless we intend to practise different behaviours, she shared what she wanted to do differently. She also shared what she needed from them, invited them to provide her with ongoing feedback and she opened herself up for questions and comments on all she had shared.

Now that takes enormous courage. It was the beginning of a complete shift in the culture of her team and the relationship she had with them. The transition wasn't perfect, but because the team appreciated her authenticity, vulnerability and good intentions, they gave her a lot more latitude to make mistakes. It also encouraged them to look at their part in the dynamic that had been playing out.

4. Giving and receiving constructive feedback

Inviting ongoing authentic dialogue and providing and receiving feedback is essential for growth and improvement in our relationships at home and at work. It is also one aspect that I see many of us avoid. Or when we do give it, because we feel uncomfortable about it, we are either not clear or direct, or we go to the opposite extreme and come across as aggressive or defensive.

When giving feedback, it is crucial to use a constructive approach that focuses on specific behaviours, highlights strengths and offers suggestions for improvement, while inviting open and authentic dialogue.

Ruth said to me many times, 'I hate conflict and will do all I can to avoid it'. As we explored these feelings, the interesting thing was it wasn't always *conflict* that was going on; she was usually just avoiding giving people feedback *in case* it turned into conflict, or in case she hurt or upset someone. I invited her to drop the word 'conflict' from her vocabulary, and instead reframe her need to give someone feedback as an opportunity for them both to learn and grow, and positively affect their relationship. We can't learn and grow if we don't know what we are doing wrong, we often do both ourselves and the other person a great disservice by staying silent.

I remember one time, not long after this, she sat down with her new boss and told him, 'I am really enjoying working for you. I particularly like that you are very clear on your expectations, and I am excited about what I can learn from you with your background in customer experience. There is one thing I am curious about, though. Lately, I have felt like when I try to talk to you about the Phoenix Project, you quickly change the subject or shut our conversation down. I have been working on this project for three years, and with all the staff changes, I have more background knowledge and understanding than anyone else here, and I feel I have a lot of value to add to the current discussions. I am wondering why you don't seem interested in my views?'

To Ruth's surprise, her manager was genuinely surprised that he had been doing this. He did share that he was feeling quite frustrated by the project. He then mentioned that sometimes he felt Ruth took a long time to make a point, so if he was time poor, he sometimes felt he had to shut Ruth down, but he said he was genuinely interested in Ruth's perspective on the project.

Here, both Ruth and her manager got some valuable feedback, and this feedback likely stopped the relationship from reaching a place of conflict, which may have happened if Ruth kept feeling shut down, and her manager kept feeling Ruth was not able to be more succinct. You can see how these concerns were feeding off each other and were likely going to get worse. Yet, in this instance, they now felt closer and understood each other better.

At work, constructive feedback, offered with curiosity, compassion and care, leads to increased employee engagement, performance and motivation. It helps foster a supportive and growth-oriented culture, enabling us all to learn from our mistakes and make positive changes.

A quick process for offering feedback

My husband and I have a process that we use for giving feedback, and I use it in my work as well.

- ◆ *Ask permission.* I always start by asking the other person if they are open to some feedback or a conversation. This allows them to let me know if they are in the right place to hear or discuss something.

- ◆ *Offer positives.* I then offer at least one, often two pieces of positive feedback, things I have really appreciated about what they have been doing lately, from a very genuine place. The reason this is so important to me, is if I can't think of something genuinely positive to say, then it is not the right time for me to be having this conversation. It shows me what frame of mind I am in, and it also gives me a place to start the conversation that puts people at ease.

- ◆ *Share what is going on for you.* Then, I will talk about something I have noticed or I am struggling with, not blaming the other person but explaining my perception and asking them questions about what is/was going on for them. For example, I recently told a team member, 'I am feeling concerned about how long it is taking you to respond to some of our customers. I am not sure what the problem is. Is it that you currently have too much on your plate and need some help, or perhaps we need to talk about priorities? Or is it something else that I am not aware of?'

- ◆ *Deeply listen.* Allow them space to fully respond. Don't listen with a focus on how you will respond, instead, as discussed on page 243, listen to really understand.

(continued)

◆ *The art of questions.* Then it's time to ask questions to understand and explore the issue together, including how you can best resolve it. There is nothing more powerful in a good conversation than great questions with a genuine curiosity to learn. Not questions that paint them into a corner or lead them to an answer you are looking for. Big, curious, open-ended questions. What would that look like for you? Help me to better understand what that felt like for you? How did what I said affect you? Can I share with you what my experience was like? What could we do differently next time?

◆ *Set clear expectations.* At the end of the conversation, make sure you are very clear on what you have both agreed on and who will be accountable for what. This is a part we often miss, and we may leave the conversation with different views on what needs to change or who is going to do what.

◆ *Check-in.* Lastly, off the back of these important conversations and the agreements we make, we need to hold ourselves accountable for what we have said we will do. Make sure you follow-up and check-in with the other person, not only around what they said they would do, but also how they are feeling.

5. Conflict resolution

Conflict is inevitable in any workplace, and how it is handled can significantly impact relationships and team dynamics. Employing evidence-based conflict resolution strategies, such as active listening, finding common ground and focusing on shared interests rather than positions, can help manage and resolve conflicts effectively.

Typically, what happens is, we both go to our corners and start to defend as we are hurt or disappointed or anxious about the impact someone's behaviours have had on us or vice versa. When I am dealing with conflict, I always try to start by remembering that there is usually a big difference between intention and impact. When we are thinking rationally, we can see that it is rare that someone has intentionally set out to hurt or upset us.

When we feel triggered by something someone has said, it's wise to pause before reacting and ask, 'Can you explain what you mean by that?' Likewise, when we notice that we have caused a reaction in someone by something we've said, we can ask, 'Is there something I can clarify for you?'

Simple curiosity can have a profound impact on the outcomes of interactions and conversations. As I mentioned previously, this involves asking a lot of open-ended questions and developing empathetic listening skills.

Some of us talk over people and take up a lot of space in the room or in our relationships. Some of us don't talk at all and don't step into the space, even when it is offered. We all need to learn how to sit somewhere in between. Few things create a feeling of care more than having someone invite us to speak and genuinely listen to us without judgement or bias. And yet, as we have already explored, it is a lot harder than it sounds. We can learn to get our ego out of the way and be genuinely curious about what that person is sharing with us when we listen to them to understand.

Gaining clarity and inviting authentic, two-way dialogue are key ingredients in handling conflict issues. First, we ask a lot of questions and genuinely practice empathetically listening to what someone else is sharing with us. Then, when it is our time to speak, it's important to practice compassionate directness and be as clear as possible. Many of us can be very ambiguous, talk too much or repeat our point over and over. This often comes from a place of nervousness, or really wanting to be heard. This can be particularly true if it's new to us to speak up, or if we are passionate about something.

Whether you are sharing an opinion, or providing or inviting feedback, take some time to prepare for what may be a difficult conversation in advance and practice being clear and succinct. Clear in what you are asking for, clear in your expectations, clear in the opinion that you are offering so that others walk away being very clear on what it is that you have said or asked for.

I recently worked with two senior leaders who were in constant conflict with each other. It had been going on for months and they had started avoiding each other. They were peers and they and their teams needed to work very closely together for the business to be successful. They liked to think they were hiding their frustrations from each other and their teams, but everybody was picking up on it and it was affecting the culture and results of both teams.

When I spoke to them individually, they were each in their own corners. They both felt very justified in why they were behaving the way they were and what the other person had done wrong. One felt the other one should 'just get over it', while the other was feeling very hurt by words that had been spoken. While they were interested in finding a truce so they could work better together, neither was initially interested in sharing what was really going on for them or fully repairing the relationship.

For me, this was a good example of what can happen when we don't address what needs to be addressed up front and we try to ignore conflict. Thankfully, in the end, through a lot of self-reflection and coaching, they both started to get very honest with themselves about their part, what they had done to contribute to the situation, albeit unconsciously and not with any intended malice. They had a long history together, years of not talking to each other about what needed to be talked about. They had very different styles, and again, unconsciously, were not aware of their lack of respect for each other's styles.

Once they stopped defending, started owning their part, and became open to sitting down together and really talking it through (from a place of genuine care and compassion, and a willingness to understand each other's needs) they were able to find a whole new relationship. At first, particularly for one, there was still a level of hurt that remained raw. However, over time they were able to rebuild their trust in each other, and importantly, have each other's backs when talking to their teams.

By incorporating these strategies and techniques into our daily interactions, we can enhance our ability to navigate workplace relationships with finesse. These approaches promote effective communication, empathy, curiosity and understanding. They enable us to build strong connections, resolve conflicts, and foster a positive and productive work environment for ourselves and others. These skills and practices, when combined with our own deep self-awareness, self-compassion and boundaries empower us to be both soft and strong as we live and lead true to ourselves.

Conscious reflection

Reflect back on these five key areas that support us to cultivate being both soft and strong in our relationships:

◆ deep listening

◆ emotional intelligence

◆ courage

◆ giving constructive feedback

◆ conflict resolution.

Which of these do you feel you are strong in, and which areas do you most need to practice and develop?

CHAPTER 15

Redefining success

When I was seventeen years old, I sat down to lunch with my dad and asked him, 'Dad, what's the meaning of life?'

With great frustration and impatience — probably because he did not know the answer and hated not knowing — he responded, 'I don't know. To work hard, be successful and take care of everyone around you'.

There's a set up for a core belief waiting to happen! And I certainly listened to that one. I suspect from a young age, I had already picked up from my parents and grandparents what they saw as successful, and quite unconsciously had a very clear perception of what success did and didn't look like in our family and in my culture.

Interestingly, as I learnt more about my dad from other adults who knew him well, while that may have been what he perceived life was about, I now understand he spent a lot of time feeling dissatisfied, philosophising and searching for meaning himself.

My dad considered himself neither a spiritual nor a religious man. In fact, he was a staunch atheist. But when he was dying of cancer at the age of fifty-three, I gave him *The Tibetan Book of Living and Dying* by Sogyal Rinpoche, which he said he found very comforting and supportive in what was understandably a deeply reflective time for him.

One afternoon, while he could still stand, we went for a gentle walk in the bush together. He looked like he wanted to tell me something important, but seemed uncertain where to begin. He started talking about the book. He explained that the book explored the art of both living and dying with awareness, compassion and wisdom, and gave him practical insights and teachings on preparing for death. It was also offering him an understanding of the nature of existence, with an emphasis on the interconnectedness of all beings and the impermanence of life and how to discover meaning in the face of mortality.

I listened intently and with some anticipation as to where this was leading. It finally came. 'I got it all wrong, Jo', he said. 'Life is not about work and achievements and what you do and how you look. It's about who you are, family, relationships, love and the little things'.

I was thirty-four and my marriage had just ended, in part because I had been so focused on becoming 'successful'. I remember feeling so furious at him for suddenly changing the goal posts on me. *What do you mean it is not about work and achievements?* It felt like that's a lot of what I had seen my parents focus on — typically at the expense of nurturing family, love and the little things.

This was a life-changing moment for me. Coupled with the fact that, in the four months I had with Dad while he was dying, he became a different man and we finally started to have the kind of relationship I had always craved from him.

And then he died. As selfish as I may sound, it felt like another betrayal, another abandonment.

But as I reflected, I wondered how painful it must have been to come to that same realisation himself, to become a different person, to get clear on what was important to him and then to die. He had been surrounded by love and family and the little things much of his life and had often been unable to fully appreciate them.

Off the back of this, not long after my dad died, I went back to Troy in the hope of reuniting our family, and learning how to do life and love differently. But it was too late. I had hurt him a lot when I left, and he had moved on.

This brought up so much grief in me and was the beginning of the rock bottom I described in Chapter 5. I am grateful to my father that it was also the beginning of me redefining what success looked like for me.

The quality of our future lives depends on the choices we make now

What does success mean to you — not just at work, but across the breadth of your life?

I asked my new client Amanda what her aspirations were for her career and for her life, and if she feels she is currently living and leading in alignment with these and her core values. She said she had never stopped to clearly articulate either her core values or her vision for *life success*. Work success, yes, but not *life success*.

Amanda is a high-performing executive in a global insurance company and has always been promoted before she even thought about what was next for herself. To meet her, you would think she is one of the most confident and capable women, and in her area of expertise, she is, but much of the time that is not how she feels on the inside, or more generally outside of her areas of expertise.

Amanda was promoted into a senior leadership role with a team much larger than she had ever managed before and given challenging financial targets to meet. She was feeling out of her depth and quite overwhelmed by the constant demands and expectations she was experiencing from others — and perhaps most importantly, the expectations to perform that she was putting on herself. Her reactive coping strategies were running her, and she was showing up as super controlling and distant to her team and colleagues, as a way of trying to unconsciously manage her own anxiety, overwhelm and need to perform. She had dropped into survival mode and was starting to unconsciously sabotage herself and her career.

Amanda also has two young children and a husband who was struggling with mental health issues after the collapse of his business. And while he decided he wanted to be a stay-at-home dad for a few years, he then wanted to focus on his own career and go back to work. She was unsure how they would juggle both. Their marriage had been struggling for a couple of years, and while they wanted to stay together, she was not sure if they were going to make it. Amanda also felt like she was missing out on important times with her two young boys and the joys of being a mum.

She and her partner were starting to resent each other. She was starting to question whether she was even any good at her job. Her confidence was tanking, which heightened her reactive tendencies. The easy, but equally impossible answer, felt like either moving companies or quitting altogether.

When we distilled her aspirations, what life success would look like for her, she said, 'Mostly I just want to lead a simple life where I like who I am, feel fulfilled by what I do, have a solid marriage and I am a present and fun mum'. Yet, she was not living in congruence with this vision of her life at all. She made daily choices, often unconsciously, that moved her further away from her definition of life success.

I suggested we spend six months together before she made any life-changing decisions. Her decision may be to take on a role with fewer responsibilities. Or it may be that she learns to lead and succeed in her current role from a new place — one where she understands herself more deeply, cares for herself, finds her boundaries and starts making different choices. Or she may choose to leave the organisation, if it is systemically broken and does not allow her to lead in a way that is congruent with her values and vision. One choice at a time, she can create a new way of showing up to life, for herself, her family and her team, of living and leading true to herself.

Another lady I worked with named Jill aspired to be the chief technology officer for a top twenty–listed global company. For her, this is what success had always looked like. As we started to focus on her life success, what was most confronting for Jill was that she became aware of what this ambition was costing her at home with her health, and the difficult relationship she was having with her children.

When I asked her why being a chief technology officer was so important to her, she said, 'Because I want to be in control. I want people to do what I tell them'. Yet, what she was finding in her current role was that this need for control and telling people what to do had cost her a recent promotion. Her overdrive and need to feel safe, which is ultimately what control is, was limiting her success at work and across all areas of her life.

I often wonder if we can truly consider ourselves successful at work if our home life or health is a mess. We need a new way to live, lead and succeed that can support us to feel successful in all areas of our lives.

I am all for women stepping into big roles; having big, bold, ambitious aspirations. In fact, I believe the world needs strong female leadership more than ever. And yet, in my experience, if we are not clear on our *why*, and if our *why* is not coming from a place of passion, purpose and service to the greater good, then it is rarely a fulfilling proposition. And even when we are clear on our *why* and it is coming from a place of passion, purpose and service, it is rarely sustainable if we have not created space and balance to look after all the areas of our lives that are important to us.

Slowing down and shifting from burnout to balance

Once she had become clear on what life success looked like for her, the first question Amanda asked me was, 'Where do I start?'

I remember the perplexed look on her face when I answered, 'As counterintuitive as it sounds, we begin by slowing down'.

Her nervous system was in constant overdrive. She was running on high-functioning anxiety, allowing herself to be pulled in a million different directions, and she was burning herself out. As both the internal and external pressure built, Amanda went harder in the never-ending hope that eventually something would change, something would give, and she would finally have the space and simplicity she craved. Running on anxiety leaves us with nowhere to rest, especially not within ourselves. Learning to rest within ourselves and our lives is the greatest gift we can give ourselves.

Sadly, we often don't slow down until we are made to: we get sick, break a leg, have a mental health breakdown, lose our job or perhaps lose someone we love. What if we don't wait for that to happen? We can lead the way. We can slow down, get clear on the life we want, and then start taking small purposeful actions toward reclaiming ourselves and our lives.

This is the journey we have been on together within this book. Firstly, knowing ourselves, why we do what we do, what fears and limiting beliefs hold us back. Then learning to care for ourselves and be true to ourselves. We now know why it is hard to live true to ourselves, and yet we are the only one who can change this. To do this, we do our inner work and learn to get comfortable feeling uncomfortable. Dare I say, even reframe and embrace feeling uncomfortable; this is how we grow and create the life we want.

During COVID, my husband and I put in a sauna and ice bath at home. He loves both, and I am not exaggerating when I say I hated both. I found the sauna way too hot and uncomfortable, and not surprisingly, at 1°C (33°F) and surrounded by ice, the ice bath was too cold. For almost a year I left him and his mates to it. And then we watched a documentary series called *Limitless* with Chris Hemsworth, and I learnt about the science and benefits of cold and hot immersion, which my husband had been telling me about, but for some reason, when Chris Hemsworth told me, I listened!

I decided to give it a try. The first time I stepped into the ice bath, I lasted twenty seconds. Everything in my body screamed to get out and it literally felt impossible for me to stay in. But I persisted, because aside from the health benefits, I realised I was practising getting comfortable with the very uncomfortable. I now love the sauna. And I now do five-minute ice baths two to three times a week. Some days are much harder than others mentally. Every single time, for the first thirty seconds, everything in me still screams, 'Get out!' But I breathe through it and settle down within myself.

Like meditation, the ice bath shows me where my head is at: if I am in a restless state or a state of ease. I practise staying with whatever is uncomfortable. We grow through taking purposeful action toward our vision, from doing something different to what we have always done, and we breathe through and stay with the uncomfortable feelings that arise within us.

I once heard someone say, 'We burn out when the way we are working is not working. Something must change: the way we work or the way we handle how we work, usually both.' Many businesses are trying to do more with less now, creating demanding and often toxic cultures that put enormous pressure on people. Across many companies and industries, the system is still broken, with many women still experiencing unconscious bias, discrimination and sexual harassment.

We may find we simply can't be who we want to be or work the way we want to work in our current environment. Or we may feel we can genuinely be part of changing the system. Either way, it is up to us to decide if we want to collapse into that pressure and let it overwhelm us, often abandoning ourselves, our needs and our families in the process. Or we change both how we work and how we handle our stress at work, ultimately practising a new way of living, leading and succeeding, where we feel more engaged and energised.

The power to do this comes from a grounded, still inner state, which we can only tap into if we slow down and create space to be with ourselves and be present in our lives. There is immense power for transformation, within us, within our teams and within our organisations when we show up fully present. This is not easy, as it takes deep inner work to be truly present.

While counterintuitive, slowing down and learning to simply *be* is the foundation to thriving. And it is hard! Harder than I ever imagined.

Partially because we live in a world that seems to prioritise and celebrate busyness. We can be such martyrs within it, too — or at least I sure can.

Then there is the problem that once you slow down, you can't hide from yourself anymore or from each other. We can't hide from the truth about ourselves, our relationships, our lives. I notice that I can crave more space and then when it arrives, or when I create it through holding better boundaries, I often find myself avoiding it or not knowing what to do with myself. Learning to be with myself and enjoy stillness has taken a lot of practice.

Comparison kills our innate confidence and sense of success

I don't know many of us who don't compare ourselves with others. I can do it from both a place of *better than* and *less than*. *Better than* can look subtle for me these days. It can take the form of judging others (either just in my head or out loud), thinking I know better, criticising others and self-righteousness. Of course, I have had different experiences and will have different opinions to others, and there are some areas where I do have more expertise than others. It is the attitude with which I bring these things that shows me something deeper is going on for me. If I am behaving defensively, or if I need you to be wrong for me to be right, or if I can't allow us to have a different opinion or experience, then underneath these thoughts and behaviours are always my own insecurities and fears. My *better than* is always driven by my *less than*.

My *less than* is a lot more obvious to me and it often comes about because I compare my insides to your outsides. When I look at someone's life and judge it as 'perfect' or think, *They are happy and have it all together because they are successful, look better, have a bigger house or drive a nicer car, make more money, have more friends, they are more talented, they have better skills, they are more intelligent* ... the list goes on!

I have coached so many people who, on the outside, look like they have it all, and what I have learnt is we all have our struggles, our own type of suffering. The people I compare myself with may be struggling with mental health issues, or have a seriously ill child, or have a family member struggling with alcohol or drugs. Or they don't get to spend any time with their kids because they work so hard or are not doing what they want to be doing, or have money issues or are in an unhappy marriage. Everyone has their own insecurities, unfulfilled dreams and struggles.

When I compare my insides (in other words, all the stories I tell myself, my insecurities and the day-to-day rollercoaster of being a human being) with other people's outsides (how they present themselves), then it kills my innate confidence and inner peace. It also kills my ability to see my own success and feel satisfied with my life. It adds to the existing story that I am not enough or what I have is not enough. And even if, on that rare occasion I meet someone who genuinely is deeply content with their life, inside and out, when I compare and judge my life against theirs, it rips me off. It doesn't honour the life I am living, the person I am and the person I am becoming. It doesn't honour, value or celebrate my authenticity.

I love that saying I mentioned previously, 'When I am pointing my finger at someone else, I am also pointing three fingers back at myself'. It works both ways. What I see in others is often a direct reflection of the parts of me that I have not become aware of or don't want to own in myself, so I project them onto others. This includes what is often referred to as the golden shadow: I see my gifts in others but can't recognise them in myself.

I have also learnt that when I feel envious of what someone else has or does or how they are in the world, that is a wonderful guide to my own longings of what might be important to me, what I might want more of in my life, what I might aspire to, not so much from a material perspective but from what they represent to me.

My practise, in all areas of life, has been to take the focus off others and to love and accept myself and my life, as it is. My wounds and my gifts. To honour, value and celebrate my authenticity and my individual journey. To practise gratitude. All as a way of cultivating and sustaining my inner confidence and innate sense of self and honouring what life success looks like for me. As I have heard said many times, happiness is not having what you want, it is wanting what you have.

Cultivating satisfaction and joy is an inside job

It has quite honestly shocked me to learn that cultivating contentment, fulfilment and self-worth is an inside job. I spent years looking outside of myself, in the hope that I would find whatever it was that always seemed to be missing, and even now, I can quickly forget that!

'When I [get the next promotion/buy a new home/get a new car/ have a partner/am skinnier/have more money] then I will be happy.'

When I ... rips us off from enjoying the life we are living right now. It takes us out of the present and it never arrives. *When I* ... is all about our inability to sit with our reality, to feel either the good or the bad that life is currently serving up. It is about our inability to be with ourselves and life, on life's terms.

We have no control over what life brings us (another shocking realisation!). Sure, we can do our best to create the external life we want. But there are also a million unforeseen circumstances that come our way, both good and bad. If we are relying on getting what we want and keeping what we want to make us feel safe, happy and worthy, then we are in for a tumultuous and often disappointing journey.

What cultivates contentment, fulfilment, self-worth and joy is the relationship we have with ourselves and the relationship we have with all that happens outside of us. How we show up to the world, how we handle change, how we bounce back from adversity, how we appreciate and feel gratitude and joy for what we do have, the choices we make, how we are in our relationships and community. This is an inside job.

Someone asked me years ago if I was content with my life and I said, 'I don't want to be content; that sounds boring. I want to have a big life that is exciting'.

I gently laugh at myself when I think of that now. That statement was coming from a place of *When I ...*, and it took me many years in therapy and meditation practice to cultivate feelings of contentment and satisfaction. Happiness is fleeting. But cultivating satisfaction allows me to truly enjoy my life success. It is such a cliché, but there is no destination. Yet, I can so quickly forget that. I love the paradox of both taking life seriously, while holding it lightly. There is so much freedom when I wear life like a light garment.

It doesn't mean I don't have goals, aspirations and big bold dreams — I do. However, my worth and joy are not tied to these. They are just part of the fun, the adventure of life.

When I look around my home and I can take in the beauty and abundance of my life, then I know I am travelling well. When my head is telling me I need a bigger house, or need to be closer to the ocean, or I need more success, or when I am comparing myself to others, then I am not travelling well. Again, this is not to say I can't aspire to these things. I can be very clear on what I aspire to, and then I let go and cultivate satisfaction with the life I currently have; it's like a graceful dance.

Key practices for cultivating a feeling of satisfaction in work and life

◆ Daily mindfulness and gratitude.

◆ Recognising and celebrating accomplishments, no matter how small, and letting in positive feedback and compliments.

◆ Daily self-compassion, particularly toward those parts of yourself that never feel enough and continuously strive for more.

(continued)

◆ Embracing challenges as opportunities for learning and growing, rather than failures or setbacks.

◆ Prioritising work-life balance and engaging in activities that nourish your soul and nurture meaningful relationships.

◆ Reflecting on your values, purpose and vision; aligning your actions with them; and pursuing meaningful work that aligns with these.

Grace, faith and letting go

As I redefined success and committed to living true to myself, one of the hardest practices for me has been letting go and letting be. Letting things happen, rather than pushing to make things happen. This is my ongoing daily spiritual practice.

I have read so many different definitions of spirituality, and I notice how often people can intertwine it with religion. While many find fulfilment in religion, my experience of it was never a positive one. The word 'god' has many negative connotations for me, some of which are from my experience of religion as a young girl, and many of which are negative projections from my relationship with my father. Just as I experienced my dad as controlling, critical and judgemental, any time I have explored having a relationship with God, I unconsciously think 'he' will be controlling, critical and judgemental. Therefore, I feel I have to get it right and be perfect to be loved by this god. And within this relationship, I also notice I am looking for God to rescue and take care of me, to stop anything bad from ever happening again, like a parent-child relationship.

I think of spirituality as my personal quest for meaning, purpose and connection to something greater than myself as well as deep within myself. It is a deeply personal and subjective experience that goes well beyond religious affiliations and rituals. Spirituality involves exploring and understanding my inner self, values, beliefs and the nature of existence. It encompasses the exploration of transcendent and transformative experiences, seeking a sense of interconnectedness with others, nature and/or a higher power. It means trusting in and being guided by a deep inner knowing and intuition: a higher consciousness that connects us all, which I choose to call *grace*. It means having faith in life, faith that no matter what happens, I will be okay. Ultimately, spirituality for me is about finding a sense of meaning, fulfilment and harmony in my life and with the world.

To cultivate my spirituality, I practise regular meditation, prayer, reflection, mindfulness and virtues, such as compassion, gratitude and love. I turn to these practices when I am holding on too tightly to something and struggling to let go, which might be to a person, a behaviour that doesn't serve me, a promotion or a vision for a different life. Or I turn to them if I am driving too hard to try to make something happen, or feeling anxious or scared about making a decision, or putting a boundary in place, or doing something new. These practices help me get still and tap into a higher self, a higher level of consciousness. They support me to feel connected and to make wiser, more self-respecting choices, which are aligned with the vision I hold for my life and myself. They allow me to surrender my wilfulness, ego, insecurities and fears.

The gift of prayer

Prayer has been very powerful for me. It doesn't matter what I pray to, although I do still often choose the moon as a feminine symbol. The act of praying, with intention and purpose, changes something within me and helps me to let go and have faith that all will unfold as it is meant to. And in some mystical way, which I will never be able to explain, it allows grace to enter my life.

When we try too hard, it creates a lot of stress. When we cultivate presence, curiosity, take purposeful action and surrender, it allows a natural inner confidence to arise from within us. When we listen to our soul and our quiet intuition, it always knows the way.

I had a beautiful experience of grace recently around this book. I was 90 per cent finished writing and I had absolutely no idea what to do next. I didn't know anyone who had published a book and had no experience myself. When I looked on the internet, it all felt overwhelming. How would I find a professional editor to look at it and give me feedback and help me get it ready for publishing? Should I self-publish or try to find a publisher? How would I find a publisher? What should I title the book? How would I market it so that as many women as possible could benefit from it?

I felt overwhelmed by all my questions, and had a sense of having to work it all out on my own, and not knowing the right way forward. It was taking up a *lot* of head space and energy. I prayed to the moon. I set the intention that I wanted to bring this book into the world, and I wanted to feel supported in this process, and I asked the moon to guide me.

Then I completely let go. I stopped thinking about it. Less than a week later, I was in my front yard gardening and my neighbour, Michael Bunting, who lives two doors up, pulled up in his car to say hi. I had not seen Michael or his wife for a long time. I suddenly remembered Michael has written three books. When I vulnerably shared with him where I was at in my own book-writing process, he generously offered me his experience and wisdom, including an introduction to his editor and publisher.

You may call this synchronicity or lucky timing or consider the statistical probability of this occurring given we were neighbours. I call it grace and divine timing. And it is only one example of the numerous ways I have felt held by grace in this book process and all other areas of my life.

I then remembered a lady named Shelly Unwin who had published several children's books with a very large and reputable publisher. But I had not seen her for over ten years and felt uncomfortable reaching out to her after all these years to ask her if she would provide an introduction for me. Then a month later, as I was starting to think about publishers again, I had a call from Shelley, completely out of the blue, asking if I would be a referee for her for a role she was pursuing. And, yes, of course, she said she would find the right person and introduce me to her publisher.

Someone said to me recently, 'You can make a choice to believe that "grace" is everywhere, or grace is nowhere'. I choose to believe it is everywhere.

I still get anxious about my book. I can still obsessively think about what I 'should' do next, usually to try to feel more in control and not have to feel my anxiety. And when this happens, I stop, breathe and slow down. I do what I need to do to settle my nervous system, which is always rest, and then I ask a higher consciousness what the next right step to take is. Often, when I am still and listen to the deep knowing within, the answer is, 'Relax now. There is nothing more to do today'.

These practices support me to stay in the present with myself and with others. They empower me to let go of the result and instead be present and enjoy my life as it is, trusting and having faith that all will unfold in perfect order and timing. These are also the practices that empower me to lead with presence and authenticity.

CHAPTER 16

Leading true to ourselves

Leadership isn't about what role you are in; it is about how you live your life. It is about living and leading true to yourself for the benefit of the greater good and influencing and engaging others in the pursuit of this collective vision. Leading true to ourselves means showing up authentically, being congruent with our values, purpose and vision, and leading others from this place of integrity. Through being both soft and strong, we empower and engage the hearts and minds of our team members and take them on the journey with us. Authenticity is revealed when what we say and do aligns with who we are and who we want to be.

It doesn't mean we don't feel anxiety and fear, it doesn't mean we don't experience self-doubt — it means we become aware of the behaviours that manifest from our fears and insecurities, and we don't allow them to run and limit us. We manage these fears while staying committed and focused on what is true for us, what we are passionate about and the impact we want to have in this world. Even when we are scared, when things don't go our way, when we make mistakes, when the 'system' we are working and living within may pressure us to do or be someone else, we stay true to ourselves.

From this place, we have the honour of being of service to the world rather than to our own egos and fears. From this place, we offer our leadership presence.

Embodied leadership presence

Great leadership is all about presence. There is arguably nothing more powerful and magnetic than a leader with a calm and purposeful presence. There is so much power in inner stillness, and yet it can be one of the most challenging strengths to cultivate. Calmness is a superpower. You have experienced those women and men who captivate a room with their presence, who do not take up excessive space in a meeting, but step in and say exactly what needs to be said at exactly the right moment. They make it look effortless. In my experience, they have often spent many years cultivating the calm within them. They have learnt, through their own deep inner work, and a commitment to their executive wellbeing, and ongoing growth, that stability comes from inside of them. They take this inner stability into every interaction.

Embodied presence means we emit a strong, authentic and influential presence through our physical, emotional and mental presence. It goes beyond just the words we speak and encompasses our entire demeanour, body language and overall energy. We not only convey our ideas and vision through words, but also through our non-verbal cues, emotions and the way we carry ourselves.

What we say is important. Words matter. Yet, typically, we tend to focus most of our attention on *what* we want to communicate instead of *how* we want to communicate. We research, we practise, we overthink what we want to say. Yet, few of us invest time and space to support our nervous system, which will have the biggest impact on *how* we will show up and say it.

It is essential to understand the vital role of our nervous system in enhancing non-verbal communication. Human beings continually read each others' nervous systems, and our tone of voice generally reflects our emotions. Whether we are interacting with family or colleagues, the lower region of our brain is consistently evaluating the safety or potential threat in our surroundings and experiences. This instinctive brainstem reaction is scientifically termed 'neuroception', as described by the respected neuroscientist Dr Stephen Porges in his Polyvagal Theory.

Neuroception serves as an unconscious gauge, constantly scanning our environments to assess the level of perceived safety. As part of our biological evolution, we developed a significant pathway of nerves known as the vagus nerve pathway. This facilitates communication between the brain and body, allowing signals to travel back and forth. This communication profoundly influences how we experience the world, people and situations we encounter, and how others perceive us.

This was brought to the forefront for me when I was asked to emcee an event by Jono Fisher. At the time, Jono was the founder of WakeUp Project, which ran some incredible events celebrating mindful leadership and living for their community of over 100 000 people. A mutual friend introduced us via email, and we decided to meet up. I was instantly taken by Jono's calmness and warmth, as well as his incredible passion to be of service to his community. We spent an hour or so getting to know each other and I left feeling like I had met a like-minded soul.

An hour later, Jono called me to ask if I would be interested in emceeing their inaugural Mindful Leadership Forum. At this event, leaders in this field came together from all over the world for a day to share their wisdom with an audience of over 900 people in Sydney.

I was completely caught by surprise. Jono had only just met me. And while I had done a handful of keynotes by that time, I had never spoken to a group that size, and I had never been an MC for an event, which is not as simple as it may sound. I asked him why he wanted me to do it, particularly given it was their inaugural event and I knew it was an important role for him. He said it was because of my authenticity and presence, the *energy* and *holding* he felt I would bring to the stage and event.

I said yes. And then I went into complete terror that I would embarrass myself and let Jono down.

Self-doubt has been a big issue for me over the years. I have noticed many times that other people often see in me what I can't see in myself. I can be very quick to focus on what I lack rather than what I bring, and then start to doubt myself. After I said yes, my perfectionist side went nuts. I studied every speaker in detail. I wrote copious notes. I created detailed speaking cards that I decided I would read out loud so I could not possibly forget a single word or get anything wrong. I over-prepared, feeding my anxiety and insecurities.

Before the event started, we had a session with all the speakers. We sat in circle and Jono invited each of us to share our intentions for what we each wanted to bring to the event. I remember feeling like a fraud in this group of wonderful human beings and highly accomplished experts in their fields. My anxiety grew.

The night before the event, my anxiety was so huge that I started to think about ways I could legitimately pull out of the event without letting Jono and the team down. I am not joking when I say the idea of running my car into a tree briefly crossed my mind. Eventually, I allowed myself to slow down, and I stopped rehearsing my scripts. I went for a long walk to help move the nervous energy that felt stuck in my body. I sat with my anxiety, breathing deeply into it, and allowed it to just be there within me and eventually pass through me.

I rang a girlfriend and spoke all my fears out loud, at times getting teary in my overwhelm. She listened and told me she understood. It made perfect sense that I would be feeling nervous getting up in front of 900 people and being responsible for setting up the speakers and 'holding' the room. At the end of the conversation, she said that there was no doubt in her mind that I would be perfectly imperfect and amazing all at the same time, and that she would love me no matter what happened. Finally, I slept.

The next morning, I woke up early, and rather than reading my script for the hundredth time, I sat in nature and meditated for twenty minutes. I prayed and set an intention for the day: *Please guide me in my thoughts, words and actions, may grace hold me and move through me to hold the speakers and guests.* I then had some protein for breakfast to help me stay grounded. I put on my favourite outfit, which felt both feminine and comfortable.

I arrived at the large event room early as they were still finishing the set up and sound check. I did a ritual that I had been taught many years prior, walking fully around the edge of the very large room, touching the wall every few metres, setting an intention and envisioning the room being wrapped in light and compassion. I do this in every room where I work with groups. I stood on the stage, reminding myself I only needed to remember the first line. The first line is critical for me, as sometimes when I am stressed and my pre-frontal cortex goes offline, I freeze up. But I have learnt that if I know the first line by heart, then grace arrives and I trust myself to show up fully and remember whatever is important to say.

And that is what I did. I showed up fully and all my anxiety disappeared. I was calm and grounded, and I loved every single minute of the day. I let go of reading my scripts, just checking them when I needed to, and instead focused on *being with* the audience and deeply listening to the speakers so I could thank them and share my take-outs and experiences of them from an authentic place.

I got a lot of wonderful feedback on how I contributed to a very successful event. The biggest compliment was Jono asking me to do it again the following year, as well as asking me to emcee their Women Leading Change event. The second year, I started losing my voice the day before the event, but I still showed up and perfectly imperfectly did the best I could until halfway through when my voice completely went, and Jono had to step in and take over. I was mortified, feeling like I had let him down, but I received only compassion and care.

Following this, I started receiving more invitations to speak in front of groups, both large and small. Every single time, I still get extremely anxious. And every single time, when I sit with my fear and anxiety, rather than trying to ignore or avoid them, they leave the moment I step on stage, and my authentic inner confidence arrives and grows. I have learnt repeatedly that I am often asked to speak, not because of my expertise (although of course that is important) but because of the presence I bring. People tell me they listen and feel inspired by how I show up. This happens when I show up true to myself and allow grace to move through me.

Support your nervous system to stand in your power

By nurturing and supporting our nervous system, we can enhance our ability to connect with others non-verbally. Prioritising practices that promote nervous system wellbeing, such as meditation, qigong, relaxation techniques and healthy lifestyle habits, can positively impact how we perceive and respond to our surroundings. Ultimately, investing in the health of our nervous system contributes to more effective non-verbal communication, fosters healthier relationships in all aspects of life and enables us to show up with leadership presence. What is *your* practice for cultivating and expanding your leadership presence?

Julianne is a highly respected expert and senior leader in a global property business. When we first met, she had just spoken at a large client event and separately to a group of over 500 staff at their quarterly town hall meeting. While people found it hard to tell her to her face, there was a lot of talk going on about how uninspiring she was at both events. It was not about what she said — there were few people who knew the topic better than her. It was about *how* she said it, how she showed up, the energy with which she arrived on stage.

When Julianne was nervous or stressed, she had the tendency to speak very fast, to say the same point repeatably and to say too much. The pitch of her voice got higher, and her tone tended to sound a little impatient and, at times, aggressive. She was often the same in smaller groups and one-on-one meetings, where her energy came across as rushed and demanding. She would often over-talk, cut people off and shut people down, albeit unconsciously.

As we explored it together, Julianne began to recognise that these behaviours came from the reciprocal interaction between her over-activated nervous system and her anxiety, which drove her need to feel in control. She needed to be seen as the expert and she felt a strong drive to move people and projects along quickly, given the pressures within the business. She realised this also mirrored back an internal pressure within her. These were also behaviours that she had cultivated in her childhood as a way of getting her needs met and managing her anxiety in a very loud and demanding family.

I suggested she had two options. First, she could learn some new skills that would support her to show up differently; however, I explained that they are typically a band-aid solution, as once she gets stressed, triggered or anxious it may be hard for her to remember to use them. Secondly, we could do some of the deeper inner work to process her anxiety and deeper fears and the ongoing practices that would support her to learn how to regulate her nervous system and *be with* her underlying anxieties. Once again, the first step was for her to learn to slow down when everything in her wanted to speed up.

I find it so interesting that the prevailing method of leadership development often focuses on our competencies, referred to as the *outer game*. Although important, it frequently falls short of generating significant change because it neglects the inner game: a leader's internal operating system; what drives us and our values, assumptions and beliefs.

It is embracing our inner work and transforming our inner game that allows us to transform our outer game and cultivate a calm presence and connect with our intuition, creativity and innovation as a leader. Deep confidence, connection, calmness and contentment all begin within us. They come from high levels of awareness, self-management, empathy and compassion. Ultimately, they come from our emotional intelligence and emotional maturity — our ability to be aware of and regulate our emotions. As we have explored throughout this book, this comes from knowing ourselves and caring for ourselves.

Alongside our deeper inner work, the number one tool for cultivating calm and presence on a day-to-day basis is our own breath. Almost every relaxation, calming or meditation technique relies on breath as a tool to calm the body and mind.

No matter where we are or what we are doing, we all have access to this tool. The only challenge is to remember to use it. That's where our daily meditation practice and regular one-minute conscious pause come in. They are like going to the gym to build up your muscles, but in this case, we are building up the muscle to slow down and take three deep breaths. We are building the muscle to connect with our inner stability and be attentive and present, which also enables us to have a choice around whether we *react* or *respond* from a place of clarity and authenticity, and show up with a calm and purposeful presence.

The feminine leadership advantage

I have mentioned numerous times that I believe the world needs more female leaders who show up authentically, and live and lead true to themselves and what they want to bring into being in this world, which is crying out for change. Women who lead with feminine principles and balance their masculine traits; who lead with both their head and their heart. Women who lead by example from a philosophy of integrated conscious leadership, to be of service to others and the greater good. Female leaders who lend their presence to answer the needs of their customers, teams and the organisation, and do so from a place of sustainable and highly effective leadership, whilst balancing their own needs and wellbeing.

This doesn't mean I believe all women should be leaders. There has been so much pressure put on women for so long to do it all, have it all and be superwomen. We have so much pressure to over-function and to put other people's needs ahead of our own. Within this, women who want to focus their time and energy on being mothers and shaping the next generation are often dismissed. Or, women who choose to not have children and instead focus on their careers, or create whatever life feels good for them, are often judged. Whatever choice we make, this is about leading our own lives true to ourselves and what calls to us.

That said, many of the women I have worked with have felt *called* to lead. It is often tied to their purpose and passion. The question I find them wanting to explore is, 'How can I do this in a way that is sustainable and honours the other areas in my life, which are also important?' The answer always comes back to:

- getting very clear on our values, purpose and vision

- recommitting every day to the practice of living in congruence with these

- holding clear and compassionate boundaries, within ourselves and with others, around what supports us and what limits us

- coming into balance with *doing* versus *being*

- discerning the difference between purpose, passion and overdrive. The energy of moving toward our purpose and vision is a lot more effortless than the driven energy and intensity of moving away from not being enough or needing to prove ourselves

- the practise of letting go and trusting deeply in ourselves, our capabilities, our talents, our intuition, our soul's longings

- accepting, and even appreciating, we will never do it perfectly; it is a lifelong journey, and there is no arriving.

For a great many of us, it is also about recognising and honouring a feminine leadership advantage, a research finding named by authors Cindy Adams and Lani VanDusen from the Leadership Circle. They coined the term in their research, 'Understanding the difference in reactive and creative orientations between female and male leaders', where they compared self-identified male and female leaders within Leadership Circle's large database of 84 000+ leaders.[36]

While there were many interesting insights and comprehensive findings, I would like to highlight these five:

◆ Female leaders, on average, demonstrate higher levels of leadership effectiveness.

◆ The data reveals that there is a 'feminine leadership advantage' across all management levels, age groups, leadership levels and cultures. This means that, when compared with their male counterparts, women leaders demonstrate significantly greater competency in nearly all areas.

◆ Women score significantly higher on the competencies underlying relational skills and perspective-taking. They also score higher in authenticity and achieving. These come from their pronounced ability to leverage caring connections to achieve productive results. Their evaluators view them as 'leaders who lead by example and are people-oriented in their approach'.

◆ Interestingly, in self-scores, women leaders view themselves with some self-doubt or humility. They tend to rate themselves lower than their evaluators, while men tend to rate themselves higher than others see them in relating and effectiveness (remember the example of the financial services organisation in Chapter 9?). This could be illustrating a theme of self-doubt and women not seeing who they really are or as others see them. Thus, female leaders underestimate their impact, and this can hinder them at some point.

◆ Perhaps not surprisingly, the two biggest potentially limiting areas for most women leaders are over playing to drive and perfection. Women leaders tend to be identified with needing to be 'better than best' in all areas.

Ouch. It's not like I don't experience this self-doubt coupled with high expectations of myself or see this in the many women I work with every single day. But boy, it is still hard to see it so clearly laid out. It is a stark reminder of how we undermine our own success, our own talents, skills, capabilities, and voice — even those of us who are already considered successful. Perhaps one good thing is the growing awareness that we are not alone in our own self-doubt, and knowing this we can take an active role in both managing our own self-doubt and lifting each other up more.

I also want to be clear that none of this is about women leaders being better than men. In fact, the research made the point, which I feel equally strongly about, that the contrast between genders in their research is not meant in any way to marginalise or make men 'wrong'. Their intent with this research is 'to develop women's strengths and areas that are holding them back and to integrate more of what is possible, uniting in inherent unity'.

I am reminded of the quote by Marianne Williamson, American author, speaker and humanitarian:

> Our deepest fear is not that we are inadequate. Our deepest fear is that we are powerful beyond measure. It is our light, not our darkness that most frightens us. We ask ourselves, "Who am I to be brilliant, gorgeous, talented, fabulous?" Actually, who are you not to be? ... Your playing small does not serve the world. There is nothing enlightened about shrinking so that other people won't feel insecure around you. We are all meant to shine, as children do ... And as we let our own light shine, we unconsciously give other people permission to do the same. As we are liberated from our own fear, our presence automatically liberates others.

Not playing small doesn't mean we need to hold the most important role in the company or our communities. Not playing small means we find and live our truth. It means we have the courage to be who it is we want to be, to say what we need to say, to let go of conforming to who we think others want us to be. Having the courage to explore the internal conflict and self-doubt that can arise when we consider stepping into our full potential enables us to recognise our worth and to embrace our capabilities.

I wouldn't say that my greatest fear is that I am inadequate — although I do have that fear. My greatest fear is that I will not be loved if I stand in my light, that I will be alone. In Chapter 1, I quoted

Robert Kegan, who said that the transformation from socialised mind to self-authoring mind is a:

> ... *tremendously empowering and inspiring stage of development as we come into our own voice. But before we get there, as we transform, there is often a lot of terror, grief and anticipated loss as we object to the norms we used to adhere to. What will be the results? Will people still love me? Will I be put out of my society, community, or organisation.*

In my experience, this is a spiritual experience, a spiritual transformation. It is not something we can wilfully change in ourselves. We get clear on who we want to be, we set an intention, we pray for support, we practise showing up in a new way and we let go of the outcome. We notice the self-doubt, the fear, the terror; we acknowledge it; we can even name it. We thank it for keeping us safe in the past and we suggest it goes out and plays in the sunshine because we have got this now. Thanks, but no thanks to the self-doubt that undermines us leading true to ourselves.

It is almost comical that when I started writing this final chapter, I was filled with self-doubt. Even though I was staring at a nearly complete manuscript on authentic feminine leadership, my inner critic screamed that I had nothing to say on the subject. My fear and self-doubt wrote the chapter, and it was very obvious to my very dear editor, Steve.

Thankfully, he put on his writing coach hat and told me exactly what I needed to hear — and what I already knew in my heart. He was clear (and spot on) in his feedback that the chapter was missing heart and soul. But then he followed that up with a loving reminder that I *did* have a lot to say on the subject.

I cried when I received his feedback. Not because he was criticising my work, but because he saw me. He saw my self-doubt and he saw something even more important: my authentic voice. He shone a light on my fear that I am inadequate, and within that, my even deeper fear of: *Is it okay for me to speak my truth, to stand in my light, to share my experience, what I see in myself and deep within the beautiful women I have the privilege of working with?*

I see and hear their self-doubt every day, including those women who are at the height of their career success, women who many others look up to. And if they don't doubt themselves at work, they doubt themselves at home or in their relationships.

We cannot push our self-doubt away and we can't make it disappear. But we can hold it with great self-compassion. As women, we have been fighting to find our authentic voice and power for centuries — and we cannot let our self-doubt run us or limit us. Instead, we can continue to show up time and time again for what we believe in and who we want to be. We can live and lead true to ourselves until it becomes second nature to us. And even if it never becomes second nature, we can still show up anyway for ourselves and for each other.

We can also support each other in this. I would never be where I am today without the incredible circle of women that I have around me. These women believed in me when I did not know how to believe in myself. These women encourage me to stand in my authentic power. I spent way too many years feeling like I had to do life on my own, there is no joy in that. May we see and support the incredible women who are all around us. Together, may we continue to grow in love and respect for ourselves and each other.

We can also fully embrace our feminine leadership advantage. This means we play to our inherent relational strengths. For many years, in my own leadership, this was a strength I overlooked and often minimised. I was very *masculine* in my style and behaviours. Trying to be like the guys, I often lost touch with my *feminine* traits, as I felt like they wouldn't be respected in my industry. Both at work and in my life in general, my journey has been to come into balance with both my healthy *masculine* traits and my mature *feminine* strengths.

I have spent many years working with women at both ends of this spectrum. Julianne, whom I introduced on page 278, was leading almost fully from her *masculine* traits: focused on tasks, achievements, strategy and systems thinking, but not investing any time into creating caring connections, fostering team play or taking people on the journey with her.

Another leader, Wendy, was leading almost fully from her *feminine* traits: focusing on relationships, often at the cost of herself, and ignoring the business strategy and outcomes required for her team and organisation to be successful.

Conscious and effective leadership integrates traits from both the *feminine* and *masculine*, allowing us to cultivate a diverse range of qualities and adapt our approach to different situations and individuals. Here, our goal is to foster inclusive conscious leadership that values collaboration, empathy, assertiveness and risk-taking, regardless of gender.

Ultimately, this isn't about our gender: it is about how we live, lead and succeed, whether we are a man, woman or gender diverse. It is about leading from a place of authenticity and balance, from within us and allowing life to move through us.

This is also key to managing the overdrive that showed up so clearly in the research, and I see in many women I work with. This often comes from a place of unreasonable expectations and perfectionism, a need to prove our worth by achieving, and an inability to find our limits and set our boundaries, much of which we have already explored. But leaders must be reminded to prioritise their self-care and find more balanced expectations of what they can and can't do, especially when they want to genuinely honour themselves and other parts of their lives.

Charlotte was such a wonderful example of a female leader who transformed her inner game after embracing the inner work and practising a new way of being. She now leads true to herself and manages her self-doubt when it arises. She now more consistently holds her boundaries, without guilt.

She is a single parent, working across global timeframes and leading a large team under constant pressure to get results. She knew if she was going to be at her best as a parent and a leader, she needed to set very clear expectations about what she could and could not do and when she was and was not available. She created a very clear vision and inspired her team, colleagues and customers with her authenticity and her care of each and every person in her team as human beings with different needs and motivations. She brought out the best in others, partnering with and empowering people and in return they went over and above for her and their collective vision.

She stopped competing with herself and with others, lowering unrealistic expectations to be the best and do everything perfectly whilst still moving toward the desired results. When things got stressful, she doubled down on her exercise and wellbeing. She learnt to say 'no'. She learnt her value as a leader was in her presence and wisdom, not in doing more to prove her worth as she had done in the past. Slowly, gently, she tamed and contained her passion and overdrive, thus creating space to rest. When we run on anxiety there is no place to rest — we all need a place to rest.

When one of her sons got very ill, she asked her organisation for three months' leave to be fully there for him, even though her fear and self-doubt had her question the impact it might have on her career and financial stability. Instead of letting this fear run her and make her decision for her, she advocated for the contribution and value she brought to the organisation and negotiated an arrangement that worked for her and her organisation.

In all areas of her life, Charlotte, perfectly imperfectly, leads by example and role models for others what 'leading true to ourselves' and showing up authentically looks like for her. She radiates her own power and respect from the inside out.

For other women I have worked with, leading true to themselves has meant stepping out of their current organisation, either to follow a more entrepreneurial path that calls to them or because they have realised that the current culture will never meet the needs of how they want to lead their life. As part of this, I always encourage women to reflect on the part she and her history may be playing in the current dynamic, so we do not simply replay it again in a new organisation. It takes courage to embrace the path to know ourselves, care for ourselves and be ourselves.

A FINAL REFLECTION

As we have explored, authenticity is not something we have or don't have. It's a practice — a conscious choice for how we want to live and lead. It is a daily practice of letting go of who we think we're supposed to be and embracing who we truly are. Or as Dr Gabor Mate describes it in his book, *The Myth of Normal: Trauma, illness and healing in a toxic culture*:

> *The pursuit of authenticity is rife with pitfalls ... authenticity is not a concept you can describe but you know when it is there ... it cannot be pursued, only embodied.*

Leading our lives authentically is no small thing. Truly being ourselves is one of the most challenging and courageous endeavours we'll ever undertake in life.

Living an inauthentic life or living with cognitive dissonance is exhausting and drains both our capacity for joy and our ability to live and love fully. However, as we embrace the lifelong transformational inner work that frees us to embody our authenticity, we are able to reveal more of who we are, own our strengths and talents; be aware of the beliefs and assumptions that can limit us; and adopt a broader set of leadership qualities necessary to show up with true inner confidence and effectively lead. By fostering a stronger sense of self-awareness and self-compassion, along with a clear understanding of our values, purpose and vision, we are empowered to fully embrace the chance to lead a life true to ourselves. This enables us to wholeheartedly dedicate our skills and abilities to leading, whatever our role, and even when confronted with cultural and societal biases and our own self-doubt.

In a world hungry for change, women hold the power to revolutionise our future. We need more female leaders unapologetically breaking barriers and shattering glass ceilings. Our unique perspectives, empathy and resilience can transform industries, fostering innovation and inclusivity. Female leaders can bring a diversity of ideas, nurturing collaboration and dismantling outdated norms and structures. We can inspire young girls to dream bigger, paving the way for a generation of trailblazers.

There is an extraordinary power in women coming together. Together, we can unleash the untapped potential and the brilliance that lies within. We can unify and ignite a world where equality and diversity thrive, where voices are amplified and where our collective potential is unleashed. Together, as we create the space to know ourselves, care for ourselves and be ourselves, while supporting each other to learn a new way to live, love, lead and succeed, we can create a different future for ourselves and our children.

May it be so.

ACKNOWLEDGEMENTS

Writing this book was hard and yet profoundly healing. It brought up every insecurity, old trauma and hurt within me. And how could it not? To grow up, show up and lead our lives true to ourselves, to truly embody this way of being, whatever is in the way needs to be seen, felt, accepted and integrated — this is how we gently forgive and love ourselves back to a whole and meaningful life. It has also been a reminder for me that we can't do this alone, and I want to thank several people who I could not have done this without.

My two incredible editors, Steve Palmer, and Melanie Dankel, who both held me in different ways and helped me to step back and find my voice when I felt lost. Jo Flynn and Leah Sparkes for reading my first manuscript and providing feedback and encouragement with their big open hearts. Michael Bunting and Shelly Unwin for their generous spirits. Roma Gastor and Heather Albrecht for their contributions and love. Karen Baikie for reviewing key psychological chapters. Robyn North-Zaman, thank you for loving me back to life before I could, and Jeanne, thank you for walking me home and holding me through it all; this would never have happened without you.

To my other girlfriends who are always there when I need them, Jules, Melli, Emma, Sim, Mandy, Amanda, Gina and Cheryn, thank you for being in my circle. And Jody, thank you for coming back.

To my mum, thank you for facing your own vulnerability and seeing my courage. To Hugo for not only loving me, but also liking me within all my imperfections as a mum. To my brother Rob for standing beside me on this journey. To Marco for all of your support when I disappeared into my book while still trying to run my business, and for showing up every day to the wonder and challenge of being in a relationship with me. And thank you Troy for your honesty and encouragement.

To all the people I did not mention in this book and all the stories I did not tell, it does not mean you are not important to me.

To all the women I have had the privilege of working with. As the beautiful quote by author and illustrator Sark says, 'The circles of women around us weave invisible nets of love that carry us when we're weak and sing with us when we're strong'. May this book weave invisible nets of love when we are struggling and sing with us in celebration of who we are. May we all be this for each other.

RESOURCES

If my story has brought up feelings about your own experience with sexual abuse or trauma, please know help is out there. The following organisations can support you in your healing journey in Australia, and there are similar organisations around the world that I would encourage you to reach out to.

- 1800 Respect (1800 737 732) is a national counselling service and is available 24 hours a day.

- Sexual Abuse and Redress Support Service (1800 211 028) provides trauma specialists offering counselling.

- Lifeline crisis support (13 11 14) is Australia's largest crisis support service.

- Fullstop Australia (fullstop.org.au/) provides trauma counselling via phone or online.

- Australian Government support services (www.respect.gov.au/services) can help you find a service specific to your state or territory.

Likewise, if my story is making you question your relationship with alcohol or drugs, there are some supports you can reach out to.

- Alcoholic Anonymous (aa.org.au) offers a program of recovery.

- ReachOut (au.reachout.com) has information on identifying whether your alcohol use is risky, as well as links to supports.

- Alcohol and Drug Counselling Online (counsellingonline.org .au) offers confidential and free counselling.

- National Alcohol and Other Drug Hotline (1800 250015) is a confidential, national service available twenty-four hours a day, seven days a week.

REFERENCES

Chapter 1

1. Lautarescu A, Craig MC, Glover V 2020, 'Chapter two –
   Prenatal stress: Effects on fetal and child brain development',
   International Review of Neurobiology, vol. 150, pp. 17-40.
2. Jan M 2023, Secure attachment style relationships and how to
   form them, Simply Psychology, https://www.simplypsychology
   .org/secure-attachment.html.
3. Center on the Developing Child n.d., Neglect, Harvard
   University, https://developingchild.harvard.edu/science/deep-
   dives/neglect/#:~:text=Science%20tells%20us%20that%20
   young,impairments%20than%20overt%20physical%20abuse.
4. Zagefka H, Jones J, Caglar A, Girish R, Matos M 2020,
   'Family roles, family dysfunction, and depressive
   symptoms', ResearchGate, https://www.researchgate.net/
   publication/347162899_Family_Roles_Family_Dysfunction_
   and_Depressive_Symptoms.

Chapter 2

5. Leadership Circle n.d., https://leadershipcircle.com/.

Chapter 3

6. Circle of Security n.d., Resources for parents, Circle of Security, https://www.circleofsecurityinternational.com/resources-for-parents/.
7. Yip J, Black H, Herbert Walker D, Ehrardt K 2018, 'Attachment theory at work: A review and directions for future research', ResearchGate, https://www.researchgate.net/publication/318150229_Attachment_theory_at_work_A_review_and_directions_for_future_research.

Chapter 4

8. Martínez-García F, Puelles L, Ten Donkelaar HJ, González A 2012, 'Adaptive brain function and evolution', Frontiers, https://www.frontiersin.org/articles/10.3389/fnana.2012.00017/full.
9. Holland K 2023, 'Amygdala Hijack: When emotion takes over', Healthline, https://www.healthline.com/health/stress/amygdala-hijack.
10. Ressler KJ 2011, 'Amygdala activity, fear, and Anxiety: Modulation by stress', Biological Psychology, vol 67, no. 12, pp. 1117–19.
11. Hanson R 2013, *Hardwiring Happiness: The new brain science of contentment, calm, and confidence*, Harmony.
12. Koster F, van den Brink E 2015, *Mindfulness-based compassionate living: A new training programme*, Routledge.
13. Kegan R 1998, *In over our heads: The mental demands of modern life*, Harvard University Press.
14. Friedman HL, Hartelius G, editors 2013, *The Wiley-Blackwell handbook of transpersonal psychology*, Wiley.
15. Pally R 2007, The predicting brain: Unconscious repetition, conscious reflection and therapeutic change, ResearchGate, https://www.researchgate.net/publication/6157413_The_predicting_brain_Unconscious_repetition_conscious_reflection_and_therapeutic_change.

16. Freedman M 2019, Mia Freedman: 'Your son growing up will feel like the slowest break up you've ever known', Mamamia, https://www.mamamia.com.au/mia-freedman-family/.

17. Healthdirect 2022, Perimenopause, Healthdirect, https://www.healthdirect.gov.au/perimenopause#:~:text=For%20most%20females%2C%20menopause%20will,for%20others%20only%20a%20year.

18. Whiteley J, DiBonaventura MdC, Wagner J, Alvir J, Shah S 2013, 'The impact of menopausal symptoms on quality of life, productivity, and economic outcomes', *Journal of Women's Health*, vol. 22, no. 11, pp. 983-90.

19. British Menopause Society 2021, 'The British Menopause Society response to the Department of Health and Social Care's call for evidence to help inform the development of the government's Women's Health Strategy, https://thebms.org.uk/2021/08/the-british-menopause-society-response-to-the-department-of-health-and-social-cares-call-for-evidence-to-help-inform-the-development-of-the-governments-womens-health-strateg/.

20. White Ribbon Australia n.d., Homepage, https://www.whiteribbon.org.au/resources/.

21. Priestly A 2014, Overt discrimination (mostly) gone, 'Gender asbestos' now the real danger in organisations, Women's Agenda, https://womensagenda.com.au/latest/eds-blog/overt-discrimination-mostly-gone-gender-asbestos-now-the-real-danger-in-organisations/.

22. Hello Sunshine 2018, How it is podcast hosted by Diane Guerrero with Glennon Doyle. Series 1, Episode 5.

23. Field E, Krivkovich A, Kügele S, Robinson N, Tee L 2023, Women in the Workplace 2023, McKinsey & Company, https://www.mckinsey.com/featured-insights/diversity-and-inclusion/women-in-the-workplace.

24. Johnson WB, Smith DG 2018, 'How men can become better allies to women, *Havard Business Review*, https://hbr.org/2018/10/how-men-can-become-better-allies-to-women.

25. Ron Kurtz quote (last page ch4).

Chapter 5

26. David A. Sbarra, Hillary L. Smith, Matthias R 2012, 'When leaving your ex, love yourself: Observational ratings of self-compassion predict the course of emotional recovery following marital separation', *Psychological Science*, vol. 23, no. 3, pp. 261-9.
27. Hiraoka R, Meyer EC, Kimbrel NA, DeBeer BB, Gulliver SB, Morissette SB 2015, 'Self-compassion as a prospective predictor of PTSD symptom severity among trauma-exposed U.S. Iraq and Afghanistan war veterans', *Journal of Traumatic Stress*, vol. 28, no. 2, pp. 127-33.

Chapter 7

28. Hutcherson CA, Seppala E 2008, 'Loving-kindness meditation increases social connectedness', *Emotion*, vol. 8, no. 5, pp. 720-4.
29. Frederickson BL, Cohn MA, Coffey KA, Pek J, Finkel SM 2008, Open hearts build lives: Positive emotions, induced through loving-kindness meditation, build consequential personal resources, *Journal of Personality and Social Psychology*, vol. 95, no. 9, pp. 1045-62.
30. Davidson R 2010, Cultivating compassion: Neuroscientific and behavioral approaches, Center for Compassion and Altruism Research and Education.
31. Emroy University 2008, Compassion meditation may improve physical and emotional responses to psychological stress, ScienceDaily, www.sciencedaily.com/releases/2008/10/081007172902.htm.
32. Burklund LJ, Cresswell JD, Irwin MR, Lieberman MD 2014, The common and distinct neural bases of affect labeling and reappraisal in healthy adults, *Frontiers in Psychology*, vol. 5, pp. 221.

Chapter 8

33. *The Connection: Mind your body* (2014) [film], Harvey S (dir), Elemental Media.

Chapter 13

34. Katie B 2019, Judge-your-neighbor worksheet, Byron Katie, https://thework.com/wp-content/uploads/2019/02/jyn_en_mod_6feb2019_r4_form1.pdf.

Chapter 14

35. Kluger AN, Itzchakov G 2022, The power of listening at work, *Annual Review of Organizational Psychology and Organizational Behavior*, vol. 9, no. 1.

Chapter 16

36. Adams C, Van Dusen L 2022, Understanding the difference in reactive and creative orientations between female and male leaders, Leadership Circle, https://leadershipcircle.com/wp-content/uploads/2022/03/Research-on-Female-and-Male-Leaders-White-Paper-2022-03-17.pdf.